ROMAN TRAGEDY

# ROMAN TRAGEDY

## *Theatre to Theatricality*

MARIO ERASMO

UNIVERSITY OF TEXAS PRESS

AUSTIN

Publication of this book has been generously assisted by grants from the
National Endowment for the Humanities, the Gladys Krieble Delmas
Foundation, the James R. Dougherty, Jr., Foundation, the Dougherty
Foundation, Rachael and Ben Vaughan Foundation, Lucy Shoe Meritt,
Mark and Jo Ann Finley, Anne Byrd Nalle, and other individual donors.

Requests for permission to reproduce material from this work should
be sent to Permissions, University of Texas Press, P.O. Box 7819,
Austin, TX 78713–7819.

♾ The paper used in this book meets the minimum requirements of
ANSI/NISO Z39.48–1992 (R1997) (Permanence of Paper).

Library of Congress Cataloging-in-Publication Data

Erasmo, Mario.
    Roman tragedy : theatre to theatricality / by Mario Erasmo.
        p.   cm.
    Includes bibliographical references (p.    ) and index.
    ISBN 0-292-70242-6 (alk. paper)
        1. Latin drama (Tragedy)—History and criticism.   2. Theater—Rome.
I. Title.
    PA6068.E73    2004
    872'.0109—dc22

                                                            2004001670

*To my mother and in memory of my father:*
laetus sum laudari me abs te, pater, a laudato viro
*(Naevius* Hector proficiscens)

# CONTENTS

# PREFACE

Any study of Roman tragedy must begin with Otto Ribbeck's *Römische Tragödie* (1875), which remains an important study of the myths and Greek precedents of Latin plays. Equally important, and perhaps more well known, is Ribbeck's *Scaenicae Romanorum Poesis Fragmenta*, vol. 1: *Tragicorum Romanorum Fragmenta* (3d ed., 1897), in which he attributes the fragments of Roman tragedy to individual dramatists and offers reconstructions of plot outlines. Since Ribbeck, monographs have discussed each of the early dramatists individually, especially on questions of Greek models and poetic style. These philological studies are important, in particular H. D. Jocelyn, *The Tragedies of Ennius* (1967), R. J. Tarrant, *Seneca: Agamemnon* (1976) and *Seneca's Thyestes* (1985), Elaine Fantham, *Seneca's Troades* (1982), and Michael Coffey and Roland Mayer, *Seneca: Phaedra* (1990), for their attention to dramaturgical detail; but for the most part, the other commentaries treat plays as texts rather than as performance events.

Recent studies on the Roman theatre examine the dramaturgical, cultural, and political contexts of performance: W. Beare's *The Roman Stage* (3d ed., 1964) remains an important general study of drama at Rome for the content and dramaturgical contexts of tragedies and comedies. Antonio La Penna's *Fra teatro, poesia e politica romana* (1979) is a collection of earlier influential articles on the content and reception of Roman tragedy. Richard C. Beacham's *The Roman Theatre and Its Audience* (1992) looks at the development of the Roman theatre and applies an examination of a dramatic production of comedy to a study of audience expectation. William J. Slater, ed., *The Roman Theatre and Society* (1996), presents essays that address questions of dramatic reception throughout the Roman Empire, but not the reception of tragedy exclusively. Shadi

Bartsch's *Actors in the Audience* (1994) examines the theatricalized contexts of Nero's reign and the later historiographic tradition of his reign, which recognized the inherent theatricality of Neronian Rome. Most recently, Richard C. Beacham, *Spectacle Entertainments of Early Imperial Rome* (1999) examines the role played by emperors as sponsors of and participants in spectacles. All of these studies provide valuable insights into the cultural contexts of tragedy, on and off the stage.

There has also been recent interest in the dramatic tradition and cultural context of historical dramas. Joining the influential study by Nevio Zorzetti, *La pretesta e il teatro latino arcaico* (1980), are the recent important studies of Harriet I. Flower, *"Fabulae Praetextae* in Context: When Were Plays on Contemporary Subjects Performed in Republican Rome?"* (1995) and *Ancestor Masks and Aristocratic Power in Roman Culture* (1996); T. P. Wiseman, *Roman Drama and Roman History* (1998), which examines rituals and historiographic sources for the existence and production of preliterary historical dramas; and Gesine Manuwald, *Fabulae praetextae: Spuren einer literarischen Gattung der Römer* (2001), which provides texts, commentary, and extensive analyses of *praetextae*.

Performance criticism for Roman tragedy, however, lags behind studies in Roman comedy. Important are Niall W. Slater's *Plautus in Performance: The Theatre of the Mind* (1985) and Timothy J. Moore's *The Theater of Plautus: Playing to the Audience* (1998), for their treatment of Plautus' plays as performance events. Important studies in Greek theatricality include Sander M. Goldberg's *The Making of Menander's Comedy* (1980) and M. S. Silk's *Tragedy and the Tragic* (1996).

The most important recent study on Seneca is A. J. Boyle's *Tragic Seneca* (1997), which considers the metatheatricality of Senecan tragedy and its later reception under the Renaissance. My work on tragedy began before the publication of Boyle's book as an attempt to synthesize the approaches taken by these textual, cultural, and performance-criticism studies, looking at the genre of tragedy as a whole, to consider the role played by theatricality in shaping Senecan tragedy. We arrive independently at the same conclusions about what Boyle terms "Seneca's actor audience," but from different routes. Boyle uses Seneca as a starting point for further discussion of the theatricality of Renaissance texts. Rather than work my way back from Seneca, I work forward, focusing on the process of how Roman tragedy became increasingly theatricalized and the role played by Roman culture in shaping the perception of theatricality on and off the stage. My approach seeks to put Seneca's plays within the dramatic tradition of Roman tragedy

rather than outside of it, contrary to the conclusion drawn by Beare
(1964, 235):

> There is no evidence that Seneca (or whoever the author was) was imitat-
> ing the old Latin tragedies; the Senecan tragedies are simply artificial im-
> itations of Greek tragedy, worked up in the style of the Silver Age, and
> they are meant to be read or declaimed, not acted.

A word about the evidence. Reconstructing aspects of Roman culture
can be difficult with the best of evidence, and the problem becomes
magnified when dealing with scant production notices of plays and fragments from tragedies that survive because of chance references or due
to their interest to lexographers. In essence, the evidence is a limited
sample of the already partial extant fragments. I follow the evidence by
examining those plays whose fragments are numerous enough for analysis or for which we have details concerning original or subsequent productions. I make cautious but informed attempts to reconstruct the cultural contexts of tragic performances for their significance to Roman
culture in general, realizing the dangers involved in under- or overstat-
ing the available evidence. My analyses must remain suggestions that I
hope will form the basis of further discussion, not conclusions.

My approach is diachronic: chapters 1 and 2 reflect the growing incorporation of a rhetoricized reality onstage, as plays begin to point to
their own theatricality, and follow a chronological order of tragic production; chapters 4 and 5 analyze the reversal of this exchange—the
permeation of theatricality first into the audience's reality as real-life
events are viewed through a theatrical lens, and second, back into the
theatre as offstage theatricality defines the dramatic action onstage, producing the metatragedies of Seneca. An analysis of the *fabulae praetextae* (chapter 3) separates these two discussions and provides a means of
observing how the audience (re)interprets historic events in relation to
the theatre.

Parts of this study took root in my dissertation at Yale University under the supervision of Gordon Williams, and I am grateful for his guidance. The following have read early drafts of parts of the manuscript,
while I was still developing my ideas; I am grateful for their encouragement and criticism: James C. Anderson, Jr., James O'Hara, Michael Put-
nam, Guy Rogers, and Vasily Rudich. A special thanks to Niall Slater
for his encouragement. I would also like to thank the anonymous refer-
ees from the University of Texas Press, who will readily see my debt to
their generosity of time in providing remarkable guidance and astute

criticism. I have followed their advice closely, but all errors remain my own. Thanks, too, to Jim Burr, Sherry Wert, and the editorial staff at the University of Texas Press for their enthusiasm and guidance for this project. My thanks to Henry Schwab Publishers for allowing me to reprint, with changes, "Staging Brutus" in chapter 4, which originally appeared as an article, "Staging Brutus: Roman Legend and the Death of Caesar," in Elizabeth Tylawsky and Charles Weiss, eds., *Essays in Honor of Gordon Williams: Twenty-Five Years at Yale* (2001). Financial assistance for my research came from the Social Sciences and Research Council for the Humanities (SSRCH) of Canada and a Yale University Dissertation Fellowship, for which I am grateful.

This study is aimed at a diverse readership interested in the Roman theatre. All Latin citations in the main text, therefore, are translated into English, and I have tried to keep Latin citations in the notes to a minimum. Unless otherwise stated, all translations are my own.

# THEATRE TO THEATRICALITY

In the *De finibus* (1.2.4), Cicero claims that Roman dramatists copied their Greek originals "word for word." If we read further in the same passage, however, Cicero states that Romans did more than merely translate from the Greek:

What strikes me first about [those who claim to despise Latin writings] is this: why does their native language not please them on serious topics when not unwillingly do they read Latin tragedies that have been translated word for word from the Greek? Indeed, who is so hostile practically to the name Roman that he would despise or reject Ennius' "Medea" or Pacuvius' "Antiope" because he claims to enjoy the very same plays written by Euripides, and hate Latin literature? "Am I to read," he says, "the 'Synephebos' of Caecilius or Terence's 'Andria,' rather than the corresponding plays of Menander?" I disagree with such people so much that, although Sophocles has written an "Electra" best, nevertheless I think the version by Atilius, however badly translated, ought to be read, whom Licinius calls an "iron writer," but all the same a writer, I think, and deserving to be read. To be sure, complete ignorance of our own poets is the sign either of total laziness or of extreme rare taste. In my opinion, no one seems sufficiently learned who is ignorant of our native authors. If we read the line from a Latin tragedy, "Would that in the forest . . .," no less eagerly than we do the same line in the Greek, would the same passages in which Plato discusses morality and happiness be less effective if translated into Latin? And what if we do not perform the mere task of translation, but taking care to preserve what was expressed in the original by those of whom we approve, we add to them our own opinions and style of composition? What reason could they offer for preferring Greek over what is brilliantly written and not merely translated in Latin from the Greek?

(*FIN. I.2.4 – 6*)

How should we interpret Cicero's remarks? The context of the passage makes it clear that Cicero was looking for a Roman *exemplum* to follow in order to justify his translation of Greek philosophy into Latin. He appeals, therefore, to the precedence of tragedians at Rome, who have already "copied" Greek literature in the form of plays. Cicero's statement early in the passage that Roman dramatists copied their originals "word for word," however, is qualified further by his insistence that Roman versions contain something more, namely their own opinion and style (*nostrum iudicium et nostrum scribendi ordinem*). Does *iudicium* refer to changes made to a play, based on the dramatist's own opinion, in order to make terms or concepts from Greek passages comprehensible to Romans, or to changes made to Greek originals that anticipated audience expectation or enjoyment, in the form of spectacle or offstage allusions? The two are not mutually exclusive.

Roman tragedy needs to be understood in its cultural context from a performance-criticism perspective: Roman tragedians *adapted* rather than translated their Greek originals, unless they were composing original Roman plays.[1] The Roman term "emulation" (*aemulatio*) in a literary context means to engage an original and improve upon it, versus mere imitation (*imitatio*), which seeks only to copy an original without any distinction.[2] Roman writers, whether engaging a Greek or a Latin model, always attempted to emulate rather than imitate their models. In the case of Greek tragedy, Roman dramatists added distinct Roman elements to make the plays intelligible to a Roman audience. In addition, Roman dramaturgy differed significantly from Greek practice: the chorus appears on the stage in Roman tragedies, not the orchestra, as in Greek plays, thus necessitating scenic and metrical changes. A Latin play for a Roman audience required the inclusion of Roman culture onstage to make a connection with the audience. From Livius' first plays, which influenced Naevius and Ennius, Roman dramatists altered Greek originals for a Roman audience—indeed, there could have been no success, in either tragedy or comedy, if there were no connection with the audience.[3]

The Roman context of performance, which differed significantly from Greek practice, gave greater access to the stage (and more importantly, to an audience) to more people on more occasions for a variety of purposes, in particular political exposure. In Athens, an annual lottery determined who would be *chorēgos* to provide the financial backing for the plays presented at the Great Dionysia. Dramatists submitted plays for competition, and prizes were awarded following the dramatic program.[4] Besides religious festivals, there were no opportunities for the production of plays by citizens for private occasions. In Rome, however, plays formed part of a greater number of *ludi,* or religious festivals, from April to November. Plays were selected by the aedile or *praetor urbanus,* and it was his prerogative to choose which plays made it onto the stage. There was no competition, and the dramatist was compensated directly by the aedile or a stage manager if his play was selected.[5] Individual Romans could also stage scenic entertainment at occasions such as triumphs, votive, and funeral games.[6] The plays performed on these occasions were selected by an individual wealthy enough to afford the costs associated with producing *ludi,* thereby allowing him greater control of the dramatic program, from the thematic appositeness of plays to the emphasis of scenes, than any Athenian could at the Great Dionysia or any other religious festival. Without the original performance dates for most plays from the early to mid-Republic, it is difficult to reconstruct an aedile's or a private individual's motivation in selecting a specific play or dramatic theme, but ample evidence survives from the late Republic and early Empire to illustrate the importance of his and the actors' role in incorporating offstage allusions into the theatre and into the plays themselves in order to shape the reception of either the plays as a whole or particular passages from them.

From a performance-criticism perspective, theatre precedes theatricality in the same way that something cannot be understood as dramatic before one defines or recognizes something as drama. We should not confuse the lavish displays found in processions that predate the arrival of theatre in Rome with the terms "theatrical" or "dramatic." Today, the terms are synonymous with "breathtaking," "unexpected," or even "exaggerated." Theatricality proper, however, is the connection of a person, thing, or event with the theatre, which is itself a combination of text, actors, and audience. Once offstage reality pervades dramatic reality, reciprocity ensues—culture informs the theatre and theatre permeates society to the extent that one identifies the dramatic in everyday life or history, as Plutarch observed on the role of Tyche as dramatist.[7] Dramatic reality is understood as relevant offstage in order to interpret actual words or actions, and it leads to the recognition of theatricality *outside* of the theatre (actions interpreted in relation to the theatre, therefore, are perceived as theatrical rather than realistic).

The theatricality of the late Republic and early Empire is only understandable as a development of the earlier tragic tradition, which made theatrical allusion sensible *outside* the theatre (versus the staged reality of *praetextae,* which made outside reality sensible *inside* the theatre). When earlier "texts" and performances were combined with contemporary productions under the late Republic, the result was the reciprocal mixing of theatre and reality. At variance with literary allusion, which depends upon a verbal or thematic echo of an earlier "text," theatrical allusion depends both upon a relationship with earlier texts and plays with similar subjects, and upon allusions arising out of previous or contemporary performances that are recognized as having significance to current production/restaging or to events offstage. How else could the earlier plays of Ennius, Pacuvius, and Accius, like the plays of Shakespeare today, remain popular and relevant to later audiences and culture in general?[8] Restaged plays with performance traditions were "used" for specific occasions to produce a correspondence between real people and mythological characters, between current events and mythological events, and between the current stage production and a previous stage production. As I explore in chapter 4, the numerous productions (new and restaged) of the Thyestes myth, in particular Augustus' choice of *Thyestes* for his triple triumph in 29 B.C.E., and the cultural context(s) of Accius' *Brutus,* especially the play's later role as an inspiration to Caesar's assassins, point to the important role previous productions played in interpretations of contemporary stagings.

The relationship between onstage and offstage reality is one of coexisting and competing realities: Onstage reality is the reality of the actors on the stage, which does not refer to or acknowledge the reality of the audience (= illusory drama).[9] Offstage reality is the reality of the audience—life going on in the audience or outside of the theatre while dramatic reality is presented onstage. One might argue that the convergence of these realities can originate from the stage or the auditorium: offstage reality may be admitted or incorporated into dramatic reality, whether by design of the dramatist or the stage manager, through props or set design (= nonillusory drama), or by the audience's perception of an allusion, whether intended or perceived. In both cases we have the emergence of metatheatre as a self-conscious construct of theatricality, which is common in Plautus' comedies: actors intentionally break the dramatic illusion of a play by acknowledging the presence of the audience within the dramatic action or by interacting with the audience in its own reality.[10]

Since the incorporation of the audience's reality onstage is apparent from the beginning of Roman tragic productions, the audience faced the interpretive challenge of "competing realities"—in other words, distinguishing between rhetoric and realism—from the earliest tragedies.[11] Character delineation and scene drawing characterize the importance of rhetoric to the Roman tragedians' approach to dramaturgy. We find the rise of self-fashioning heroes who make the audience question the existence of the actors' "rhetoricized" stage reality. In Pacuvius' *Antiopa,* for example, shepherds are steeped in rhetoric and sneer at the very rusticity that should characterize their actual, and hence dramatic, existence, and in Accius' *Medea sive Argonautae,* a shepherd describes a ship that he has never seen before in language that reflects his ignorance. Such observations are, of course, from a modern dramatic "realism" point of view, but the problem that concerns us here is that the audience's reality is at odds with the dramatist's use of rhetoric, since, from a dramatic point of view, the question of whether such speech or characterization is convincing or appropriate arises when one should be focusing on the dramatic action of the play.

The term "metatheatre" has been understood differently by classicists: Gentili used the term to signify "plays constructed from previously existing plays."[12] Slater, however, broadens the definition of metatheatre to account for the performance contexts of plays: "Theatrically self-conscious theatre, i.e. theatre that demonstrates an awareness of its own theatricality."[13] Here, performance criticism helps us to supplement a philological analysis of Roman drama. Metatheatre may emerge from the play itself: allusions to personalities or events outside of the theatre or to the dramatic action of the play are needed to understand the play. If the relevance of the allusion was not inherent to the text or theme of the play, it could be supplied by an actor who interpolated or emphasized a line through gestures, or by the audience, which understood relevance whether intended or not. Cicero provides a ready example of comic actors' incorporation of the audience's reality into their own:

For when the comedy *Pretender* was being performed, so I recall, the whole actor's troupe shouted in unison, staring at the face of the foul man: "This, Titus, is the limit and end of a vicious life." He sat lifeless, and he, a man who earlier was accustomed to filling his own assemblies with the clamor of singers, was himself thrown out by the voices of singers themselves. And since mention was made of spectacles, lest I should omit anything, in the great variety of opinions there was not a single place in which

what the poet wrote did not seem to have relevance to our own time, because it did not escape the audience altogether or the actor himself gave
emphasis.

(*SEST.* 55)

It may be easy for comic actors to improvise somewhat fluid dramatic
texts and alter performances, but how could tragic actors make apposite allusions in plays that were, in some cases, at least a century old?
Were these allusions voluntarily made by the actors performing in a
tragedy, or did they reflect the views of the praetor? The most notable
examples occurred in July 59 B.C.E., when Pompey was attacked with
the line: "In our misery, you are great" (*nostra miseria tu es magnus*),
and at the *ludi Apollinares* of 57 B.C.E., when the tragic actor Aesopus
altered dramatic texts to rouse the audience for the recall of Cicero.

Events surrounding the latter performance deserve fuller attention.
On the day of the performance, the senate was deliberating on Cicero's
recall at the Temple of Virtue, but news of the senate's decision reached
the theatre and the stage (*ad ludos scaenamque*) only after the audience
had assembled and presumably just prior to the delivery of the opening
lines of Accius' *Eurysaces*.[14] In any case, neither the audience nor the actor knew the result of the senate's meeting until the last minute, raising
the question of whether Aesopus made provisions beforehand, depending on the outcome, as to what lines he would emphasize and interpo-
late, or whether his actions were spontaneous. Many lines from Accius'
play were highlighted—Aesopus, for example, pointed to the assembled
senators and knights with a line alluding to Cicero: "Who aided the republic with determined soul, upheld it and stood with the Achivi" (*qui
rem publicam certo animo adiuverit, / statuerit steterit cum Achivis*),
and he was encored when he added, "In doubtful circumstance, he
did not doubt to offer his life nor spare his person" (*re dubia / haut du-
bitarit vitam offerre nec capiti pepercerit*).[15] Apparently, the audience
applauded this line so much that it neither noticed nor considered the
implications for the drama being staged when Aesopus interpolated his
own tribute to Cicero: "Our great friend, friend in this great war, en-
dowed with great genius" (*summum amicum summo in bello summo ingenium praeditum*). Later in the same play, Aesopus added lines from
Ennius' *Andromache* in which Andromache addresses Eetion: "O father—I saw all these things in flames. By the immortal gods! (*O pater—
haec omnia vidi inflammari. pro di immortales!*). Returning to the text
of the *Eurysaces* again, Aesopus pointed to all sections of the theatre, in

6

effect making all members of the audience members of the cast, and declaimed with force: "O you ungrateful Argives, undutiful Greeks who are forgetful of a kindness!" (*O ingratifici Argivi, immunes Graii immemores benefici!*), and "You allow him to be an exile, you secured his expulsion, you suffer him to be in exile" (*exculare sinitis, sistis pelli pulsum patimini*).

The importance of Aesopus' interpolations is twofold. First, Aesopus demonstrates how a fixed dramatic text, significantly tragedy rather than comedy, could be turned into a topical performance text (= nonillusory drama). Unlike the mime, which incorporated a large amount of improvised material, the mythical themes and characters of tragedy confined the actor, but did not entirely prevent him from altering the text to suit his purposes. Second, the audience on this occasion received news of Cicero's recall while seated in the theatre just before the performance began, making it primed to read allusions and accept interpolations referring to Cicero. In semiotic terms, this can be explained as a tension between dramatic and performance texts.[16] The dramatic text is the play written by the dramatist, while the performance text is that which is actually delivered onstage with actors' deletions or interpolations. In the late Republic, the distinction between intended meaning (authorial intent) and understood meaning (audience interpretation and topicality regardless of authorial intent) was sharply perceived by the audience, with the latter exercising more influence outside of the theatre and leading to a recognition of theatricality off the stage, in society at large.[17]

What happens, however, when the flow is reversed and the audience's reality, in the form of historical dramas, enters the stage? Was there, for example, a recognition of the dramatic fallacy of "realism" that what one is seeing is not what actually happened, even when historical persons did participate? Since real or historic people become characters in plays, the dramatizing of events alters the perception of on- and offstage reality and intentionally breaks down the separation between the stage and the audience (= nonillusory drama). This is especially the case if a character representing a real person is onstage watching "himself" in the audience or vice versa, or if a real person, whether or not he is in the audience, is alluded to onstage. As I explore in chapter 4, Pompey used the spectacle of the triumphing Agamemnon in a restaging of Accius' *Clytemnestra* as a pretext (and substitution for a *praetexta*) to "restage" his own triumph, with enormous consequences for the use of tragedies as allusive commentaries of contemporary politics.

Where does dramatic allusion end? At what point is offstage reality,

7

when it occupies the stage, recognized as "dramatic" rather than "realistic," especially when the audience's reality is perceived as a theatricalized reality? The distinction is difficult to pinpoint, especially when the distinction itself is intentionally blurred, as in the case of Nero, who performed onstage wearing masks, including those of his own likeness.[18] Suetonius, furthermore, reports that the audience had difficulty in distinguishing theatre from reality, even while seated in the theatre watching Nero perform onstage, since it was not sure even then when Nero was "acting."[19] It can be no surprise, therefore, that later historians viewed Nero's reign as "theatrical," deliberately suggesting that there was no difference between Nero's behavior and interpretation of that behavior, on and off the stage.[20]

The incorporation of theatricality onto the stage leads to the creation of Seneca's metatragedy, in which the characters acknowledge their own theatrical reality as they incorporate the audience's own theatricalized reality into their own. Boyle's "actor-audience" arrives on the Senecan stage via theatricalization of tragedy and contemporary rhetoric. Following the murder of her children, for example, Seneca's Medea remarks that her actions cannot be considered a crime since they were not witnessed by Jason (*Med.* 986–994). In other words, Medea needs Jason to supply the text and the context for her actions. The spectators in the audience are irrelevant in a drama where characters have become their own audience. Where exactly does one draw the line between theatre and reality?

Just as tragic texts and the dramatic traditions of certain plays were achieving a remarkable level of intertextuality, the curtain rose on the writing of new tragic plays. This was due in part to the enormous success of pantomimic productions, but one must also take into account waning Imperial patronage and the role that rhetoric and theatricality played in exhausting the genre, and perhaps even in alienating the audience. Even if dramatists wanted to write tragedy after Seneca, could dramatic reality successfully compete with the theatricality of offstage reality to attract an audience? The implications of this question will be considered through a study of the evolution of tragedy to metatragedy and the cultural importance of theatricality on and off the stage.

# ONE

# CREATING TRAGEDY

## LIVIUS ANDRONICUS

*mirum videtur quod sit factum iam diu?*

(LIVIUS *AJAX MASTIGOPHORUS* FRAG. I)

Does it seem wonderful because it was done a long time ago?

So a character in Livius' tragedy asks of the value of an early deed in relation to the present. Should something be admired solely because of its age, or rather because it possesses some other quality besides antiquity to deserve commemoration in the present? Perhaps the character realized that the question actually requires an understanding of the present, against which the value of an earlier event can be measured. Livius' plays, already ancient by the late Republic, are important for more than their antiquity. As the first Roman dramatic works, they influenced the form of drama that was to follow, but their relative neglect, even in Cicero's day, has obscured their contribution to the Roman theatre.

If we look forward from the perspective of Livius, rather than back from the perspective of Senecan tragedy, we find that Livius' plays are at once examples of theatre and metatheatre that greatly influenced the plays of Naevius and Ennius, and later those of Pacuvius and Accius, in which the audience's reality (and later theatricalized reality) comes to alter the perception of dramatic reality onstage. The reciprocity of these realities on and off the stage during the late Republic and early Empire contributed to the metatheatricality of Seneca's plays, but his plays emerge as products of the tradition rather than as aberrations. It is unlikely that members of Seneca's audience, experiencing just a small part of it, would have recognized a linear pattern to this development, but our vantage point gives us an opportunity to analyze the entire tradition of tragic productions at Rome.

The history of Roman tragedy and Latin literature begins in 240 B.C.E., when Livius Andronicus presented the first tragedy (together with a comedy?) at Rome.[1] Unfortunately, the title of this play cannot be recovered from the known plays of Livius. We do know that this tragedy was an adaptation of a Greek play and was presented at the games celebrating the end of the first Punic War.

The future dramatist had arrived in Rome as a prisoner taken in the capture of Tarentum in 272 B.C.E., when he was only a boy in the service of Livius Salinator. A native Greek speaker, Livius must have acquired Latin at Rome, where he was a schoolteacher. Depending on the order of composition, experience with Greek adaptation may have come from his translation of the *Odyssey* for a classroom text, which he rendered in the native Saturnian verse.

By adapting a Greek tragedy, Livius was transferring an established Greek dramatic tradition to Rome, creating the Roman theatre.[2] The occasion implies a ready audience, but not one that would have had any experience viewing a tragedy written in Latin. Unfortunately, we do not know whether Livius presented a tragedy before this date. If Livius was approached with the commission due to his reputation as a poet for his *Odyssia,* this was his first attempt at writing a play. If Livius had presented a play or plays prior to this date, then he had had the more difficult burden of attracting an initial audience for a novel, if not highly experimental, form of entertainment.[3] In either scenario, we cannot answer the question of why a tragedy was included in the victory celebrations on this date and for this occasion.

What were the first steps toward developing a tragic theatre in Rome? From the beginning, one finds a tension between Greek plays written centuries earlier for a Greek audience and Greek plays adapted for a Roman audience. Livius altered his Greek originals to make elements within the plays intelligible to his Roman audience through changes in dramatic format and content, thereby creating a distinctly Roman tragic theatre. Livius' innovations were not immediate, but rather evolved from actual stage experience. Since Livius presented the first play ever produced at Rome, whether for this or an earlier occasion, he must have organized or assisted in organizing everything from scratch: seating, stage construction and props, costumes, and perhaps the training of Greek actors in Latin. Livius also introduced far-reaching changes to the format of tragedies, most importantly the assigning of *cantica,* or recitative arias, to an actor, rather than to the chorus, which meant that the chorus did not provide the musical interludes between acts, as on the Greek stage. This change both reduced the chorus' role significantly and resulted in the unrealistic expression of emotion by actors who sing in complicated meters rather than speak in a natural way in trimeters or senarius verse throughout the play.

Livius initially acted in his own plays—a circumstance reminiscent of the career of Aeschylus. The strain on Livius' vocal cords, however, was later alleviated by the introduction of an offstage singer who would sing the *cantica* for him, allowing Livius to concentrate on acting and dialogue parts. The evidence is not clear but, at least initially, this seems to refer only to the leading role played by Livius.[4] The effect of having the lead actor(s) gesticulating onstage while someone else sang offstage was to make an already unrealistic depiction of human interaction onstage even further removed from the audience's experience outside of the theatre.

The custom of having other characters join principal actors in duets and trios, common in later tragedy and comedy, may have originated with Livius as well. These *cantica* must have been enormously successful, since their use was immediately exploited by Naevius and soon after by the comic dramatists Plautus and Caecilius Statius.[5] The diminished role of the chorus furthermore altered the architectural needs of Roman tragedy, since actors rather than the chorus now provided the lyric components of drama.[6]

Too little remains of the fragments of Livius' tragedies to reveal the rigidity of style, which Cicero compared to a sculpture of Daedalus, claiming that Livius' plays were not worth a second reading.[7] Cicero was usually full of praise for the older poets, especially Ennius, so his condemnation of Livius' poetry is startling.[8] Cicero's comment nonetheless contains a clue to the reception of Livius' tragic works in the late Republic: "they are not worth a second read" implies that they were no longer to be seen onstage. Perhaps the dominance of tragic plays by later dramatists also cut short the popularity on the stage of Livius' tragic plays, but not before he had acquired a reputation as a tragedian.[9]

As with the plays of the other early dramatists, few fragments of Livius' plays survive, often only a single line.[10] The greatest number of surviving fragments come from the *Aegisthus.* Eight fragments from this play exist, yet it is unclear whether Livius used Aeschylus' *Agamemnon* or Sophocles' *Aegisthus* as a model. The dramatic action centers on the return of Agamemnon, with Cassandra, to Mycenae after the fall of Troy, and his murder and Aegisthus' subsequent usurpation of power.

Fragments 1 and 2 describe the sack of Troy and the voyage back to Greece. The speakers of these lines are unknown. The alliteration of *p*'s in fragment 1 and *c*'s and *s*'s in fragment 2 point to the influence of *carmen*-style verse techniques.[11]

(1)

> nam ut Pergama
> accensa et praeda per participes aequiter
> partita est.

> For after Pergama
> had been burned, and the booty was divided equally
> among the participants.[12]

(2)

> tum autem lascivum Nerei simum pecus
> ludens ad cantum classem lustratur.

> Then the frisky flat-nosed flock of Nereus
> frolicking to our song encircled the fleet.

Fragment 3 portrays a character, perhaps Aegisthus, as a stock tyrant onstage,[13] overstepping the bounds of nature and civilization, through a gluttonous appetite for pleasure or power:

(3)

> iamne oculos specie laetavisti optabili?

> Have you, by now, delighted your eyes with a desirable sight?

Fragments 4 and 5 describe the return of Agamemnon and Cassandra to Mycenae:

(4)

> nemo haece vostrorum ruminetur mulieri!

> Let no one of you rehash this to the woman!

(5)

> sollemnitusque †adeo ditali laudem lubens.

> Solemnly and freely (he offered) praise to god.

Details of the murder of Agamemnon are described in fragments 6 and 7, perhaps by Cassandra:

(6)
... *in sedes conlocat se regias:*
*Clytemestra*[14] *iuxtim; tertias natae occupant.*

He seats himself upon royal thrones:
Clytemnestra is next to him; their daughters occupy the thirds.

(7)
*ipsus se in terram saucius fligit cadens.*

Falling, he dashed his wounded self onto the ground.

In fragment 8, in his command to servants(?) to remove Electra (*hanc*), Aegisthus behaves like a tyrant, but his self-identification with his *maiestas* points to a Roman, rather than a Greek, concept:

(8)
*quin quod parere ⟨mihi⟩ vos maiestas mea*
*procat, toleratis temploque hanc deducitis?*[15]

Rather, that which my majesty orders you
to obey, tolerate it and lead this woman from the temple?

With the death of Agamemnon, Aegisthus and Clytemnestra emerge triumphant at the end of the play and, as in Aeschylus' version, seem to succeed unpunished. Did Livius choose this play because the mythological characters were known to his audience, or was it because the themes of power, betrayal, and usurpation evoked universal responses? Since Livius was establishing the theatre at Rome, his choices in plays played a large role in shaping his audience's perceptions of and expectations for tragedy.

How did the various elements of the first Roman audience of literary productions react to such an explosive beginning? If Livius was presenting a tragedy for the first time in 240 B.C.E., seeing a "Greek" play in Latin was a novel experience to many in his audience. Even to military personnel and government officials who had seen Greek plays performed in southern Italy, the production of a tragedy in Latin at Rome would have been a novelty, especially with Livius' operatic innovations. It is a matter of debate whether it was the opportunity to see a Greek play performed in Latin rather than in Greek that attracted Hiero II of

Syracuse, who visited Rome in 237 B.C.E. in order to view the spec-
tacles/plays.[16]

Livius, through his bold literary innovations, introduced a poetic vo-
cabulary, expressed Greek concepts in a Roman way, lessened the role
of the chorus, and established the *canticum* format—necessary first
steps toward the development of a distinct Roman tragic theatre. Livius'
success is further measured by the almost immediate appearance of a rival, Naevius, who followed Livius' lead in dramatic form and content.
From a semiotic perspective, Livius' innovative approach to adapting
Greek tragedy, in particular his use of *cantica* by a professional singer or
actors rather than the chorus, ensured that, from the beginning of the
Roman theatre, dramatic reality was not a reflection of offstage reality
(who, after all, sings their joys and fears?), but rather a construct of recognizable human experiences expressed in an unrealistic way. This sus-
pension of offstage reality demonstrates that the audience needed to be
selective in its response to dramatic reality: this action is realistic; however, that one is not, but rather is theatrical. Livius, therefore, lay the
groundwork for both theatre and metatheatre at Rome.

## NAEVIUS

The second tragedian at Rome, Gnaeus Naevius (c. 270–c. 199 B.C.E.),
faced a dilemma: should he reject Livius' innovations and present a tragedy on the Greek model, or adopt the format introduced by his precursor? Naevius chose the latter course, maintaining the diminished role of
the chorus and the use of *cantica* sung by characters, thereby continuing
the "unrealistic" dialogue format. He also contributed some innovations of his own. Naevius staged his first tragedy in Rome in 235 B.C.E.,
only five years after Livius presented his first play.[17] As the author of
both tragedies and comedies, he must have learned his dramatic technique as a member of Livius' audience at least sometime between 240
and 236/5 B.C.E.

The lack of secure dates makes it impossible to identify which plays
of Livius were staged before Naevius began his dramatic career in 235
B.C.E. There is no reason to assume Livius produced all of his plays before 235 B.C.E. For the sake of convenience it is easier to imagine a linear progression and to assume that some of Livius' plays were produced
before Naevius', although for plays written after 235 B.C.E. the converse
is equally possible. The original dates of production for Naevius' plays
are unknown, and one can date the restaging of his plays on only one

occasion—the *Equos Troianus,* which was presented at the dedication of Pompey's theatre in 55 B.C.E. Others may have enjoyed a vogue in the late Republic, but the sources are silent.

The titles of Naevius' plays reveal a fondness for mythological material associated with the Trojan War cycle: *Andromache*(?),[18] *Equos Troianus, Hector proficiscens, Hesione,* and *Iphigenia.*[19] His only other known tragedies, the *Danae* and *Lycurgus,* appear to be examples of *contaminatio,* the fusing of plots from different originals.[20] From a dramaturgical point of view, this raises an important question concerning the audience's knowledge and reception of the technique: does *contaminatio* require the audience to recognize this fusion, or can it just enjoy the result without knowing anything about the process? If the recognition of the technique is required, then Naevius inserts yet another interpretative for the audience to consider as it follows the dramatic action on the stage.

The writer of both tragedies and comedies in his youth, Naevius turned to epic in his old age and composed in saturnians—the meter used by Livius in his own epic, the *Bellum Punicum,* which described the mythological origins and contemporary history of the Punic Wars.[21] Yet in his *Vita,* Naevius is remembered as a *comicus* rather than a tragedian.[22] His skill as a comic writer is also noted by Volcacius Sedigitus, who places him third in his list of top comic writers at Rome. Many of the characters common in the plays of Plautus first appeared in Naevius' plays.[23] Part of his fame as a comic writer may rest on his famous lampoons, such as the one suggesting that the Metelli owed their political power to chance rather than intelligence: *fato Metelli Romae fiunt consules.* This supposed feud with the Metelli earned him their rejoinder—*malum dabunt Metelli Naevio poetae*—and eventually led to imprisonment and exile in 201 B.C.E., but the evidence surrounding this episode is inconclusive.[24] According to Cicero, Naevius' Old Comedy–style attack against figures of state served as a warning to later poets at Rome.[25]

Naevius' contributions to the creation of a Roman theatre were many. In addition to the practice of *contaminatio,* Naevius introduced a new dramatic genre with specific Roman content called the *fabula praetexta.* Themes of his historical drama deal with remote legendary or quasi-historical subjects, such as his *Romulus sive Lupus,*[26] or with the military success of his patron, such as his *Clastidium,* which described M. Claudius Marcellus' victory over the Insubrian Gauls in 222 B.C.E. The *Clastidium* brought a contemporary figure and theme and, more important for the further development of metatheatricality, introduced offstage realism to the tragic stage.[27] Moreover, those members of the audience who personally knew the person being depicted onstage could weigh whether that depiction was accurate and whether the events portrayed or related were historically correct.

As with the case of Livius, few fragments survive from Naevius' tragedies. Of those that do survive, the fragments from the *Danae* reveal aspects of the metatheatricality of Naevius' tragedies difficult to recover elsewhere. The play contains Roman elements: *cantica, carmen*-style verse techniques, and specific Roman concepts drawn from the audience's world, such as that of a *pater familias*. The Greek model or models for the *Danae* are unknown, but possibilities include Sophocles' *Acrisius, Danae*(?), and *Men of Larissa,* and Euripides' *Danae.* If the plot of Naevius' play was culled from more than one of these plays, as the fragments suggest, then we have *contaminatio* in a tragedy, in which case one cannot rule out the possible influence of Livius' *Danae.*

The basic outline of the myth is as follows: Acrisius, fearing an oracle that a grandchild would kill him, imprisons his daughter Danae, who is then loved by Jupiter in the form of a shower of gold. Danae and her resultant son, Perseus, are locked in a chest and put out to sea by Acrisius, and they drift until they finally reach Seriphus.

Eleven fragments of Naevius' *Danae* survive, but they are difficult to place within the dramatic action of the play. The action seems to center on events after the rape of Danae, when Acrisius punishes her with imprisonment and exile for the birth of Perseus. Fragment 1 may describe either Jupiter or Acrisius:

(1)
*omnes formidant homines eius valentiam.*

All men fear his power.[28]

In fragment 2, the speaker (Danae's father?) defends or mocks Danae's current/former condition and invites another character (and the audience) to look at Danae:

(2)
*contempla placide formam et faciem virginis.*[29]

Examine quietly the shape and beauty of a virgin.

(3)
*excidit orationis omnis confidentia.*

All confidence of speech was lost.

Does Acrisius accuse Danae of promiscuity in fragment 4?

(4)

*eam nunc esse inventam probris compotem scis.*

Now you know that she was caught a friend to filth.

In fragment 5, Danae seems to recount how Jupiter seduced her in what appears to be a euphemism for sex. The emphasis on Danae's hand recalls a Roman wedding ceremony, for which the hands of the betrothed were joined to signify their union:

(5)

*auri rubeo fonte lavere ⟨me⟩ memini manum.*

I remember that I washed my hand in a redness of gold.

Does fragment 6 contain Danae's complaint on the unfair treatment of women, or Acrisius' fears of gossip concerning Danae's pregnancy?[30]

(6)

*desubito famam tollunt, si quam solam videre in via.*

Straightaway do men start a scandal, if they see a woman alone in the street.

In fragment 7, Acrisius justifies his punishment of Danae:

(7)

*quin, ut quisque est meritus, praesens pretium pro factis ferat.*

Indeed, just as each man deserves, let him have the reward for his deeds.

Danae protests her innocence in fragment 8:

(8)

*indigne exigor patria innocens.*

Innocent, am I unworthily driven from my homeland.

Is fragment 9 a reference to Semele?

(9)

*. . . quae quondam fulmine icit Iuppiter.*

(She whom) Jupiter once struck with a thunderbolt.

Fragments 10 and 11 describe Danae's appeals to Jupiter for help and his apparent response:

(10)

*manubias suppetiat pro me.*

Let him send forth attending slaves on my behalf.

(11)

*suo sonitu claro fulgorivit Iuppiter.*

Jupiter flashed with his own loud thunder.

It is only when the poetry and dramatic works of Naevius and Livius are held up in comparison with the more sophisticated poetry of Ennius and the later Republican poets that they appear deficient in poetic syntax and language.[31] Cicero compares Naevius' poetry with that of his successor Ennius rather than with that of his precursor Livius, thus suggesting that Naevius' style anticipated Ennius' innovations more than it reflected Livius.[32] Yet Naevius' success should be based on his adoption of Livius' innovations to the genre and on his furthering of metatheatrical elements. With Ennius, rhetoric is further exploited as tragedy becomes even more open to offstage culture, culminating in the heavily rhetoricized plays of Pacuvius and Accius. Only after the establishment of a theatre can the concept of theatricality be recognized by the audience and applied to the interpretation of offstage events.

## ENNIUS

Ennius experienced an early and formative contact with Greek culture owing to his birthplace at Rudiae in southern Italy. According to Suetonius, the proximity of his birthplace to Greek culture made him *semigraecus.*[33] Ennius himself boasted that he had three souls as a result of his broad cultural exposure: *Ennius tria corda habere sese dicebat quod loqui Graece et Osce et Latine sciret.*[34] Like Naevius, he served in the military.[35] Afterward, Ennius was brought to Rome from Sardinia by M. Porcius Cato in 204 B.C.E.[36] He lived on the Aventine close to the Temple of Minerva and, like Livius, taught for his livelihood. After Cato, Ennius received the patronage of M. Fulvius Nobilior, and he cultivated the friendship of many important men of state, like the elder Scipio Africanus.[37]

Ennius' literary output was prodigious. In addition to writing tragedy and comedy, Ennius further developed Naevius' innovations in historical epic with his *Annales*. He also wrote a poem about Scipio Africanus, four books of satires, and various treatises. Ennius wrote many successful tragedies concurrently with his *Annales*, the last of which, the *Thyestes*, dates to 169 B.C.E.[38]

Ennius' tragedies bring a recognizable Roman world onto the stage, which contributed to the growing reciprocity between onstage and offstage reality begun by Naevius. Like Naevius, Ennius wrote *praetextae* and incorporated specific Roman elements into his tragedies. Fuller development of metatheatrical allusions by Ennius leads to the growing recognition of theatricality off the stage. If Romans could see themselves on the stage, it was inevitable that they would recognize theatrical allusions off the stage. To this end, Ennius paved the way for Pacuvius and Accius to exploit rhetoric further and anticipate the blurring of on- and offstage reality during the late Republic and early Empire.

Metatheatrical allusions to the audience's reality abound in Ennius' tragedies, in a way that recalls the mixing of Greek and Roman customs common in Roman comedy. In his *Iphigenia*, for example, Ennius alters his Euripidean model (446–449) to people the stage with Romans when Agamemnon laments the impending sacrifice of his daughter:

> *plebes in hoc regi antistat loco: licet*
> *lacrumare plebi, regi honeste non licet.*[39]

> Common people are better than their king in this:
> the people may cry, but the king may not with dignity.

By drawing on the audience's knowledge of Roman class distinctions, Ennius imbues Agamemnon with Roman aristocratic personality traits.[40] Later in the same play the chorus, rather than Achilles, as in Euripides, stresses the politically charged Roman concepts of *otium* and *negotium*:[41]

> *otio qui nescit uti . . .*
> *plus negoti habet quam cum est negotium in negotio.*
> *nam cui quod agat institum est †in illis† negotium*
> *id agit, ⟨id⟩ studet, ibi mentem atque animum delectat suum:*
> *†otioso initio† animus nescit quid velit.*
> *hoc idem est: em neque domi nunc nos nec militiae sumus.*
> *imus huc, hinc illuc; cum illuc ventum est, ire illinc lubet.*
> *incerte errat animus, praeter propter vitam vivitur.*[42]

He who does not know how to use leisure . . .
has more of work than when there is work in work.
For to whom a task has been set, he does the work,
desires it, and delights his own mind and intellect:
in leisure, a mind does not know what it wants.
The same is true (of us); we are neither at home or in the battlefield;
we go here and there, and wherever there is a movement, we are
    there too.
The mind wanders unsure, except in that life is lived.

Considering his style and expression more refined than those of Livius and Naevius, Ennius sought to distance himself and his poetry from their works:[43]

scripsere alii rem
vorsibus quos olim Faunei vatesque canebant
cum neque Musarum scopulos [. . .]
nec dicti studiosus quisquam erat ante hunc.
nos ausi reserare. . . .[44]

 Others wrote history
in verses that once the Fauns and seers used to sing
when neither the mount of the Muses [. . .],
nor was there anyone learned in literature before him.
We dared to unlock. . . .

Despite protests to the contrary, Ennius' epic, like his tragedies, betrays an admiration for the form of tragedy developed by Livius and Naevius[45]—in particular, the reduced role of the chorus in favor of *cantica,* with full exploitation of *carmen*-style verse techniques. In the *Alexander,* for example, Cassandra's piteous speech describing her mantic state makes heavy use of alliteration and assonance. One also finds a *figura etymologica,* two words of the same root meaning in noun and verb form (*fatis fandis*), and a *versus quadratus,* an archaic verse meter, in the final line:

sed quid oculis rapere visa est derepente ardentibus?
ubi illa paulo ante sapiens †virginali† modestia?

mater, optumatum multo mulier melior mulierum,
missa sum superstitiosis hariolationibus;

†neque† me Apollo fatis fandis dementem invitam ciet.
virgines vereor aequalis, patris mei meum factum pudet,
optumi viri. mea mater, tui me miseret, mei piget.
optumam progeniem Priamo peperisti extra me. hoc dolet:
men obesse, illos prodesse, me obstare, illos obsequi.[46]

But what did she seem to see suddenly with burning eyes?
Where is she who was so recently wise with virgin modesty?

Mother, a better woman by far than the best women,
I was driven by superstitious prophecies;
Apollo stirs me [not] unwilling, in my mad state, by fate foretold.
I feel shame before virgins my age, my deeds cause my father, the best of
    men, shame.
Mother, I pity you, despise myself.
Except for me, you have given birth to the best offspring for Priam. That
    grieves me:
I injure, they protect; I oppose, they follow.

In the *Andromeda,* the description of the slain sea monster is full of alliteration and assonance:

alia fluctus differt dissupat
visceratim membra, maria salsa spumant sanguine.[47]

A wave separates and spreads other
torn-apart limbs, the salty sea froths with blood.

This resembles the *carmen*-style technique apparent in the *Chresphontes,* where Merope laments the fate of her husband Cresphontes:

neque terram inicere, neque cruenta convestire corpora
mihi licuit, neque miserae lavere lacrimae salsum sanguinem.[48]

Neither was I allowed to sprinkle earth, nor to cover the bloody bodies,
nor to wash the blood with the salt of a pitiful tear.

In the *Phoenix,* one surprisingly finds an unknown speaker stating impressively, if only for sheer linguistic manipulation,

†stultus est qui cupida† cupiens cupienter cupit.[49]

He is foolish who desires desirously, desiring with a desirous (heart).

A speech by Phoenix (to Amyntor?) from the same play contains examples of wordplay (*virum/virtute; adversum adversarios*) and puns (*innoxium, obnoxiosiae,* and *nocte*):

> *sed virum vera virtute vivere †animatum adiecit†*
> *fortiterque †innoxium vocaret† adversum adversarios.*
> *ea libertas est qui pectus purum et firmum gestitat;*
> *†aliae† res obnoxiosiae nocte in obscura latent.*[50]

> But for a man to live with true courage
> and to call (himself) guiltless bravely before the foe.
> This is liberty when he conducts his life pure and firm;
> other harmful things lie in obscure night.

More examples of Ennius' dramatic technique and metatheatrical allusions are apparent in the *Medea exul* than in any other surviving play. Once again, a listing of the fragments and analysis of their dramatic features provides a more useful means of measuring the dramatic action and the role played by metatheatrical elements within the play. A listing of the play's fragments will also provide a basis for comparing Accius' *Medea sive Argonautae* in chapter 2.

The *Medea exul* is based upon the *Medea* of Euripides, set in Corinth, in which Medea, hearing of Jason's marriage to Creon's daughter, plans her revenge by killing his bride, murdering her own children, and fleeing to Athens. It is very likely that Ennius wrote a second play about Medea, called *Medea,* based on Euripides' *Aigeus,* whose action is set in Athens after the events of Corinth. It is doubtful that Ennius would have combined all the events of Corinth and Athens into one play.[51] The fragments that survive provide valuable insights into Ennius' dramaturgy, especially on the matter of his play's relationship to Euripides' original.

The first fragment, in senarii, is a speech by Medea's nurse, who wishes that the ship *Argo* had never reached Colchis and initiated the terrible course of events that followed. We know from the opening lines of Euripides' play that this speech formed the opening lines of Ennius' play:[52]

> (1)
> *utinam ne in nemore Pelio securibus*
> *caesa accidisset abiegna ad terram trabes,*
> *neve inde navis inchoandi exordium*
> *cepisset, quae nunc nominatur nomine*

*Argo, quia Argivi in ea delecti viri*
*vecti petebant pellem inauratam arietis*
*Colchis, imperio regis Peliae, per dolum.*
*nam numquam era errans mea domo efferret pedem*
*Medea animo aegro amore saevo saucia.*[53]

Would that the fir timbers had not fallen to earth,
cut from the Pelian grove with axes,
and that no initial building of the ship had begun,
which is now called the *Argo,*
since conveyed on her, the select Argive men
were seeking the golden fleece of the Colchian ram,
through trickery, by order of King Pelias.
For never would my mistress Medea, sick at heart and wounded by a
    savage love,
erring, have set foot outside her house.

Ennius alters the opening lines of Euripides' play in several ways. He lists the events of the *Argo*'s voyage chronologically; he omits the detail that the Argive heroes rowed the ship themselves, thereby making their social station comprehensible to a Roman audience; and he changes the *Argo*'s timber from pine to fir, which was in contemporary use in Rome. Ennius adapted rather than adopted Euripides' text.[54] In Euripides' version, the emphasis is on the arrival at Iolcus, rather than the departure from Colchis. Roman elements in versification include heavy alliteration and assonance, and a *figura etymologica, nominatur nomine.*

Fragment 2 seems to correspond to the scene in Euripides' play in which Medea confronts Jason (lines 465–519), but curiously, Ennius uses the conversational senarius, rather than the musically accompanied verse that one might typically expect in such a highly emotional scene:

(2)
*quo nunc me vortam? quod iter incipiam ingredi?*
*domum paternamne? anne ad Peliae filias?*

(JOCELYN, 217–218)

Where now shall I turn? What journey shall I begin to undertake?
To the home of my father? Or to the daughters of Pelias?

In fragment 3, Medea addresses the matrons of Corinth, rather than the generic women found in Euripides. The first line is omitted in Jocelyn's text for metrical reasons, but I include it as a line that may be corrupt, but that, due to the *carmen*-style features, seems to preserve the context of the lost original, especially the elevated social and married status of Medea's addressees and their domicile on an *arx*, which corresponds to the Palatine Hill in Rome, rather than the city of Corinth: [55]

(3)
[*quae Corinthum arcem altam habetis matronae opulentae optimates,*]
*multi suam rem bene gessere et publicam patria procul;*
*multi qui domi aetatem agerent propterea sunt improbati.*

(JOCELYN, 219–220)

[You rich, optimate women who dwell on the hill of Corinth,]
many are the men who have conducted their own and the [re]public's
business well far from their homeland;
many are the men who spent their lives at home and accordingly earned
no esteem.

The highly alliterative *sententiae* following Medea's address express Roman ideas of foreign *provinciae,* typical of the jurisdictions given to contemporary magistrates, again showing adaptation rather than translation. They also reveal Medea's knowledge of public life, which betrays her status as an unconventional woman with masculine traits.

Fragment 4 comes from the dialogue between Creon and Medea, in which Medea tries to allay Creon's fear of her:

(4)
*qui ipse sibi sapiens prodesse non quit nequiquam sapit.*

(JOCELYN, 221)

The wise man who is not able to help himself is wise for nothing.

In fragment 5, the Nurse speaks about Medea's misery:

(5)
*cupido cepit miseram nunc me proloqui*
*caelo atque terrae Medeai miserias.*

(JOCELYN, 222–223)

Now a desire has seized poor me to speak
to the sky and earth about Medea's miseries.

Fragments 6–10 correspond to the scene in which Medea confronts Jason about his imminent marriage to Creon's daughter and his betrayal of their own implicit marriage bond. Jason's accusation of sexual motives in fragment 6 are central to his position that he was tricked into accepting Medea as a wife:

(6)
*tu me amoris magis quam honoris servavisti gratia.*

(JOCELYN, 224)

You saved me more for the sake of love than for honor.

In fragments 7–9, Medea informs the chorus of the significance of her conversation with Jason, which has just ended, and alludes to her intention of killing Jason, Creon, and the princess to exact vengeance. The use of the word *blandiloquentia* in fragment 7 makes it clear that deception played a role in securing Medea a place in Jason's expedition:

(7)
*nequaquam istuc istac ibit; magna inest certatio.*
*nam ut ego illi supplicarem tanta blandiloquentia*
*ni ob rem —*

(JOCELYN, 225–227)

There is no way that the business will go there; great is the struggle.
For would I have begged him as a suppliant with such sweet expressions unless because. . . .

(8)
*qui volt quod volt ita dat ⟨semper⟩ se res ut operam dabit.*

(JOCELYN, 228)

He who makes a wish, that wish always turns out according to the attention he gives to it.

Fragment 9 contains Medea's intentions to exact her revenge, and the *versus quadratus* in the final line adds a ritualistic air to her threats and belie her status as a sorceress in possession of superhuman powers:

(9)
*ille traversa mente mi hodie tradidit repagula*
quibus ego iram omnem recludam atque illi perniciem dabo
*mihi maerores, illi luctum, exitium illi, exilium mihi.*

(JOCELYN, 229–231)


That man has given the means to me today
with which I shall unbolt all my anger and I will give harm to him,
sorrows to me, for him grief, disaster for him, exile for me.

Ennius preserves the shocking simplicity of Euripides' famous line:

(10)
*nam ter sub armis malim vitam cernere*
*quam semel modo parere.*

(JOCELYN, 232–233)


For I would prefer to wage my life three times under arms
than only once to give birth.

In fragment 11, the chorus, which now knows of Medea's intent to kill her children, prays to Jupiter after she has left the stage:

(11)
*Iuppiter tuque adeo summe Sol qui res omnis inspicis*
*quique tuo lumine mare terram caelum contines*
*inspice hoc facinus prius quam fit. prohibessis scelus.*

(JOCELYN, 234–236)


Jupiter, and you, rather, highest Sun who see all things
and who embrace the sea, the earth, and the sky with your light,
look upon this deed before it comes to pass. Prevent a crime.

The Paedagogus addresses the Nurse in fragment 12:

(12)
*antiqua erilis fida custos corporis,*
*quid sic te extra aedis exanimatam eliminat?*

(JOCELYN, 237–238)


Ancient faithful guardian of your mistress' person,
why have you come outside of your house, breathless?


Fragment 13 is out of dramatic context here and seems to come from Ennius' second play about Medea, which is set in Athens—unless, of course, this is an example of *contaminatio* and the play is set in both Corinth and Athens. The city of Athens is pointed out to Medea:

(13)
*asta atque Athenas anticum opulentum oppidum*
*contempla et templum Cereris ad laevam aspice.*

(JOCELYN, 239–240)


Look upon Athens, an ancient and wealthy city,
and look to your left upon the Temple of Ceres.

The mixture of Greek (Athens) and Roman (Ceres) elements in this fragment are reminiscent of the fictional world of Roman comedy, which is a composite of the two cultures.

The contexts and placement of fragments 14–16 are very difficult to determine. In fragment 14, Medea says goodbye to her children, who do not appear in Euripides' version; therefore Ennius heightens the pathos of the scene for a Roman audience, which comes through even in the image of Medea's hands intertwined with those of her sons, since we know those very hands will soon take their lives:

(14)
*salvete optima corpora.*
*cette manus vestras measque accipite.*

(JOCELYN, 241–242)


Farewell, best of souls.
Give your hands and accept mine.

Fragment 15 contains an address to Helios, Medea's grandfather:

(15)
*sol qui candentem in caelo sublimat facem.*

(JOCELYN, 243)

Sun, you who lift your shining face in the sky.

Medea's love for Jason is mentioned in fragment 16, and the internal repetition of words signifying a heart (*cordis . . . corde*) calls particular attention to her amorous desires, if not her sexual appetite:

(16)
*utinam ne umquam †mede† cordis cupido corde pedem extulisses. . . .*

(JOCELYN, 244)

[Medea,] would that you had never set out with desirous heart. . . .

The context of fragment 17 is unclear as well:

(17)
*fructus verborum aures aucupant.*

(JOCELYN, 245)

Ears yearn for the fruit of words.

These fragments make it clear that Ennius adapted his Greek original in many important ways to make the dramatic action and characters intelligible to a Roman audience, as in the alteration of Greek concepts and the elevation of social status of the Argive heroes and the Corinthian women in the *Medea*. Metatheatrical allusions make Ennius' play at once Greek and Roman. Greek characters are transformed into Romans in a drama, which, while ostensibly unrealistic and set in the timeless spaces of Greek mythology, nevertheless was as accessible as contemporary Rome.

THE AUDIENCE

Interpretation of tragedy requires interpreters in the audience. The "audience" of the earliest tragic productions was, of course, not a monolithic group, but one that was composed of various diverse groups. There has been much effort to identify the social groups in the audiences of the third

28

and second centuries B.C.E., and to determine the influence that each group exerted on scenic productions in particular and popular culture in general. The upper classes, for example, are commonly associated with tragedy; the lower classes, however, are associated with Plautine comedy and the native Italian Atellana and mime.[56] It is important to stress that tragedy and comedy shared not only meter, language, and mythical subject matter, but also an audience, as the concurrent development of the two genres after 240 B.C.E. shows. Both groups continued to attend all types of scenic entertainment throughout the Republic. Otherwise, what need would there have been for legislation governing the seating arrangements of the theatre according to public rank and class? Moreover, the aristocracy took an interest in performance spaces.[57]

Related to the question of the audience's composition is that of the level of its cultural sophistication. As Charles Gorton states, "The general history of drama from 240 B.C. has been summed up as 'the hellenizing of the Roman stage' (Jocelyn [1967], 12–23). The vital first forty or fifty years had been a time of healthy rankness with an audience blessedly ignorant of rules and schools."[58] However, the evidence of tragic and comic texts points to genres built upon fully developed Greek models, which in itself suggests that the audience's interpretive abilities were not expected to grow gradually with the emerging theatre, but rather were expected to be in place from the beginning, as witnessed by the inclusion of metatheatrical elements in the earliest plays. A confused or unsatisfied initial audience would have been difficult to attract to subsequent productions. Yet within the first forty or fifty years, Livius, Naevius, and Ennius attracted and retained an audience for a variety of dramatic works, which suggests that the audience was not ignorant of either thematic material or metatheatrical elements that were in keeping with its taste for rhetoric. Allegory, on the dramatic level, does not seem to have been above the sophistication of the audience, especially before the availability of written literary texts.[59] Indeed, the audience may have been first introduced to allegory through theatrical productions.

The audience of Plautus' comedies seems to have been acquainted with myths through previous exposure to the performance of Latin tragedy.[60] It is difficult to find specific verbal parallels between tragic and comic texts because of the paucity of fragments, yet some verbal echoes are detectable. Ennius' tragedies provide some clues to the interrelationship. Line 932 of the *Bacchides,* for example, is considered a parody of a line from Ennian tragedy. Plautus' *o Troia, o patria, o Pergamum, o Priame periisti senex* in its context points to a parody of tragedy, but its model can be made specific by comparing it to Ennius' *o pater, o patria, o Priami domus.* Other examples have been collected by Ribbeck.[61] Comic parody, however, is not limited to tragedy only, and an example from the *Annales* has been offered in support of Plautus' exploitation of Latin poetry for comic material: *o Tite, tute, Tati, tibi tanta tyranne tulisti,* which seems to be parodied in the *Pseudolus* (191 B.C.E.): *io te te, turanne, te te ego, qui imperitas Pseudolo* (702).[62] The use of *turanne* and the alliteration of *te* and *t* sounds continues in the lines following 702, but this line itself does not seem sufficient to assign the Ennian line as its model.

Fraenkel, however, in his *Plautinisches im Plautus,* argues that the Chrysalus passage (925–978) in the *Bacchides* of Plautus is largely a free composition by Plautus himself and is based neither on a Greek model nor on a specific tragic precedent.[63] Yet this passage alludes to tragedy and provides an extended parody of a tragic scene, which is presented in a way that assumes the audience's knowledge of events surrounding Troy's destruction, including the roles played by heroes such as Agamemnon, Menelaus, and Ulysses. Furthermore, this tragic parody trivializes the mythical event by likening it to Chrysalus' attempts to raise money, and it further parodies the fall of Troy by presenting Chrysalus in the guise of a hero, in attendance at the battle itself. While buffoonery can always be appreciated by various members of the audience, this scene can best be understood by an audience versed in the specifics of events around Troy and the tragic circumstances of its fall. The tragedies dealing with the Trojan cycle would have provided this information.[64]

The fragments from the plays of Livius, Naevius, and Ennius illustrate that the stage was not the exclusive domain of actors, unconnected with the reality of the audience. Ennius' rhetorical skill contributed to the perception of offstage theatricality in that only once actors say and do things appropriate to the theatre can they be quoted and imitated offstage and recognized as theatrical. The involvement of the audience or the inclusion of the audience's reality on the tragic stage points to metatheatre developing concurrently with the theatre itself: the recreation of the audience's reality onstage leads to a perception of theatre, whereas the recreation of stage reality or the framing of offstage reality in relation to the theatre leads to a perception of theatricality offstage. In chapter 2, I consider the plays of Pacuvius and Accius, examining the effects of this reciprocal theatricality between the stage and the audience and role played by rhetoric to produce tragedies that call attention to their own theatricality.

# THEATRICALIZING
# TRAGEDY

*aiunt Accium interrogatum, cur causas non ageret, cum apud eum in tra-*
*geodiis tanta vis esset optime respondendi, hanc reddidisse rationem,*
*quod illic ea dicerentur quae ipse vellet, in foro dicturi adversarii essent*
*quae minime vellet.*

(QUINTILIAN *INST.* 5.13.43)

They claim that when Accius was asked why he did not plead cases, when
in his tragedies there was such a talent of refuting excellently, he gave the
reason that in his plays the characters said whatever he wished, but in the
law courts his opponents would say things he would not wish.

Accius' clever response that whereas he could put speeches into the
mouths of his characters, but not into those of his opponents in the law
courts, points to similarities in style, beyond argumentation, between
the rhetoric of the forum and that of the tragic stage recognized by those
audience members posing the question.[1] The reciprocity between the
theatre and the forum leads to the recognition of theatrical elements
in oratory and of rhetorical elements in the theatre—the orator as actor
and the actor as orator—and accordingly, the perception, and in this
case the self-identification, of theatre spectators with a forum audience.[2]
What emerges is an audience, whether in the theatre or in the forum,
that is attuned to role-playing and able to identify with rhetorical personalities and constructs. As a result, public figures, whether or not they
actively encourage a connection between themselves and the theatre, are
identified as role-playing; for such figures, even attending a show becomes a political and theatrical act in that they could be applauded or

hissed by the audience or targeted by actors from the stage.[3] Persons become personas.

Despite Ennius' use of rhetoric to effect metatheatrical allusions to the audience's reality, the extent to which his audience applied their perception of theatricality to modes of expression or to the interpretation of events offstage is uncertain. However, examples of the audience's perception and promotion of theatricality offstage are numerous for the period following the original presentation dates of Pacuvius' and Accius' plays. Cicero, for example, presents himself as an actor on the world stage:

> *sic obtinui quaesturam . . . ut omnium oculos in me unum conlectos esse arbitrarer, ut me quaesturamque meam quasi in aliquo terrarum orbis theatro existimarem.*[4]

> So I held the office of quaestor . . . in such a way that I thought the eyes of all were concentrated upon me alone, and that I considered myself and the office as if they were in some theatre of the world.

Even before Cicero's role in the Catilinian conspiracy, he was eager to draw attention to the dramatic nature of his actions by presenting himself as an actor upon the world political stage, as though he were "starring" in his own *praetexta*.[5] The theatricality of Cicero's pose is reinforced by many examples in the late Republic of the confusion between theatre and reality. Plutarch records that in Parthia (not Rome), Crassus' head was incorporated into a production of Euripides' *Bacchae* following the Battle of Carrhae, near the actual battle site. When the actor playing Agave entered the stage carrying Crassus' head at that point in the play when Pentheus' head is displayed, the actual slayer of Crassus, who was in the audience, stood up and took credit for the deed, rather than let the actor speaking Agave's lines do so, thus confusing theatre and reality to produce metatheatre on many levels: the audience's (offstage) reality was incorporated into the dramatic production with audience intrusion into an already nonillusory drama. Plutarch likens this banter between audience and actor to an *exodium,* or after-play, which in the time of Cicero usually consisted of a mime presentation following the production of a tragedy (*Crass.* 3.3). But unlike an exodium, in which actors and audience expect an exchange, here we have the creation of a new performance text during an actual performance—the audience watches the assassin interact with the author portraying Agave; the actor(s) onstage watch the assassin and other members of the audience interact and alter the dramatic text. Later, in the spirit of a mime *exodium,* Augustus, on his deathbed, asked if he had performed well in the mime of life (Suet. *Aug.* 99), thus suggesting that his life could be equated with a drama and transforming those standing by his bed into a theatre audience.

Cicero extends the metaphor of the forum as theatre by presenting a trial as a stage performance: *introitus fuit fabulae Clodianae (Att.* 1.18.2), thereby giving ordinary actions and events an extraordinary or theatrical emphasis. Moreover, as also cited in the introduction, Cicero quotes from tragedies in his speeches and self-identifies with actors portraying mythological roles.[6] For example, he associates himself with Medea when he quotes from Ennius' *Medea, quo nunc me vortam?* in a speech on the potential conviction of his client Murena, and again later in a letter to Atticus concerning his strained relationship with Antony in 49 B.C.E.[7]

Allusions to the theatre arising from the forum could also come from the audience, as in the case of the orator Hortensius, whose effeminacy earned him comparisons with a mime actress.[8] The gestures of those off-stage began to resemble the gestures of actors onstage, since the term "theatrical" now applied to both actors on the stage and spectators/ actors in the audience.[9] Reception by the theatre audience gave political/public figures "cues" on how to shape their public personas or images, or to guide the public's perception of their actions, though not without risk, since identification and applause could result in *infamia* and *turpitudo* in what Parker describes as the "semiotics of failure."[10]

The perpetuation of offstage theatricality affects the audience's perception of dramatic reality (the theatre's illusion of offstage reality), leading to the paradoxical question, "Is this realistic?" when what is being asked is whether the action on the stage accurately reflects the theatricality of reality off the stage (or the audience's perception of it). Boyle has characterized Seneca's plays as (metatheatrical) tragedies that "point to themselves as verbal and performative constructs of the theatrical imagination," calling them "language theatricalised," but traces of this metatheatricality are already apparent in the plays of Pacuvius and Accius.[11] These dramatists present a dramatic reality that has at once connections to and differences with the theatre (world of actors) and the *cavea* (world of the audience) as it points to its own theatricality. This chapter examines how the audience's increasing awareness of theatricality offstage is due in part to the reciprocal theatricality between rhetoric and drama onstage in the plays of Pacuvius and Accius. What emerges is tragedy theatricalized.

## PACUVIUS

Pacuvius, the nephew of Ennius, was born at Brundisium in 220 B.C.E. and died in 130 B.C.E. Little is known about his career except that he was a dramatist of modest output in the circle of Laelius, and that he was also a painter.[12] The *Vita* of Pacuvius states that in addition to painting he sold plays, but this must be a reference to a dramatist's customary practice of selling plays to aediles.[13] Pacuvius earned a reputation in antiquity as a *tragoediarum scriptor* not because he excelled in writing tragedy over other dramatic and literary genres, but because he was the only early tragedian who limited himself strictly to the writing of tragedies.[14]

In his critique of the plays of Pacuvius and Accius, Quintilian focuses on the use of language, however deficient by his contemporary standards, to express serious thought and to present dignified characters:

> *tragoediae scriptores veterum Accius atque Pacuvius clarissimi gravitate*
> *sententiarum, verborum pondere, auctoritate personarum. ceterum nitor*
> *et summa in excolendis operibus manus magis videri potest temporibus*
> *quam ipsis defuisse. virium tamen Accio plus tribuitur; Pacuvium videri*
> *doctiorem qui esse docti adfectant volunt.*

(QUINT. *INST.* 10.1.97)

> The tragedians Accius and Pacuvius are the most noteworthy of the old writers for the seriousness of their reflections, the weight of their words, and the dignity of their characters. But the lack of elegance and polish in the revision of their works is a shortcoming more of their times rather than of themselves. Nevertheless, of the two, Accius is more rigorous; Pacuvius is considered more learned by those who aspire to learnedness.

Quintilian's interests lie in oratorical rhetoric, so his silence on the effect of their language on the dramatic action of their plays should not surprise us. The chance survival of fragments seems to point to an emphasis of rhetoric over plot, since the large number of riddles, philosophical discourses, and graphic descriptions overshadows, perhaps unfairly, whatever events of the plot we can reconstruct from the fragments. While caution is needed to avoid oversimplification of a complex issue, the dramatic contexts of surviving rhetorical passages point to a heightened awareness of the role of language for character delineation and metatheatrical allusion, perhaps at the expense of an economical dramatic narrative.[15]

If stage actions do begin to resemble token gestures, then we are faced with the following dilemma: does theatricality intrude on the theatre's illusion of offstage reality, or does theatricality on the stage reflect the growing awareness and perpetuation of theatricality off the stage? A character in Pacuvius' *Dulorestes* recognizes the power of rhetoric and seems to be threatened by words more than by actual violence:

> *. . . primum hoc abs te oro, minus inexorabilem*
> *faxis; ni turpassis vanitudine aetatem tuam.*
>
> *oro, nive plectas fandi mi prolixitudinem.*[16]
>
> . . . First, I beg you to make me less unyielding;
> do not spoil your age with falsity.
>
> I beg you, do not weave a complexity of speech for me.

The power of words to persuade and deceive is recognized by the speaker, who tries to remove the danger of rhetoric by confronting his or her interlocutor in a sort of preemptive strike. These appeals point to the vulnerability of the speaker and to the cleverness or deceptiveness of the unknown interlocutor, who takes on the role of an orator. This suggests that at least at one point in the play, the dramatic action centered on a rhetorical exchange or philosophic speech, yet at what cost to the audience's understanding of the play's main narrative?[17] If a character onstage was vulnerable to persuasion, so, too, was the audience. Bilinski, for example, argues that Pacuvius' sympathy for the plebs in the *Dulorestes* and the *Chryses* contributed to the Sicilian slave revolt.[18]

The audience's reaction to the presentation or questioning of Greek philosophical ideas within the larger context of the play's dramatic action is also a question.[19] The fragments of Pacuvius' *Armorum iudicium*, for example, point to an extended treatment of the debate between Ajax and Odysseus, but this debate is a central feature of the myth and may even reflect the prominence of the debate scene in Aeschylus' play (*Hoplon krisis*). Since Pacuvius' play does not survive, however, certainty is impossible.[20] Similarly, in the *Teucer*, the central focus of the play seems to be Teucer's defense to his father Telemon of his actions in the death of his brother Ajax.[21]

Pacuvius did not strive for complete audience identification with his characters in that he used the archaicizing language of his dramatic precursors and coined some odd expressions to elevate his poetry from contemporary expression. In the *Medus*, for example, Medea says, *possum ego istam capite cladem averruncassere* ("I can avert that harm from your person"), in language derived from archaic prayer formulas;[22] and from the *Teucer*, the well-known description of a herd of dolphins: *Nerei repandirostrum incurvicervicum pecus* ("the flat-snouted humpnecked herd of Nereus").[23] Lucilius satirizes Pacuvius for using convoluted expressions in his prologues: *verum tristis contorto aliquo ex Pacuviano exordio* ("Truly a downer from some convoluted prologue of Pacuvius").[24] Lucilius gives the impression that all of Pacuvius' prologues were convoluted, but there is no way to know whether such a criticism applies to other parts of the play. Pacuvius' use of wordplay, however, served a dramaturgical purpose, as it does in Accius' plays, since it contributed to psychological realism in his character-drawing. Cicero, for example, was stirred by the emotional range allowed to the actor expressing Telemon's rage in the *Teucer*.[25] Also, in his celebrated *Iliona*, the speech by the Umbra that begins

> *mater, te appello, tu, quae curam somno suspensam levas*
> *neque te mei miseret, surge et sepeli natum ⟨tuum⟩ . . .*

> Mother, I call you, you who lighten your care with deep sleep
> do not pity me, rise and bury your son . . .

elicited audience sympathy and was famous in antiquity.[26] This passage also attracted notoriety since the actor Fufius actually fell asleep in his performance of the play.[27]

The effect of this language was to make the text more complex and engaging to the audience, however removed it was from everyday experience. Nowhere is this more apparent in the extant fragments than in a *canticum* on Fortune from an unknown play, possibly the *Dulorestes*:

> *Fortunam insanam esse et caecam et brutam perhibent philosophi,*
> *saxoque instare in globoso praedicant volubilei.*
> *id quo saxum impulerit fors, eo cadere Fortunam autumant.*
> *insanam autem esse aiunt, quia atrox incerta instabilisque sit:*
> *caecam ob eam rem esse iterant, quia nil cernat quo sese adplicet:*
> *brutam, quia dignum atque indignum nequeat internoscere.*
> *sunt autem alii philosophi, qui contra Fortuna negant*
> *ullam miseriam esse, temeritatem esse omnia autumant.*
> *id magis veri simile esse usus re apse experiundo edocet:*
> *velut Orestes modo fuit rex, factust mendicus modo.*[28]

Philosophers claim that Fortune is unsound, blind, and dumb,
and they say that she stands on a rolling ball of stone.
Where chance hurls that stone, there, they claim, Fortune lands.
Unsound, they say, is Fortune since she is fierce, uncertain, and unstable:
Blind, they repeat, since she does not know where she steers herself:
Dumb, because she cannot discern between what is worthy and
    unworthy.
There are other philosophers, however, who counter that there is no
    misery in Fortune,
but that rashness is present in all things.
That this is more similar to the truth, practice teaches by experience:
just as once Orestes was a king, but then was a beggar.

Within the analysis of the opposing philosophical views, ideas are arranged with paratactic precision, with an emphasis on argumentation. The three main qualities of Fortune, *insanam, caecam,* and *brutam,* are analyzed in order, and the appearance of these words at the beginning of three consecutive sentences points to strict parataxis in the style of archaic *carmen*. The emphasis, however, does not seem to be on Fortune, but rather on the various philosophical arguments.[29] The *canticum* format suggests that the passage was sung or recited at a key moment in the play, but the emphasis on the definition of Fortune seems to undercut its effectiveness in describing the fate of Orestes. The simile begins, however, just where this fragment ends, so perhaps the remainder of the speech focused more on Orestes than is apparent.

An examination of the extant fragments of the *Antiopa* reveals a play where Pacuvius uses rhetoric/sophistic debate to delineate character. The Greek model for the *Antiopa* was Euripides' play of the same name. The myth of Antiopa revolves around her rape by Zeus, after which she fled from her father Nycteus, king of Boeotia, to Sicyon, where she married Epopeus. Upon Nycteus' death, his brother Lycus and his wife Dirce punished Antiopa by killing Epopeus and imprisoning her. At some point in her journey, Antiopa gave birth to twins, Amphion and Zethus, whom she exposed but who were discovered and raised by shepherds. It was while fleeing prison that Antiopa was accidentally reunited with her sons, who helped her punish Lycus and Dirce for their crimes. In Pacuvius' play, Amphion and Zethus are adult herdsmen who bide their time in sophistic debate until the chance arrival of their hitherto unknown mother, Antiopa. Amphion and Zethus betray an education at odds with their circumstance, recalling the overeducated shepherds of bucolic poetry. Upon discovering their mother's identity, the twins punish Dirce, who has attempted to recapture her.[30]

The surviving fragments are somewhat difficult to place within Euripides' play.[31] The most problematic fragments are the lines in which Antiopa reveals her identity to the twins, since it is unclear whether they should be placed before or after Dirce's arrival onstage.

Fragment 1 informs the audience of the twins' identity:

(1)
*Iovis ex Antiopa Nyctei nati ⟨duo⟩.*[32]

(RIBBECK, 1)

[Two] sons of Jupiter by Antiopa, daughter of Nycteus.

A playful insult from one twin to the other seems to be the context of fragment 2:

(2)
*loca horrida initas.*[33]

(RIBBECK, 3)

It is you who enter uncouth places.

As with the Euripidean model, the play contained an extended philosophical debate between the twins about music in which Zethus included a long digression on wisdom and the usefulness of virtue.[34] If a debate on music were not relevant to the dramatic action, a digression on wisdom and virtue would seem even more unnecessary. We do not know whether the rest of the play's dramatic action was overshadowed by philosophical debate/character delineation.

In fragment 3, Amphion poses a riddle to the chorus of city-dwellers (*Astici*), who were perhaps present in this scene as judges to the debate between Amphion and Zethus:

(3)
{*Amphio*} *quadrupes tardigrada agrestis humilis aspera,*
*brevi capite, cervice anguina, aspectu truci,*
*eviscerata inanima cum animali sono.*
{*Astici*} *ita saeptuosa dictione abs te datur*
*quod coniectura sapiens aegre contuit:*

38

*non intellegimus, nisi si aperte dixeris.*
*{Amphio} testudo.*[35]

(RIBBECK, 4)

{Amphio} It is four-footed, slow-moving, rustic, lowly, coarse,
with a small head, snake-like neck, harsh to look at,
gutted, soulless yet with living sound.
{Astici} So thickly hidden with words is this riddle given
that someone wise would barely find it by guessing
unless you speak openly.
{Amphio} A tortoise-lyre.

This seven-line pun illustrates the emphasis of rhetoric in character delineation, but whether this appeared in a series of puns, with brother pit-
ted against brother, is unknown.

Fragments 4–6 come from Antiopa's speech, or series of speeches,
in which she relates the punishment she has endured from Lycus and
Dirce. One cannot assume, however, that these lines immediately preceded the revelation of her identity at this point in the play.

(4)
*. . . perdita inluvie atque insomnia. . . .*

(RIBBECK, 5)

. . . ruined by filth and sleeplessness. . . .

(5)
*frendere noctes, misera quas perpessa sum.*

(RIBBECK, 6)

Gnawing nights that I, wretched, endured.

(6)
*. . . fruges frendo solidas saxi robore.*

(RIBBECK, 7)

. . . I ground the thick grain with a hard rock.

The context and placement of fragment 7 is unclear, but the emphasis
on the physical effects of the sun is different from the usual appeal, in

tragedy, to the sun as witness to some crime. The passage seems more appropriate for a scientific or philosophical treatise, such as Accius' *Praxidicus,* which contained astrological information and agricultural advice.

(7)

> ... *sol si perpetuo siet,*
> *flammeo vapore torrens terrae fetum exusserit:*
> *nocti ni interveniat, fructus per pruinam obriguerint.*

(RIBBECK, 8)

> ... the sun, if it were unrelenting,
> burning with flaming gases, would scorch the fruit of the earth:
> unless it interrupted the night, fruit would freeze through frost.

Fragment 8 seems to be a speech by Antiopa, but the addressee is unknown:

(8)

*minitabilitlerque increpare dictis saevis incipit.*

(RIBBECK, 9)

S(he) began to scream threateningly with beastly words.

In fragment 9, Zethus(?) orders Antiopa and others (*vos*) away from the animal pens:

(9)

*nonne hinc vos propere ⟨e⟩ stabulis amolimini?*

(RIBBECK, 10)

Why don't you quickly remove yourself from the stables?

Fragment 10 seems to come from a speech by the shepherd who discovered the twins as infants on Mount Cithaeron. The shepherd's inability to solve the mystery contrasts sharply with the intelligence of the educated twins:

(10)

*sed cum animo attendi ad quaerendum, quid siet?*

(RIBBECK, 11)

But I focused with my mind on the problem (of) what it is.

Dirce arrives onstage with a second chorus of Maenads in pursuit of Antiopa in fragment 11:

> (11)
> *. . . cervicum*
> *floros dispendite crines.*[36]
>
> (RIBBECK, 12)

> . . . upon your neck
> let your flower-like curls fall.

Antiope addresses her sons in fragment 12, but whether her identity had been revealed until this point is unclear:

> (12)
> *salvete, gemini, mea propages sanguinis!*
>
> (RIBBECK, 13)

> I greet you, twins, offspring of my blood!

In fragment 13, Antiopa describes the filthy state in which she was kept as Dirce's captive, but since she is actually depicted as filthy, the description can only echo the obvious evidence of her current state:

> (13)
> *. . . inluvie corporis*
> *et coma prolixa impexa conglomerata atque horrida.*
>
> (RIBBECK, 15)

> . . . with filthy body
> and tangled hair uncombed, lumpy and shaggy.

The final fragment appears to be a Latinized spelling of Zethus' name but reveals little more:

> (14)
> *Setum. . . .*
>
> (RIBBECK, 16)

The play most likely ended with the punishment of Dirce, but it is unknown whether in Pacuvius' version, the death of Dirce was anticipated or reported in a messenger speech. For the title character, Antiopa, the play's ending can be interpreted as a restoration comedy, in that she is reunited with her sons, and a revenge drama, in that she is instrumental in the punishment of Dirce.

Self-expression, identification, and sophistic problem-solving seem to form the plot of the drama itself. Rhetoric removes the dramatic reality of the play from the audience's world to a metatheatrical (re)-creation of it. The play's emphasis on identity, in particular the twins' self-expression and self-identification through rhetoric and Antiopa's revelation of her identity to her sons, anticipate Seneca's "theatricalized word." We also find this in Pacuvius' *Teucer,* where Teucer's revelation of his identity to his father leads to his exile. Rhetoric, in these plays, becomes a dramatic tool by which to create character and advance the plot.

Ancient responses to Pacuvius' plays and dramatic technique were mixed. Lucilius found the awkward and obscure elements of Pacuvius ridiculous, mocking the famous Nereus passage from the *Teucer, Nerei repandirostrum incurvicervicum pecus* ("the flat-snouted humpnecked herd of Nereus") with the comment, *lascivire pecus Nerei rostrique repandum* ("to frolic [with] the flat-snouted herd of Nereus").[37] The plays of Pacuvius, however, enjoyed a vogue in the late Republic, with restagings of the *Antiopa* and the *Teucer,* perhaps due to the perpetuation of offstage theatricality that Pacuvius' plays helped to create. According to Cicero, Pacuvius was the best of the Republican tragedians.[38] Cicero in fact claimed that he preferred Pacuvius' *Odysseus* to Sophocles' in the *Niptra.*[39] Horace and Quintilian admired the Hellenism of Pacuvius' plays and called him *doctus.*[40] Persius, however, writing during the Empire, called the *Antiopa* "warty," making a pun on the filthy appearance of Antiopa in the play.[41]

## ACCIUS

Lucius Accius (170–c. 86 B.C.E.) was born at Pisaurum, the son of a freedman. Although his fame in antiquity was achieved as a writer of tragedies, the literary breadth of Accius resembles that of Ennius. Accius wrote, among numerous other works, the *Didascalia,* in which he traced the history of Latin literature from the first plays of Livius Andronicus to his own. Appreciation for Accius' style was not universal. Lucilius,

Accius' contemporary, mocked his style as he had Pacuvius'.[42] Accius' style as a tragedian was called *altus* by Horace (Ep. 2.1.56) and *animosus* by Ovid (*Am.* 1.15.19), yet later criticism of his rhetoric focused more on his language and the rhetorical devices of his speeches than on their effectiveness in portraying character and advancing the plot. The lampooning of Accius' plays by Novius and Pomponius in their farces may point to the audience's preference for comic farce.[43] Accius was no longer in vogue by the time of Tacitus, since in the *Dialogus de oratoribus,* the plays of both Accius and Pacuvius are referred to as "moldy."[44] Perhaps this fall from popularity was due to an end to the perception and fostering of a theatricalized reality encouraged by Nero both on and off the stage, which Accius' plays had come to represent.

The extant evidence identifies Ennius most often as a precursor to Accius.[45] For example, Accius followed both Ennius and Livius in composing an *Achilles* and an *Andromeda,* but Ennius alone in composing an *Alcmeo,* an *Athamas,* a *Hecuba,* a *Medea,* and a *Telephus.* Plays that first appeared only in Livius' work include the *Aegisthus* and the *Tereus.* The only play that Accius has in common with Pacuvius is the *Armorum iudicium.* Accius also continued the tradition, shared with Pacuvius, of writing *praetextae,* the *Brutus* and the *Aeneadae sive Decius,* which are examined in chapter 3.

Accius looked to new models and translated freely, often "contaminating" the plots of many tragedies, as suggested by such titles as *Agamemnonidae, Epigoni,* and *Phinidae.* Like his precursors, Accius continued to write plays with war themes—for example, there are eight plays based on the Theban Wars and fourteen plays based on the Trojan War—but he also looked to material that was seemingly unused previously, such as episodes from the *Iliad* (*Epinausimache* and *Nyctegressia*) and the *Argonautica* (*Medea sive Argonautae*).[46] From a political viewpoint, Accius' plays may have been sympathetic to the aristocracy, which, if true, would reverse Pacuvius' perceived sympathy with the plebs.[47] But it is also possible that the audience perceived a sympathy or bias inherent in plays revolving around tyrants.

In Accius' tragedies, we find the same use of rhetoric for character delineation as in Pacuvius' *Antiopa.* Perhaps it is an accident of survival, but it seems that almost all of the passages dealing with deception and persuasion emphasize the harmful effects of rhetoric.[48] Accius seems to draw attention to the art of persuasion as much as to its ill effects. In the *Astyanax,* for example, a character voices a sinister view of the profit motives of soothsayers, which evokes a similar sentiment voiced in Sophocles' *Oedipus:*

*nil credo auguribus, qui auris verbis divitant*
*alienas, suas ut auro locupletent domos.*[49]

Not at all do I trust augurs, who enrich the ears of
others, so that they can enrich their own homes with gold.

We find deception through rhetoric again in the *Agamemnonidae*, in
which a character complains about the use of lies for personal gain. Accius' pun on the words *composita* and *componas* on a shared meaning
of balance, the one literal and the other figurative, and the apposition of
*dicta* and *factis* point to irony since the speaker also knows how to
speak for effect:

sic

*multi, animus quorum atroci vinctus malitia est,*
*composita dicta e pectore evolvunt suo,*
*quae cum componas dicta factis discrepant.*[50]

Thus

many, whose hearts are conquered by acute spite,
roll out balanced tales from their own heart,
which do not balance when you weigh words against deeds.

Finally, in the *Deiphobus*, a character complains of a torrent of words
(from Odysseus?) designed to deceive. The apposition of *praesentem*
and *praesens* again betrays an ironic use of rhetoric on the part of the
aggrieved party:

*vel hic qui me aperte effrenata inpudentia*
*praesentem praesens dictis mertare institit.*[51]

Or he who, in a burst of open shamefulness
to my face, planned to drown me, facing him, with words.

Accius' seeming dialectic with rhetoric seems to reflect his audience's
experience outside of the theatre, in particular the growing audience
awareness and exploitation of a theatricalized reality off the stage that I
examine in chapters 3 and 4. This reciprocal relationship between the
theatre and the audience's perception of reality outside of the theatre,
whether due to the plays of Accius, or in part to Varius' *Thyestes* or
Ovid's *Medea*, may have anticipated and shaped how Neronian Rome
interacted with the theatre. Metatheatre was already replacing theatre,

thereby placing the plays of Seneca within the development of tragedy rather than outside it.

The similarities between Accian and Senecan drama are striking—like Senecan drama, the extant fragments of Accius' plays feature many passages containing the use of spectacle to effect pathos. Since we cannot witness a production of Accius' plays, we must focus on descriptive rather than physical spectacle, what Beacham calls "verbal violence" and "descriptive gore," such as scenes revolving around murder, cannibalization, and mutilation.[52] A correspondence has been detected between Livius' *Aegisthus* and the *Agamemnon* of Seneca, but Seneca's play may owe even more to the *Clytemnestra* of Accius, therefore suggesting that Seneca may have been drawn to metatheatrical elements in Accius' plays and included them in his own.[53] Seneca may have also been drawn to Accius through the intermediate filter of Varius Rufus and Ovid, leading one to ask whether Accius' development of tragic rhetorical style lent itself best to Ovid in his *Medea*.[54] Although Quintilian praised the play as an example of Ovid's success when his native talent was restrained, we can only infer from Ovid's other works the extent to which rhetoric defined his (and his characters'?) approach to dramaturgy.[55] Through spectacle, Accius exploits the "theatricalized word" to present tragedy that is at once theatricalized and metatheatrical.

It is an irony of the Roman theatre that not a single play survives whole from the most famous Republican tragedian. Equally unfortunate is the disappearance of his treatise, *Pragmatica,* which contained Accius' views on dramaturgical issues and, perhaps, character delineation. Despite these losses, the extant fragments of the *Medea sive Argonautae* illustrate Accius' use of rhetoric in character delineation and the presentation of a theatricalized reality onstage that we find in Pacuvius' plays.

The surviving fragments of the *Medea sive Argonautae* bear a remarkable resemblance to the story found in Apollonius Rhodius (*Argonautica* 4.303 ff.), in which Medea murders her brother Apsyrtus, who was leading an expedition of Colchians against the Argonauts. The play covers events (too many?) following the Argonauts' theft of the Golden Fleece. After Jason and Medea, with the Argonauts, flee Colchis, they land briefly at the mouth of the Ister River to discuss a plan of attack against Medea's brother Apsyrtus, who is pursuing them with a fleet of Colchians. They resolve that Medea, under false pretenses, should request a meeting with her brother in order to murder him. Some conjecture a play by Sophocles as the possible model, but that play's fragments, which reveal that Apsyrtus was portrated as a boy, suggest instead the version of the myth in which Medea kidnaps her brother and throws pieces of his cut-up corpse to delay the Colchian fleet.[56] One cannot rule out that the *Medea sive Argonautae* was an original composition by Accius in which he dramatized a story found in Greek epic, since, as noted above, he appears to have based two of his plays upon episodes in Homer's *Iliad.*

The play opens with the arrival of the Argo, which terrifies a barbarian shepherd(s) who has never seen a ship before. Although this is the first extant fragment, it may not come from the actual first lines of the play. As with the philosophical debates in Pacuvius' *Antiopa,* the shepherd's speech does not seem to advance the plot in the most economical way, but rather seems to point to its own metatheatricality. As the only ship the shepherd has ever seen, the passage reflects his inability to describe the Argo in known terms. Thus the bizarre expressions reflect his confused state. The shepherd's speech also contains distinct Roman elements such as heavy alliteration, assonance, and a reference to the Italic woodland god Silvanus, all of which are blended with a Hellenistic fondness for obscurity.

(1)

{Pastor}                    *tanta moles labitur*
*fremibunda ex alto ingenti sonitu et spiritu.*
*prae se undas volvit, vortices vi suscitat:*
*ruit prolapsa, pelagus respargit reflat.*
*Ita dum interruptum credas nimbum volvier,*
*dum quod sublime ventis expulsum rapi*
*saxum aut procellis, vel globosos turbines*
*existere ictos undis concursantibus:*
*nisi quas terrestris pontus strages conciet,*
*aut forte Triton fuscina evertens specus*
*supter radices penitus undante in freto*
*molem ex profundo saxeam ad caelum erigit.*[57]

(RIBBECK, 1)

{Shepherd}                    Such a great heap glides
roaring from the sea with a horrifying sound and hiss;
it churns the waves before it, and stirs eddies with force;
it rushes headlong, and sprays and blows upon the sea.
So that now you would think that a thundercloud, ripped, had rolled,
now that a seized rock was hurled high to the winds
or rainstorms, or round-balled waterspouts

against the coming waves;
unless the sea stirs some land-based disaster,
or by chance Triton overturning a cave with his trident
under the roots deep in the swelling waves
raises a rocky heap from the seabed to the sky.

(2/3)
*sicut lascivi atque alacres rostris perfremunt*
*delphini, item alto mulcta Silvani melo*
*consimilem ad auris cantum et auditum refert.*

(RIBBECK, 2/3)

Just as [excited] and eager dolphins let out a snort from their beaks,
similar to the woodland tune of Silvanus,
it carries a song and sound to my ears.

Before the shepherd can process the sight of the ship and compare it to
phenomena known to him, such as the effect of a thundercloud or a
hurled globe, he reacts to the sight and sound of the mysterious object.
The comparison of the Argo to a monster is effective if the ship's bow
had been painted with eyes.

(4)
*ego me extollo in abietem, alte ex tuto prospectum aucupo.*

(RIBBECK, 4)

I raise myself onto a fir tree, and take in the sight from a safe height.

Fragment 5 may designate the meeting place of Medea and Apsyrtus:

(5)
*apud vetustam turrem. . . .*

(RIBBECK, 5)

At the ancient turret. . . .

(6)
*vagant, pavore pecuda in tumulis deserunt.*
*⟨a!⟩ qui vos pascet postea?*

(RIBBECK, 6)

... They wander, and desert the flock on the hillside out of fear.
Alas! Who will pasture you from now on?

In fragments 7 and 8, Jason seems to explain the ship and the various
stages of civilization to the shepherd(s). It is not clear how, if at all, such
a discussion would advance the plot:

(7)
*prima ex immani victum ad mansuetum applicans.*

(RIBBECK, 7)

First, tamed from their savageness, they pursue cultivating pursuits.

(8)
      *... ut tristis turbinum*
*toleraret hiemes, mare cum horreret fluctibus.*

(RIBBECK, 8)

... in order to endure the dismal storms
of hurricanes, when the sea shivered with waves.

Fragment 9 seems to come from a speech by Medea describing her plan
to lure Apsyrtus by false pretenses and echoes the use of sophistry for
deception:

(9)
*nisi ut astu ingenium lingua laudem et dictis lactem lenibus.*

(RIBBECK, 9)

Unless so that I may praise his nature with clever tongue and trick him
with soft words.

Fragment 10 is difficult to assign:[58]

(10)
*exul inter hostis, exspes expers desertus vagus.*

(RIBBECK, 10)

Among enemies, homeless, hopeless, helpless, a deserted wanderer.

(11)

*. . . perite in stabulo frenos immittens feris.*

(RIBBECK, 11)

. . . expertly applying bridles to the beasts in the stable.

In fragment 12, Apsyrtus or another character may be addressing Medea, but it is possible that this fragment actually belongs to another play:[59]

(12)

*tun dia Mede's, cuius aditum exspectans pervixi usque adhuc?*

(RIBBECK, 12)

Then are you godlike Medea, whose arrival I have lived in hope for until
   now?

The dramatic context of fragments 13 and 14 is unclear, but it is possible that they come from a speech by Jason corresponding to *Argonautica* 395ff., where he calms Medea, saying that her fears of being abandoned by him are unfounded. The glibness of Jason's words is reflected in the legal metaphor *causandi*:

(13)

*qui potis est refelli quisquam, ubi nullust causandi locus?*

(RIBBECK, 13)

Who is able to be refuted when there is no chance for pleading one's
   cause?

Fragment 14 evokes a sophistic debate of proof through argumentation; even though the proof here is visual, it is described as spoken:

(14)

*principio extispicium ex prodigiis congruens ars te arguit.*

(RIBBECK, 14)

First of all, the art of examining entrails through portents argues against
   you.

After the murder of Apsyrtus and the flight of Jason and Medea, Aeetes laments the death of his son. Aeetes' presence in the play is surprising, since nowhere in Apollonius' version does Aeetes pursue the Argonauts.

(15)
*lavere salsis vultum lacrumis. . . .*

(RIBBECK, 15)

To wet my face with salty tears. . . .

(16)
*pernici orbificor liberorum leto et tabificabili.*

(RIBBECK, 16)

I am made childless by the swift and rotting death of my children.

In fragment 17, the chorus (of shepherds?) laments the unpredictability of life:

(17)
*fors dominatur, neque vita ulli*
*propia in vita est.*

(RIBBECK, 17)

Chance rules, nor in life can anyone
call life one's own.

As with Pacuvius' *Antiopa,* rhetoric removes the dramatic reality of the play from the audience's world to a metatheatrical (re)creation of it.

Theatre productions of tragedy did not end in the Republic only to be revived by Seneca.[60] Accius may have been the last great "professional" Republican writer of tragedies, but a string of authors writing for the stage "part-time" kept new productions of tragedy on the stage under the early Empire, side by side with reproductions of Republican plays.[61] These writers include C. Julius Strabo, Cassius Parmensis, C. Asinius Pollio, Varius Rufus, Ovid, Cornelius Balbus, Pomponius Secundus, and the author of the *Hercules oetaeus.*[62] Tragedy also enjoyed an authorship and audience/readership outside of the theatre as a form of private poetry written by, among others, Cicero, who translated Aeschylus' *Prometheus Unbound;* Julius Caesar, who composed an *Oedipus;* Augustus, who penned an *Ajax;* and Quintus Cicero, brother of the orator, who wrote four plays in the space of sixteen days while on campaign. None of these compositions, however, was intended for stage production. Theatre productions nonetheless continued to be immensely popular under the Empire, even though tragedy was produced on a smaller scale than productions of pantomime and Atellane farces, as the widespread construction of theatres throughout the Roman world attests.[63]

Revivals of the "classics," especially the plays of Ennius, Pacuvius, and Accius, in the late Republic, and the corresponding influence of mime productions, altered the relationship between the earlier productions and contemporary theatre reproductions. With fewer original productions on the stage from Sulla onward, allusions arising from previously staged plays took on contemporary relevance, thereby producing a dichronic theatre experience for an audience already sophisticated in dramatic allusion. Chapter 3 explores the semiotic consequences of the "competing realities" of the stage and the audience in the staging of *praetextae.* The opening program of Pompey's theatre, which included visual referents to his triumph, demonstrated to public figures exploiting the stage how the restaging of previously produced plays and the inclusion of the audience's reality could become relevant. The blending of the audience's own reality with the dramatic reality of the play led to the double interpretation of stage action: play means this (as it relates to the play's plot) and this (as it alludes to cultural/offstage personalities and events). Therefore an ambiguity between intended message and audience perception emerges, as well as a reciprocity between metatheatre and reality, on and off the stage, that finds ultimate expression in the plays of Seneca.

## THREE

# DRAMATIZING HISTORY

*spectatum veniunt, veniunt spectentur ut ipsae.*

(OVID *ARS AMATORIA* I.99)

They come to see, they come that they themselves may be seen.

Ovid's jesting interpretation of the reasons why women attend the theatre illustrates how the audience itself provided as much "theatre" as the stage did.[1] But what if the barrier between actor and audience were removed in a production of a *fabula praetexta* or historical tragedy to reveal someone from the audience represented onstage, whether or not he is seated in the audience during performance? From a performance-criticism perspective, when offstage reality pervades dramatic reality, in the case of *praetextae*, reciprocity ensues, resulting in the semiotics of competing realities: one identifies "real" persons and events onstage, and conversely, one interprets persons and events from everyday life in relation to characters and dramatic situations from the theatre.[2] The dramatization of historical or contemporary events alters the perception of reality, both on and off the stage, and intentionally breaks down the separation between the stage and the audience (= nonillusory drama). The question becomes: is what we are viewing onstage "real"?

Since the *praetexta* presented events drawn from the audience's cultural history, both remote and contemporary, the result was a play whose dramatic format was drawn from tragedy but whose content was drawn from reality itself. The dramatic genres of tragedy and literary *praetextae* developed concurrently, which means that the developing definition and perception of theatre and metatheatre are equally inter-

52

twined.[3] This chapter considers the reciprocity of "realities" in the production of *praetextae* from a dramaturgical perspective: the dramatizing of history (the way dramatists reproduce or present reality onstage) and the staging of history (the effect on the audience of viewing reality onstage). The production of *praetextae* contributed to the recognition and perpetuation of theatricality offstage, in particular under the late Republic and early Empire, that further removes the barrier between stage and audience.

## THEATRICALITY OF HISTORY

The *fabula praetexta,* or historical drama in Roman dress, was so termed after the *praetexta,* the purple-bordered toga worn by magistrates and senators.[4] The term "historical drama" is misleading, however, since *praetextae* also include legendary and quasi-historical plays, which to contemporary Romans represented history, whether family or state, rather than fiction. *Praetextae* celebrated the careers of aristocratic men of state and were privately commissioned for private and/or public performance on a number of possible occasions: triumphs, funerals, votive games, temple inaugurations, and public festivals.[5] *Praetextae* were not bought by the aediles, as in the case of tragedies. These plays depended on the patronage of a very small number of statesmen who had poets in their circle of dependents. We cannot, therefore, attribute the small number of these plays to artistic failure. Nor can we gauge their popularity on the same scale as tragedy.[6] In no modern sense were these historical plays "national" simply because their subjects also formed part of Rome's "political" history. Roman history—in essence, the history of the city of Rome—was composed of aristocratic family anecdotes about the military and political activities of their ancestors that were simultaneously events in Rome's own history.[7] Aristocratic family celebrations and national commemoration, therefore, overlapped.

Naevius is credited with introducing literary *praetextae* at Rome, but his plays were most likely preceded by nonliterary forms of drama, including *praetextae.*[8] Prior to Naevius, we know of six Greek historical plays: Phrynicus' *Sack of Miletus* and *Phoenissae;* Aeschylus' *Persians;* Moschion's *Themistocles* and *Phereus;* and the anonymous *Gyges/Candaules* tragedy, whose date is insecure.[9]

La Penna divides *praetextae* into two groups: plays having to do with the early history and myth of Rome, and those having to do with contemporary aristocratic achievements.[10] Of all these plays, only fragments exist, with the exception of the *Octavia,* which survives whole. The mythological/historical plays include the *Romulus sive Lupus* of Naevius;[11] the *Sabinae* of Ennius; the *Aeneadae sive Decius* of Accius, which enacted the self-sacrifice of Decius Mus at the Battle of Sentinum against the Samnites and Gauls in 295 B.C.E.; Accius' *Brutus,* written for D. Junius Brutus Callaicus for an unknown occasion, celebrating the expulsion of the Tarquins from Rome in 509 B.C.E.; the *Brutus* of Cassius Parmensis, apparently on the same theme; and the *Aeneas* by Pomponius Secundus.[12] These last two plays form a contrast to the contemporary and historical *praetextae* of Pseudo-Seneca's *Octavia* and Curiatus Maternus' *Cato* and *Domitius,* written much closer in time to their subjects than the Republican historical plays.

Plays about contemporary aristocratic achievements include Naevius' *Clastidium,* written to celebrate M. Claudius Marcellus' winning of the *spolia opima* over Vidumarus earlier in 222 B.C.E.; Ennius' *Ambracia,* written for M. Fulvius Nobilior in 187 B.C.E.; and the *Paullus* of Pacuvius, celebrating Aemilius Paullus' victory over King Perseus of Macedon at Pydna in 168 B.C.E. The *Paullus* was possibly staged in 160 B.C.E. at the funeral games of Paullus, together with Terence's *Adelphoe* and the second failed production of the *Hecyra.*[13] The last known Republican *praetexta* was the *Iter* or *Journey,* which was written by L. Cornelius Balbus in 43 B.C.E., but this play was never produced in Rome.

Ancient evidence concerning the definition of *praetextae* is complicated by the fact that few ancient sources actually witnessed the performance of such a play. The creation of the *praetexta* and native comedy, as Latin dramatic forms celebrating Roman deeds rather than Greek ones, was a source of literary pride for Horace (*Ars P.* 285–294), but he does not describe typical features of the plays or their production onstage:

*nil intemptatum nostri liquere poetae,*
*nec minimum meruere decus vestigia Graeca*
*ausi deserere et celebrare domestica facta,*
*vel qui praetextas vel qui docuere togatas.*

(ARS P. 285–288)

Our poets have left nothing untried
nor have they deserved the least praise for deserting Greek paths
and for celebrating native accomplishments,
whether they produce the historical drama or Roman comedy.

Cicero (*Fam.* 10.32) preserves a contemporary reaction to an actual performance of Balbus' *Iter* that I analyze from a semiotic perspective below, but he does not define typical features of the genre. Other notices are late and rely on dramatic texts for their information. The grammarian Diomedes, for example, writing his *Ars grammatica* in the late fourth century C.E., defines in a rather cursory note the difference between *praetextae* and tragedy in the following way:

> The first type is [presented] in togas, which are called *praetextatae,* in which the business of generals is conducted and affairs of state, and Roman kings and generals are brought onstage, in the dignity and high rank of the characters, just as in tragedies . . . the *togata praetextata* differs from tragedies, because in a tragedy, heroes are brought onstage, just as Pacuvius wrote tragedies under the names of heroes Orestes, Chryses, and names similar to these, Accius did the same; in the *praetextata,* however, Roman kings or generals are brought onstage, just as plays written on Brutus, Decius, or Marcellus.[14]

Diomedes states that the transactions of generals and public affairs were the themes of *praetextae,* seemingly without making a distinction between the plots of plays celebrating contemporary aristocratic achievements and mythological/historical plays. Furthermore, Diomedes writes that "the business of generals is conducted and affairs of state" are enacted onstage (*imperatorum negotia aguntur et publica*), but this could mean anything from the preparation for a battle to its conclusion, including its reenactment, as well the presentation of events of Roman/state interest (and of historic consequence). Diomedes' silence on differences in plot between tragedy and *praetextae* perhaps indicates that the format of *praetextae* was essentially similar to that of tragedies and therefore required no comment.

The main distinction that Diomedes draws between *praetextae* and tragedies is the presentation of characters—heroes in tragedies, like Orestes and Chryses, and kings and generals in *praetextae.* Of the plays he lists, the king Tarquin appears in Accius' *Brutus* with the first consul L. Junius Brutus. In the *Decius* (transmitted to us with the title *Aeneadae sive Decius*), the consul and general Decius Mus appears, while M. Claudius Marcellus appears in Naevius' *Marcellus* (*Clastidium*). Other plays not listed by Diomedes in which aristocrats may appear as characters include Ennius' *Ambracia,* with the likely appearance of a character portraying M. Fulvius Nobilior, and Pacuvius' *Paullus* (but it is unclear from the fragments whether Aemilius Paullus appeared as a character onstage). Tarquin and Brutus may have appeared in Cassius Parmensis' *Brutus*. Plays in which kings appear that are also absent from Diomedes' list include Romulus in Naevius' *Romulus sive Lupus* and Ennius' *Sabinae*, and Aeneas in Pomponius Secundus' *Aeneas*. In Pseudo-Seneca's *Octavia*, Nero, the ghost of Agrippina, and Octavia appear. Diomedes emphasizes the dignified depiction of kings and generals in *praetextae*, which points to an encomiastic treatment of the protagonists' accomplishments.[15]

Diomedes makes no distinctions between the Republican and the Imperial *praetextae*. However, many similarities and differences in the treatment of historical material and the relation of this material to contemporary culture become apparent when the plays are viewed according to their dates of composition.[16] Since only one Imperial *praetexta* survives whole, any discussion must center on the *Octavia*, but the evidence surrounding other plays suggests that the tone of the plays was no longer encomiastic but rather was critical of perceived imperial oppression. This change in tone represents an important change to the genre and deserves further examination. From a dramaturgical perspective, the relation of plays to actual events or the audience's knowledge of those events depends on both authorial intent and the audience's interpretation of onstage allusions to offstage events.

In his *Life of Romulus* (8), Plutarch observes the theatricality of events surrounding the legend of Romulus and Remus, which seemed scripted for the stage by Chance:

> Although most details are related by Fabius and Diocles of Peparethus, who seems to have been first to describe the founding of Rome, to some their dramatic and fictitious elements are a cause for suspicion; but one should not be incredulous seeing how much a poet Chance is, and when we consider that the Roman state would not have attained its current power, had it not possessed a divine origin and no small number of paradoxes.

We also find this mirroring of theatricality in everyday events expressed in Livy. The story of the two Tullias and their two Tarquin husbands that ends in two murders and the murder of a king is described as an example of the sort of crime found in tragedy (*sceleris tragici exemplum*, 1.46.3). Since offstage events mirror the theatre in irony, reversals of fortune, and heroic suffering, should they not be easily transferable onto the stage and perceived as "real"? Recreating legends with obscure or conflicting details onstage, such as Aeneas' arrival in Italy or the contest between Romulus and Remus, would provide a wide scope for drama-tists since events cannot be completely recovered, thereby making mul-tiple versions possible, and perhaps even desirable. The recreation of contemporary historical events onstage, however, poses certain prob-lems: stage events cannot stray too far from "real" events, especially when living or near-contemporary persons are portrayed onstage, ob-served by contemporaries in the audience.[17] Where does one draw the line between theatre and reality?

The relation between historical events and their recreation onstage involves the distinction between illusory and nonillusory drama, but identifying which elements the audience would have considered fictive or unrealistically presented is difficult since we cannot reconstruct an en-tire *praetexta* from the middle or late Republican period. However, one way to recover which scenes may have appeared onstage, and perhaps how they were staged, is to compare similar material in historiographic accounts. Book 15 of Ennius' *Annales,* for example, which was the orig-inal ending of the poem, covers the same material—the Aetolian cam-paign of M. Fulvius Nobilior—as his *praetexta,* the *Ambracia.*[18]

Ennius was in his sixties when composing Book 15, therefore he wrote his epic during his career as a dramatist. We do not know which of his accounts surrounding events at Ambracia was presented publicly first, knowledge of which could influence an understanding of the ver-sion that followed. Unfortunately, any comparison of these fragments, which are analyzed from a dramaturgical perspective later in this chap-ter, with the four surviving passages of the *Annales* Book 15 is diffi-cult, since the surviving fragments of the *Annales* describe the siege of Ambracia itself, whereas the surviving fragments of the play do not. Parallels to Ennius' account in the *Annales* are found in Pacuvius' later *praetexta,* the *Paullus,* in which the siege of Pydna resembles the descrip-tion of Ambracia's siege in Ennius' *Annales;* but this does not pre-clude the possibility that Pacuvius also alluded to passages found in the *Ambracia.*[19]

The surviving fragments of the siege of Ambracia in the *Annales* con-cern siege warfare and battlefield descriptions and may provide clues as to the material around which Ennius based his play.

(1)
*malos defindunt, fiunt tabulata falaeque. . . .*

(SKUTSCH, 388)[20]

They took down the beams, floors and towers went up. . . .

(2)
*occumbunt multi letum ferroque lapique*
*aut intra muros aut extra praecipe casu.*

(SKUTSCH, 389–390)

Many fell to death by sword and rock
either inside or outside the walls in headlong fall.

(3)
*undique conveniunt velut imber tela tribuno:*
*configunt parmam, tinnit hastilibus umbo,*
*aerato sonitu galeae, sed nec pote quisquam*
*undique nitendo corpus discerpere ferro.*
*semper abundantes hastas frangitque quatitque.*
*totum sudor habet corpus, multumque laborat,*
*nec respirandi fit copia: praepete ferro*
*Histri tela manu iacientes sollicitabant.*

(SKUTSCH, 391–398)

From all sides the spears, just as a rainstorm, hailed upon the tribune:
they pierce his shield, the knob creaks against the spears
and the helmets with a grinding sound, but no one was able,
though striving on all sides, to tear apart his body with the sword.
Always did he break and quake many a spear.
Sweat covers his whole body, and he fights hard,
nor is there much breathing room: under a sea of steel
the Histri harrass him hurling spears from their hands.

(4)
*arcus ubi aspicitur, mortalibus quae perhibetur. . . .*

(SKUTSCH, 399)

When he spies the bow, which by mortals is called. . . .

The sack of the city and Nobilior's triumphal return to Rome and
subsequent dedication of the Temple of Hercules Musarum give a teleo-
logical end to the *Annales,* which opened with the sack of Troy and Aeneas' departure for Italy.

The relation of historical content found in the *Octavia,* an Imperial

58

play, to known historical events is easier to assess due to the survival of the entire text.[21] The play contains poetic elements such as the compression of events, the contents of speeches, and the figurative language of poetry, but it contains very little that contradicts historical fact.[22] It also contains historical information, in large quantity, not found in any other historiographical source.[23] The author of the *Octavia* could only have known this information if the play was written near in date to the events it describes. Therefore, the author is unlikely to have relied upon contemporary written sources, but may have been an actual witness of or a participant in the events described. No other literary source mentions that Nero waited until Poppaea became pregnant before having Octavia executed.[24] The correct titles of characters are used; for example, Agrippina is called Augusta at lines 328 and 748, a title that was eventually conferred upon Poppaea.[25] The *monumentum* of Acte is mentioned at line 196.[26] The *damnatio memoriae* of Agrippina is mentioned at line 611. Neither Suetonius, Tacitus, nor Dio mention that Nero accepted the title of *pater patriae*, as noted in the *Octavia* in line 444.[27] The author also incorporated selections from Seneca's prose work *Consolatio ad Helviam,* which Seneca quotes as he enters the drama.[28] Thus, Seneca the character is made to resemble the historical Seneca as closely as possible.

Another clue to the staging of *praetextae* is found in passages that allude to similar passages in Greek tragedy. The correspondence, for example, between Euripides' *Phoenissae* lines 571–576, Jocasta's speech to Polyneices, and Hersilia's speech to her father Hersilius in Ennius' *Sabinae*—*cum spolia generis detraxeritis, quam inscriptionem debetis?*—may indicate similar staging or scene contexts.[29] We also find allusions to Greek tragedy in a play that in turn serves as referent to another play, producing multiple, simultaneous allusions to multiple versions. Aeschylus' *Persians,* for example, serves as a model for at least one passage in the surviving fragments of the *praetextae,* in particular the dialogue between Atossa and the Chorus (176–225) in Aeschylus' *Persians* where the queen describes her dream, and the passage of Accius' *Brutus* where Tarquinius Superbus asks a *vates* to interpret the omens. The content of the passages is not identical, but there is a parallel between the omens involving competition and their interpretation:

Βα.  πολλοῖς μὲν ἀεὶ νυκτέροις ὀνείρασιν
     ξύνειμ', ἀφ' οὗπερ παῖς ἐμὸς στείλας στρατὸν
     Ἰαόνων γῆν οἴχεται πέρσαι θέλων,

ἀλλ' οὔτι πω τοιόνδ' ἐναργὲς εἰδόμην
ὡς τῆσ πάροιθεν εὐφρόνης· λέξω δέ σοι.
ἐδοξάτην μοι δύο γυναῖκ' εὐείμονε,
ἡ μὲν πέπλοισι Περσικοῖς ἠσκημένη,
ἡ δ' αὖτε Δωρικοῖσιν, εἰς ὄψιν μολεῖν,
μεγέθει τε τῶν νῦν ἐκπρεπεστάτα πολὺ
κάλλει τ' ἀμώμω, καὶ κασιγνήτα γένους
ταὐτοῦ, πάτραν δ' ἔναιον ἡ μὲν Ἑλλάδα
κλήρωι λαχοῦσα γαῖαν, ἡ δὲ βάρβαρον·
τούτω στάσιν τιν', ὡς ἐγὼ 'δόκουν ὁρᾶν,
τεύχειν ἐν ἀλλήλησι, παῖς δ' ἐμὸς μαθὼν
κατεῖχε κἀπράϋνεν, ἅρμασιν δ' ὕπο
ζεύγνυσιν αὐτὼ καὶ λέπαδν' ὑπ' αὐχένων
τίθησι· χἠ μὲν τῆιδ' ἐπυργοῦτο στολῆι
ἐν ἡνίαισί τ' εἶχεν εὔαπκτον στόμα,
ἡ δ' ἐσφάδαιζε καὶ χεροῖν ἔντη δίφρου
διασπαράσσει καὶ ξυναρπάζει βίαι
ἄνευ χαλινῶν καὶ ζυγὸν θραύει μέσον.
πίπτει δ' ἐμὸς παῖς, καὶ πατὴρ παρίσταται
Δαρεῖοσ οἰκτίρων σφε· τὸν δ' ὅπως ὁρᾶι
Ξέρξης, πέπλους ῥήγνυσιν ἀμφὶ σώματι.
καὶ ταῦτα μὲν δὴ νυκτὸς εἰσιδεῖν λέγω·
ἐπεὶ δ' ἀνέστην καὶ χεροῖν καλλιρρόου
ἔψαυσα πηγῆς, σὺν θυηπόλωι χερὶ
βωμὸν προσέστην, ἀποτρόποισι δαίμοσιν
θέλουσα θῦσαι πελανόν, ὧν τέλη τάδε·
ὁρῶ δὲ φεύγοντ' αἰετὸν πρὸς ἐσχάραν
Φοίβου, φόβωι δ' ἄφθογγος ἐστάθην, φίλοι·
μεθύστερον δὲ κίρκον εἰσορῶ δρόμωι
πτεροῖν ἐφορμαίνοντα καὶ χηλαῖς κάρα
τίλλονθ'· ὁ δ' οὐδὲν ἄλλο γ' ἢ πτήξας δέμας
παρεῖχε· ταῦτ' ἔμοιγε δείματ' ἔστ' ἰδεῖν,
ὑμῖν δ' ἀκούειν. εὖ γὰρ ἴστε, παῖς ἐμὸσ
πράξας μὲν εὖ θαυμαστὸς ἂν γένοιτ' ἀνήρ,
κακῶσ δὲ πράξας, ουχ ὑπεύθυνος πόλει,
σωθεὶς δ' ὁμοίως τῆσδε κοιρανεῖ χθονός.

Χο.  οὔ σε βουλόμεσθα, μῆτερ, οὔτ' ἄγαν φοβεῖν λόγοις
οὔτε θαρσύνειν· θεοὺς δὲ προστροπαῖς ἱκνουμένη,
εἴ τι φλαῦρον εἶδες, αἰτοῦ τῶνδ' ἀποτροπὴν τελεῖν,
τὰ δ' ἀγάθ' ἐκτελῆ γενέσθαι σοί τε καὶ τέκνωι σέθεν

καὶ πόλει φίλοις τε πᾶσι. δεύτερον δὲ χρὴ χοὰς
γῆι τε καὶ φθιτοῖς χέασθαι. πρευμενῶς δ' αἰτοῦ τάδε,
σὸν πόσιν Δαρεῖον, ὅνπερ φὴις ἰδεῖν κατ' εὐφρόνην,
ἐσθλά σοι πέμπειν τέκνωι τε γῆς ἔνερθεν ἐς φάος,
τἄμπαλιν δὲ τῶνδε γαίαι κάτοχα μαυροῦσθαι σκότωι.
ταῦτα θυμόμαντις ὢν σοι πρευμενῶς παρήινεσα,
εὖ δὲ πανταχῆι τελεῖν σοι τῶνδε κρίνομεν πέρι.

QUEEN: With many nocturnal dreams, I have lived as soon as my son, gathering his army, left to conquer the Ionian land, but never before have I seen such a vivid vision: I will describe it to you: there appeared to me two women—the one dressed in Persian clothes, the other in Doric—who in size and beauty excelled us, now, by far, and being sisters, cast by lot for their father's land—one receiving Greece and the other Asia, the barbaric land. A quarrel breaks out among them, or so it seemed to me, then my son, perceiving this, tries to control and calm them. He yokes them to a chariot and places a bridle around their necks. One towered proud with her mouth obeying her reins, but the other struggles and rips the reins with her hands and, without a bridle, seizes the chariot and breaks the yoke in two. My son falls, while his father Darius, standing by, pities him, but Xerxes, seeing him, tears his robes from his body. These were my night visions. After I arose, I washed my hands in a fair-flowing spring, and wishing to offer sacrifice to guardian deities, I approached the altar, when I sighted an eagle fleeing to the precinct of Apollo—I stood struck dumb with fear. Then I saw a falcon swoop down on him, in flight, and pluck his head with his talons. The eagle did nothing but cower, hare-like. These were the visions I saw that you now hear. Mark my words, should my son succeed, he would be a man admired, but should he fail, no city will hold him. In any case, safe, he will rule this land.

CHORUS: Queen mother, we do not wish to give you fear or confidence with our words. Supplicate the gods, if you see some omen, to avert these things so that blessings may be brought to you and your son, your city, and your friends. First, you must pour libations to Earth and to the dead. Beg your husband Darius, of whom you just dreamed, to bring up to light that which will turn out well for you and your son but to keep evils in darkness, beneath the earth. Being prophetic, I kindly encourage you to be of good cheer that all will turn out well.

Atossa's dream of the two women representing Persia and Greece anticipates Xerxes' defeat. The second omen of the eagle attacked by a hawk, seen by Atossa once she has awakened, further anticipates Greek victory. Both omens are incorrectly interpreted by the Chorus, thus providing some dramatic irony to an otherwise predetermined and known end to the play.

In Accius' *Brutus,* we also find a dream followed by a second omen seen by Tarquin once he is awakened, both of which anticipate his overthrow. The *vates* or priest who interprets the omens, however, predicts the outcome more accurately than did the Chorus in Aeschylus' play and provides the audience with a pun alluding to Brutus' feigned ignorance:

> TARQUINIUS: *quoniam quieti corpus nocturno impetu*
> *dedi sopore placans artus languidos,*
> *visum est in somnis pastor ad me adpellere*
> *pecus lanigerum eximia pulchritudine;*
> *duos consanguineos arietes inde eligi*
> *praeclarioremque alterum inmolare me.*
> *deinde eius germanum cornibus conitier,*
> *in me arietare, eoque ictu me ad casum dari:*
> *exin prostratum terra, graviter saucium,*
> *resupinum in caelo contueri maximum*
> *mirificum facinus: dextrorsum orbem flammeum*
> *radiatum solis liquier cursu novo.*[31]

> TARQUIN: Since then, at night's urging, I gave my body
> to peaceful rest, soothing my tired limbs with sleep,
> a shepherd, in a dream, seemed to drive toward me
> a woolly flock of exceptional beauty;
> two kindred rams were chosen,
> and I slaughtered the nobler of the two.
> Then the ram's brother butted with its horns
> and rammed at me, and by that blow, I fell.
> Then, lying on the ground on my back, seriously hurt,
> I saw a great and marvelous deed in the sky:
> the fiery radiating disk of the sun
> melted to the righthand side on a new path.

> VATES: *rex, quae in vita usurpant homines, cogitant curant vident*
> *quaeque agunt vigilantes agitantque, ea si cui in somno accidunt*
> *minus mirum est, sed di in rem tantam haut temere inproviso offerunt.*
> *proin vide ne quem tu esse hebetem deputes aeque ac pecus*
> *is sapientia munitum pectus egregie gerat,*
> *teque regno expellat; nam id quod de sole ostentum est tibi,*

*populo conmutationem rerum portendit fore*
*perpropinquam. haec bene verruncent populo! nam quod ad dexteram*
*cepit cursum ab laeva signum praepotens, pulcherrume*
*auguratum est rem Romanam publicam summam fore.*

VATES: Sire, what things men perform, ponder, worry over, and see in
   their lives
and what they do and busy themselves with when awake, if these things
   occur to one in a dream,
it is less a cause for wonder, but in such a great matter the gods offer
   you something unforeseen and not for nothing.
Be on guard lest the man whom you think is at the same time as dumb
   as a sheep bear
is a heart eminently fortified with wisdom,
and expels you from your kingdom; for that which was shown to you
   regarding the sun
portends a change of affairs for the people
in the near future. May these things turn out well for the people! For,
   since the powerful portent
took its course to the right hand-side from the left, most wonderfully
did it foretell that the Roman state would be supreme.

By alluding to Atossa's dream, Accius draws parallels between Tarquin
and Atossa: both are identified as cultural "others" from the point of
view of Greeks and Romans, respectively, and both are prescient of their
defeats by a superior opponent. A successful scene in Aeschylus' play is
adapted by Accius to express the impending overthrow of Tarquin, not
as historical fact but as effective drama.

Parallels are found, in turn, between Accius' *Brutus* and Pseudo-
Seneca's *Octavia,* especially between Tarquin's dream and Poppaea's
dream (711–739), in which Poppaea's former husband Crispinus is
killed by Nero; the Nurse's reponse (740–755), which echoes the
Vates' speech; and Octavia's sacrifice to avert the omens of her dream
(756–761):[32]

POPPAEA: *confusa tristi proximae noctis metu*
*visuque, nutrix, mente turbata feror,*
*defecta sensu. laeta nam postquam dies*
*sideribus atris cessit et nocti polus,*
*inter Neronis vincta complexus mei*
*somno resolvor; nec diu placida frui*

*quiete licuit. visa nam thalamos meos*
*celebrare turba est maesta: resolutis comis*
*matres Latinae flebiles planctus dabant;*
*inter tubarum saepe terribilem sonum*
*sparsam cruore coniugis genetrix mei*
*vultu minaci saeva quatiebat facem.*
*quam dum sequor coacta praesenti metu,*
*diducta subito patuit ingenti mihi*
*tellus hiatu; lata quo praeceps toros*
*cerno iugales pariter et miror meos,*
*in quis resedi fessa. venientem intuor*
*comitante turba coniugem quondam meum*
*natumque; properat petere complexus meos*
*Crispinus, intermissa libare oscula:*
*irrupit intra tecta cum trepidus mea*
*ensemque iugulo condidit saevum Nero.*
*tandem quietem magnus excussit timor;*
*quatit ora et artus horridus nostros tremor*
*pulsatque pectus; continet vocem timor,*
*quam nunc fides pietasque produxit tua.*
*heu quid minantur inferum manes mihi*
*aut quem cruorem coniugis vidi mei?*[33]

POPPAEA: I am disturbed, Nurse, by my fearful vision
of last night and, borne by a distraught mind,
I have lost my senses. For when the pleasant day
had yielded to the black stars and the sky of night,
held by the embrace of my Nero,
I fell asleep; nor did I enjoy
a peaceful sleep for long. A sad crowd
seemed to fill my bedroom: Latin mothers
with disheveled hair wept and beat their breasts;
and among the ceaseless sound of a trumpet,
the fierce mother of my husband was shaking
a flickering torch with a threatening gaze.
Compelled by fear, I follow,
when all of a sudden, right before me,
the earth gaped wide-open, where I fell headlong
and spotted and marveled at my marriage bed
onto which I settled. I saw my former husband
and his son approaching with some friends;

Crispinus hastened to seek my embrace
and to taste forgotten kisses:
when Nero suddenly burst into my room
and buried a deadly sword into his throat.
At last great fear shook me from my sleep;
a frightful tremor took over my face and limbs
and shook my heart; fear would have checked my voice,
which your faith and loyalty has now brought forth.
Alas, what do the infernal shades hold in threat for me,
and why did I see my husband's blood?

NUTRIX: *quaecumque mentis agitat intentus vigor,*
*ea per quietem sacer et arcanus refert*
*veloxque sensus. coniugem thalamos toros*
*vidisse te miraris amplexu novi*
*haerens mariti? se movent laeto die*
*pulsata palmis pectora et fusae comae?*
*Octaviae discidia planxerunt sacros*
*inter penates fratris et patrium larem.*
*fax illa, quam secuta es, Augustae manu*
*praelata clarum nomen invidia tibi*
*partum ominatur, inferum sedes toros*
*stabiles futuros spondet aeternae domus.*
*iugulo quod ensem condidit princeps tuus,*
*bella haud movebit, pace sed ferrum teget.*
*recollige animum, recipe laetitiam, precor,*
*timore pulso redde te thalamis tuis.*

NURSE: Some force drives the intentions of the mind,
a quick sensation, sacred and ancient, sends these things
through sleep. Do you wonder that you saw your husband
and marriage beds while in the embrace
of your new husband? And that disheveled hair
and breasts struck by hands appear on this happy day?
They were lamenting the separation of Octavia
from the sacred Penates of her brother's house and the household gods
   of her father's.
That torch carried by Augusta Agrippina, which you followed,
portends that famous name given to you
from envy, and the infernal bed promises the stable future of an eternal
   house.
The fact that your *princeps* husband buried a sword into his throat

means he will not incite new wars but will sheathe his sword in peace.
Collect your courage, restore your peace of mind, I beg,
put away your fear and return to your bedroom.

POPPAEA: *delubra et aras petere constitui sacras,*
*caesis litare victimis numen deum,*
*ut expientur noctis et somni minae*
*terrorque in hostes redeat attonitus meos.*
*tu vota pro me suscipe et precibus piis*
*superos adora, maneat ut praesens status.*

POPPAEA: I decided to seek the temples and sacred altars
to beg divine power, with sacrifices,
to avert the threats of the night and my dream
and to turn the terror upon my enemies.
Offer prayers on my behalf and worship the gods
with sacred prayers, so that the present calm remains.

By drawing a parallel between Poppaea and Accius' Tarquin, Pseudo-Seneca presents Poppaea as a modern-day tyrant who must be overthrown. The tone of Accius' depiction of Tarquin has become more critical in Pseudo-Seneca, since Nero himself appears in Poppaea's dream to destroy a rival and funereal imagery is interpreted by Poppaea's nurse as festive. We can also see an allusion to the original passage in Aeschylus, in that Atossa, a concerned witness to events, is replaced by Poppaea, an active participant in the political struggle between Nero and Octavia that will determine her future. There is also a progression to the omen in the various versions: from personifications of Greece and Asia, to sacrificial animals, to Nero killing Poppaea's first husband, Crispinus. Tarquin's dream of a sacrifice becomes a sacrifice and prayer for Poppaea, once awakened, to avert the omens of her dream, resulting in multiple and simultaneous allusions to various versions.[34]

Elements from Roman comedy also appear in the *Octavia,* in particular, the characteristically Plautine features of extended monologues spoken in the presence of other characters. The most noticeable parallel use of this device occurs in the opening lines of the *Octavia* and the *Stichus* of Plautus, where the character Pamphila voices a similar sentiment in a dramatic context similar to the *Octavia.*[35] The play opens with a monologue of Antipho (1–57, followed by his orders to servants, 58–67). His daughters Pamphila and Panegyris converse (68–74), after which Antipho speaks another monologue, unbeknownst to them (75–87). After Antipho's second monologue, Pamphila says: *certo enim mihi paternae vocis sonitus auris accidit* ("Truly the sound of my father's voice comes to my ears").[36] In the Octavia, after an opening monologue by Octavia (1–33), Octavia's nurse enters to describe her charge's problems (34–56). Octavia, who is in the palace, cries out (57–71) and prompts the Nurse to say: *vox en nostras perculit aures / tristis alumnae . . . ?* (72–73: "Does the voice of my unhappy child reach my ears . . . ?"). These parallels suggest further ways in which historical dramas share dramatic elements with the tragic and comic stage.

Significant differences do exist, however, between Republican and Imperial *praetextae*. Whereas the Republican legendary plays, as distinct from the triumphal plays, were written about events and historical figures far removed from the date of composition of the play, the Imperial legendary plays, except for the *Aeneas* of Pomponius Secundus, are barely separated in time from their subjects—by only a few years in the case of the *Octavia*, and just over a century in the cases of the *Domitius* and the *Cato*.[37]

Another difference between the Republican and Imperial plays relates to their tone and the occasions for which they were composed. The Republican legendary plays such as the *Brutus* and the *Decius* were written to glorify the descendants of famous political and military figures, while the Republican triumphal plays celebrated the military victories of those who had triumphed over defeated tribes, such as the *Ambracia,* the *Clastidium,* and the *Paullus.* The latter were commissioned for special events; therefore they did not become vehicles by which dramatists could voice political dissent. The Imperial plays, again with the *Aeneas* being a possible exception, were not commissioned to glorify the deeds of a public figure, but rather were written as criticisms of Imperial oppression, whether by the Julio-Claudians or the Flavians, through the presentation of a play about an ancestor or other historical/contemporary figure that alluded to perceived tyrannical behavior, such as the *Octavia,* the *Domitius,* and the *Cato.* The *Octavia* is also an occasion to commiserate with Octavia and Nero's victims—especially, it seems, Britannicus, who is given a eulogy in the description of his funeral.[38]

Categorization is difficult, however, when considering the plays as essentially overt criticisms of Imperial power. The two Imperial *praetextae* of Maternus and his two "barbed" mythological plays may be extreme cases, since it is not likely that Secundus' *Aeneas* was written as criticism.[39] This does not mean that the *Aeneas* was not perceived as such by an audience, which could introduce a prejudiced interpretation (*interpretatio prava*) whenever it liked. As drama, the plays were probably not entirely composed of vitriolic attacks with little dramatic action. Any anti-tyrannical sentiments contained in the plays were probably communicated through apposite innuendo within the larger dramatic action.[40] The rule of the Caesars provided enough scope for effective drama.[41]

Some *praetextae*, therefore, allude to earlier Greek historical plays, Greek tragedy, earlier Latin *praetextae*, and contemporary figures and events, producing simultaneous allusions to multiple referents. Offstage reality becomes an allusive referent, as does a previously staged version of a play. The breakdown of the illusion between the stage and the audience leads to the framing and perception of historical events in terms of previously produced tragedies, thereby contributing to an awareness of the theatricality of contemporary offstage events. This marks a continuation of the theatricalization of tragedy under Pacuvius and Accius, but the level of comprehension needed to interpret these complex intertextual and interperformance allusions has increased, and so, too, has the possibility of interpretations unintended by a dramatist or producer. Most important for the restaging of a previously produced play is the simultaneous allusion to the original context of the play, including any allusions that arose from the earlier version or occasion. An analysis of the semiotics of competing realities arising from *praetextae* will shed light on the reception of tragedies considered in chapter 4 and the effect of this theatricality on the plays of Seneca.

## STAGING HISTORY

The *praetextae*, as dramatic recreations of reality onstage, are informed by cultural events performed by historical and contemporary figures but presented in a dramatic, rather than a realistic, setting. Examining *praetextae* from a dramaturgical perspective illuminates the semiotic effects of an audience's viewing history onstage, especially the treatment of the protagonist onstage. It is impossible to reconstruct actual stagecraft, so I focus on the semiotic reception of *praetextae*, especially the semiotics of competing realities, from evidence gleaned from performance cues arising from texts. Extant fragments determine which plays can be examined, and enough fragments survive to analyze plays from each group: early history (Accius' *Aeneadae sive Decius*), contemporary aristocratic achievement (Ennius' *Ambracia*), and an Imperial play (Pseudo-Seneca's *Octavia*).

The legend behind the *Aeneadae sive Decius* is well known. Based on descriptions of episodes surrounding the self-sacrifice of Decius Mus in

Livy (10.27ff.) and Polybius (2.19), the following is a brief synopsis of events that form the backdrop of the play but that may not reflect the actual thematic content of the play. The consuls Q. Fabius Maximus and P. Decius Mus and their armies engage in battle a coalition of Samnites and Gauls at Sentinum in 295. On the right wing Fabius drives back the Samnites, but on the left wing the Gauls with their chariots scatter the Roman cavalry. Decius, as his father before him, sacrifices himself, with the result that the cavalry recovers itself; with the aid of reinforcements from Fabius, the Samnites and Gauls are defeated and their leader Gellius Egnatius slain.

The fragments of the *Aeneadae sive Decius* that survive reveal that the central action of the play may have concerned the interaction between Fabius and Decius. The play ended with the self-sacrifice of Decius. In fragment 1, a messenger informs the generals that the enemy is quiet:

(1)
*nihil neque pericli neque tumulti est, quod sciam.*[42]

There is neither any danger nor disturbance of which I know.

A description of the fighting is given in fragment 2:

(2)
*clamore et gemitu templum resonit caelitum.*

With an uproar and a groan does the temple of the heaven-dwellers resound.

Fabius orders Decius to take the left wing:

(3)
*vim Gallicam obduc contra in aciem exercitum:*
*lue patrium hostili fusum sanguen sanguine.*

Lead your force in battle line against the Gallic troops;
atone the blood of our fathers with the shed blood of our enemy.

In fragments 4–5, the priest, Marcus Livius, occupies the stage, seeking omens from his sacrifice, which he interprets to Decius; but it is not clear how this scene was staged or whether any of the speeches were shared between speakers:

(4)

*te sancte venerans precibus, invicte, invoco,*
portenta ut populo patriae verruncent bene.

You holy and unconquered one, offering prayers do I invoke you
to let the portents promise well for my people and my homeland.

(5)

*et nunc quae deorum segnitas? ardet focus.*

And now what neglect of the gods? The hearth burns.

An indecisive battle follows, after which Fabius and Decius debate their
next move in fragments 6–7:

(6)

*quod periti sumus in vita atque usu callemus magis.*

[FABIUS:] Since we are skilled in life and we are more experienced by
custom.

(7)

*fateor: sed saepe ignavavit fortem in spe expectatio.*

[DECIUS:] I confess, but often hope has paralyzed a brave man from
hope itself.

A chorus of Gauls marches onto the stage, signaled by the anapaestic
meter, announcing their presence on the field of battle, but it is unclear
whether an actual battle was enacted onstage:

(8)

*. . . Caleti voce canora*
fremitu peragrant minitabiliter.

. . . The Caleti, with sonorous voice,
march threateningly with a din.

In fragment 9, Fabius questions three deserters from Clusium to dis-
cover the movements of the enemy:

(9)

*dice, summa ubi perduellum est? quosum aut quibus a partibus*
gliscunt?

Tell me, where is the height of the insurrection? In which direction or
    from what area
does it grow?

In fragments 10 and 11, Decius returns to the stage and resolves to sacrifice himself:

(10)
*quibus rem summam et patriam nostram quondam adauctavit pater.*

With which my father once increased our supreme power and native
    land.

(11)
*patrio exemplo et me dicabo atque animam devoro hostibus.*

Through my father's example, even I will dedicate and sacrifice my life
    to the enemy.

A messenger or soldier from the Samnite/Gaul camp surrenders due to
Decius' sacrifice:

(12)
*castra haec vestra est: optume essis meritus a nobis.*

The camp is yours: you are deserving of our best.

Whether or not the play included a mock battle onstage, the fragments raise some questions about how the play may have been produced
and whether scenes such as the fighting preceding the battle of Sentinum,
the decisive battle itself, and Decius' sacrifice took place onstage. The
enemy appeared onstage at least twice, when Fabius questioned the deserters and when the Gallic chorus marched across the stage on the way
to battle. Whatever other role the chorus played in the dramatic action
cannot be recovered.[43]

The *Ambracia* survives in only four fragments.[44] While the play covers the same material as Book 15 of Ennius' *Annales,* the same events
are not described. What little that does survive points to a drama that
has much in common with the dramatic action of the *Aeneadae vel
Decius,* but little to do with the arousal of tragic sympathy for the defeated Istrians. The exact placement of fragments is far from certain.
Fragment 1 of the *Ambracia* may describe the physical condition of a
messenger or even an Aetolian sympathetic to the Roman cause:

(1)

*esse per gentes cluebat omnium miserrimus.*[45]

He was determined the most wretched of men everywhere.

In the second fragment, two characters converse before the arrival of a third:

(2)

*bene mones, tute ipse cunctas caute; o vide fortem virum!*

You advise well, you yourself are delaying; O behold the brave man!

It seems probable that this line introduces the arrival of Nobilior onstage. It is not clear whether the chorus acknowledges the advice of a character or whether two characters, and not the chorus, converse before Nobilior's arrival. In terms of dramatic action, Warmington places this fragment last among the four surviving fragments, but without comment.[46] However, it is possible that Nobilior's arrival occurred after a preliminary description of the capture of Ambracia and a glorification of his role in the campaign.

An argument in favor of a late arrival is the opportunity for an extended encomium of the victor's achievements prior to his arrival onstage, and perhaps also in lieu of his extended participation in the drama itself. Another scenario may be an arrival sometime before the siege of Ambracia and again after the fall of the city, at which point his valor would be described by other characters. However, one cannot rule out the possibility, in the light of Diomedes' assertion that Roman generals appeared onstage, that his appearance was neither brief nor understated, but that he could have appeared onstage at length, and possibly even in a reenactment of a battle.

The hypothesis of a late arrival is based partly upon the model of Aeschylus' *Persians* (which was by no means the only model or option available), where after the questioning of the chorus by Queen Atossa, a lengthy messenger speech precedes the arrival of Xerxes. It could be argued that since Xerxes was not an Athenian and therefore not a member of the audience, there was no political reason for a late arrival onstage but rather a dramatic one—Xerxes could only appear onstage in a miserable state after the description of his defeat. Unfortunately we do not know whether Themistocles was brought onstage in the *Sack of Miletus,* another possible model.[47] In the fourth century B.C.E., Moschion put on two historical tragedies, a *Themistocles* and the *Phere-*

*ans.*[48] It seems that Themistocles did appear onstage in the *Phereans,* but by this time Themistocles was a historical figure, not a contemporary member of the audience.

Fragment 3 may come from a messenger speech describing the lawlessness of the Aetolians:

(3)

⟨*iam*⟩ *agros audaces depopulant servi dominorum domi.*

At home, the reckless slaves despoil the fields of their masters.

(4)

*. . . et aequora salsa veges ingentibus ventis.*

. . . And you churn the salty sea with immense winds.

Warmington suggests "The dangers of the Adriatic?" for a possible context of fragment 4.[49] The speaker is addressing an elemental force that can stir up the waves of the sea. The most likely dramatic scenario would be an address by Nobilior to Neptune, in thanksgiving for a safe passage over the Adriatic, or a request at the end of the play for a safe return to Italy. Since the dramatic action took place at Ambracia, either scenario is possible.

If the play was produced at Nobilior's triumphal games and/or on an occasion such as his votive games in 186 B.C.E. or the dedication of the Temple of Hercules Musarum, then Nobilior may have been a member of the audience.[50] If, indeed, this was the case, and an actor portraying him was onstage, he would have watched a character representing himself onstage while the audience would have seen both Nobiliors—the one in the audience and the one onstage.

How would the Roman audience have reacted to the representation of living persons on the stage?[51] The evidence for both the depiction of contemporary figures onstage and the reaction of the audience is far from conclusive. Cicero in *De re publica* writes that it was not pleasing to ancient Romans either to praise or to insult anyone onstage, but it is clear from the context that Cicero has comedy rather than tragedy in mind.[52]

Of the mythological/historical plays that Diomedes lists, the *Brutus* and the *Decius,* the legendary figures of L. Junius Brutus and Decius Mus had been dead long before the date of production, therefore occasioning a different reaction to seeing contemporary public figures onstage. As with the *praetextae* of Curiatus Maternus, such as the *Cato* and the *Domitius,* the characters depicted in the *Octavia* were dead at the time the play was written. The dramatic action of the *Octavia* is set in 62 C.E., yet the date of composition is more than seven years later. Octavia is mostly onstage in the first half of the play, yet she practically disappears in the second half except for three fairly brief speeches.

The effect on the audience of viewing an actor portraying a subject seated in the audience at the same performance was touched on above in connection with Nobilior's *Ambracia,* but since Nobilior's presence could not be attested with certainty, the semiotic implications could not be taken further. In the case of L. Cornelius Balbus' *Iter* or *Journey,* however, we have an audience member's account of the production at which Balbus was seated in the audience while an actor portrayed him onstage.[53] This was a play that Balbus apparently wrote himself to mark his journey to Pompey's camp at Dyrrachium in 49 B.C.E. at the beginning of the civil war to win L. Lentulus over to Caesar's side. (Balbus, however, missed Lentulus.) Balbus' play was staged in Gades, at his own expense, but it was never produced in Rome. We know from a letter dated June 43 B.C.E. that C. Asinius Pollio wrote to Cicero that Balbus was seated in the audience and that he was moved to tears during the performance:

> *illa vero iam ne Caesaris quidem exemplo, quod ludis praetextam de suo itinere ad L. Lentulum pro consule sollicitandum posuit, et quidem, cum ageretur, flevit memoria rerum gestarum commotus. . . .*[54]

In other respects, he did not follow Caesar's precedent, since, during his games, he put on a play (*praetexta*) about his journey to the Proconsul L. Lentulus to convince him to change sides, and moreover, when the play was being performed, he wept, moved at the memory of his accomplishments.

It is not clear what *res gestae* (record of his achievements) moved Balbus to tears, whether it was a recreation of some part of the journey or his success at penetrating the camp. Pollio did not approve of Balbus' behavior, but it is unclear whether it is due to Balbus' writing of a play to record his mission or Balbus' reaction to the play. Did Balbus write too large a role for himself in the drama or greatly exaggerate events surrounding his journey and the role he played? Did he express excessive pride in crying in public at his own achievements? (*Commotus* suggests an excessive reaction seen to draw attention to himself.) Perhaps the cause of Pollio's objections are not so much that Balbus' status changed from ordinary to extraordinary through dramatic representation, but that Balbus himself was responsible for this portrayal, since his composition of a play about himself was unprecedented even by the examples set by Julius Caesar (*illa vero iam ne Caesaris quidem exemplo*).[55] Later in the letter, Pollio further expresses his distaste at Balbus' behavior by painting his treatment of a Roman soldier who refused to enter the gladiator school at Gades in a tyrannical light.[56]

It is important to note that Pollio reports Balbus' reaction without commenting on the substance of the play or how the rest of the audience received the play. One senses that Pollio's eyes were fixed on Balbus rather than on the production onstage. Cicero only read the dramatic text of the play, which was being disseminated among his circle; therefore he cannot offer firsthand knowledge of the performance text, or of the audience's reaction to the play or to Balbus' reaction to it. The barrier between the stage and the audience is removed if Balbus, as both dramatist and a member of the audience, could see himself portrayed onstage—and more importantly, if the audience could see him both onstage and in the audience. From a semiotic perspective, the blurring of theatre and reality results in a peculiar dynamic: the audience is watching Balbus watching himself onstage, thereby producing a simultaneous spectacle at two different locations within the theatre.

The possible production of *praetextae* at funerals is controversial and produces semiotic challenges of its own. Dupont has argued that the performance of a play about the deceased was an important feature of funerals, especially following the disposal of the deceased's remains outside of the *pomerium* of Rome.[57] Flower, on the other hand, questions the evidence for the production of a play at a funeral, since it would detract from the procession and *laudatio* and would depend on the feasibility of the deceased's family commissioning a play on short notice.[58] If *praetextae* were performed at funerals, we may not be dealing with plays written expressly for the occasion. Even in the instance of plays produced on earlier known occasions, whether at festivals or at votive games, the production of a play that would reinforce any praise found in the *laudatio* could be desirable and effective, especially if we are dealing with a play that is already paid for and that would reinforce the deceased's accomplishments by alluding to the occasion of that earlier production. The evidence is far from conclusive. A look at the semiotics of funerals, in particular at the role of actors in portraying the deceased and the implications of interpreting real and dead figures, is relevant.[59]

The main literary source for a typical funeral of a male aristocrat under the Republic is the Greek historian Polybius, writing in the second century B.C.E.:

> Whenever any illustrious man dies, he is carried at his funeral into the forum to the so-called *rostra,* sometimes conspicuous in an upright posture and rarely reclined. Here with all the people standing round, a grown-up son, if he has left one who happens to be present, or if not some other relative, mounts the *rostra* and discourses on the virtues and successful achievements of the dead. . . . Next after the interment and the performance of the usual ceremonies, they place the image of the departed in the most conspicuous position in the house, enclosed in a wooden shrine. This image is a mask reproducing with remarkable fidelity both the features and the complexion of the deceased. On the occasion of public sacrifices they display these images, and decorate them with much care, and when any distinguished member of the family dies they take them to the funeral, putting them on men who seem to them to bear the closest resemblance to the original in stature and carriage. These representatives wear togas, with a purple border if the deceased was a consul or praetor, whole purple if he was a censor, and embroidered with gold if he had celebrated a triumph or achieved anything similar. They all ride in chariots preceded by the fasces, axes, and other insignia by which the different magistrates are wont to be accompanied according to the respective dignity of the offices of state held by each during his life; and when they arrive at the rostra they all seat themselves in a row on ivory chairs. There could not easily be a more ennobling spectacle for a young man who aspires to fame and virtue. For who would not be inspired by the sight of the images of men renowned for their excellence, all together and as if alive and breathing?[60]

Since the rituals that Polybius describes took place before cremation or interment, the deceased was, in essence, a seated member of the audience among his ancestors at his own funeral. What is fascinating to Polybius, and to us, is the central role played by ancestors in the funeral ceremony. As participants, the deceased ancestors assume the *imagines* or death masks and symbols of public office that are stored in the home and reclaim their former identities and roles among the living. The focus shifts from the recently deceased to his ancestors as spectators, thereby creating a theatre of the dead in the audience, if we remember that our word for theatre comes from the Greek verb θεαô, meaning "to watch." This results in concurrent or multiple layers of generations, with the most recently deceased subsumed by the group. One must note, however, that this group is composed entirely of men. It is the spectacle of the ancestors participating in the funeral of their descendants that catches Polybius' attention and serves a didactic purpose for their younger descendants in the audience.

Turning from the audience to funeral rituals surrounding the deceased, the funeral *pompa,* or procession, which included the wearing of masks and/or the carrying of ancestor busts, led to a *rostra* upon a constructed platform upon which the corpse was placed. Polybius assumes that his readers are familiar with details surrounding interment and the "usual ceremonies." For the funerals of nobles, these platforms were probably located in the Forum Romanorum, but this location is controversial since it depends on a single reference in the *Ab urbe condita* of the historian Livy and may not be the exclusive location.[61] Since *ludi scaenici* or scenic productions were performed at some funerals, in addition to gladiatorial combats, a stage was necessary, but it is not clear from our evidence whether the platform doubled as a stage (with corpse on it?), or whether a stage was set up in sight of the platform. If the stage was in sight of the corpse—a configuration that recalls the placement of temporary stages in the early Republican period directly in front of temples within sight of the god or goddess being celebrated, with the temple steps doubling as theatre seats.[62] As Polybius reports, a mime then represented the deceased symbolically in the audience at the eulogy and at any *ludi scaenici,* among family members of the deceased and surrounded by men (mimes?) imitating his dead male ancestors, who also wore masks of ancestral *imagines.*[63] When not in use for funeral ceremonies, death masks or busts were displayed in the atria of Roman homes for occupants and visitors alike to see.[64] In addition, these dead ancestors drove to the forum in chariots and sat in a row on ivory chairs (Polyb. 6.53). Since these chairs were the symbolic seats of gods, the use of them by the deceased's dead ancestors points to a blurring of the dead with the divine for funeral games and other *ludi.* This ritual was later exploited by the Julio-Claudians to advertise the immortality of the emperor.

Further details surrounding the custom of "playing dead" come from Diodorus Siculus, who describes the funeral of Lucius Aemilius Paullus in 160 B.C.E., giving details similar to Polybius' account of a typical aristocratic funeral with the added detail that mime actors, rather than relatives, were hired to portray the deceased's dead ancestors:

Those Romans who by reason of noble birth and the fame of their ancestors are preeminent are, when they die, portrayed in figures that not only are lifelike as to features but show their whole bodily appearance. For they employ actors who through a man's whole life have carefully observed his carriage and the several peculiarities of his appearance. In like fashion, each of the dead man's ancestors takes his place in the funeral procession, with such robes and insignia as enable the spectators to distinguish from the portrayal how far each had advanced in the *cursus honorum* and had had a part in the dignities of the state.[65]

It is significant that Diodorus mentions that the mime actors imitate the carriage and appearance of the deceased, which suggests that these actors could earn a living as participants in funerals to supplement their stage roles. Moreover, it suggests that members of the aristocracy welcomed professional actors in their midst to portray their ancestors despite the low social standing of actors in general at Rome. This interaction must have been intimate enough for actors to observe the character traits of the deceased on more than one occasion, since Diodorus claims the mime's observation was made throughout the deceased's life. Presumably members of the aristocracy did not alter their behavior in the mime's presence or fear caricatures after death at their own funerals.

In addition to Diodorus, the biographer Suetonius also claims that it was the custom (*mos*) for a mime actor to imitate the deceased in appearance and carriage, which he had observed throughout the lifetime of the deceased, in order for the deceased to be a participant in his own funeral. The connection between mime actors and funerals was so strong that the death of Augustus was held to be foreshadowed by the appearance of a mime actor on his throne. At the funeral of the emperor Vespasian, Suetonius reports that the mime actor Favor, imitating Vespasian in "actions and words," joked about the emperor's stinginess:

> sed in funere Favor archimimus personam eius ferens imitansque, ut est mos, facta ac dicta vivi, interrogatis palam procuratoribus, quanti funus et pompa constaret, ut audit sestertium centiens, exclamavit centum sibi sestertia darent ac se vel in Tiberim proicerent.

(*VESPASIAN* 19.2)[66]

But at the funeral, the arch-mime Favor bearing his likeness and imitating his former actions and words, as is the custom, openly asked the procurators how much the funeral and procession cost. When he heard 10,000,000 sesterces, he shouted that they should give him 100,000 sesterces and throw his body into the Tiber.

Suetonius presents his reader with a paradoxical description of death and the dead. On the one hand, the emperor is dead, but on the other, he is a participant in his own funeral ceremony. What is not clear is whether the mime mocked the emperor in the presence of his corpse. This paradox presented the viewer with the option of accepting the dead as actually alive or, conversely, denying that the deceased had ever actually died. A reciprocal relationship exists, therefore, between death ritual and theatrical allusion recognized by an audience that not only acknowledges the death of the deceased but also perpetuates a figurative living status for the dead and his deceased ancestors.[67]

Sources are silent as to what happened after the funeral ceremonies. Was there a procession back to the deceased's house to deposit the deceased's death mask and those of his ancestors once again in the atrium, or did the actors hand over the masks and clothing and thereby surrender the identities of the deceased and his ancestors immediately following cremation or interment? The former seems more likely, especially if the actors gathered at the deceased's home to collect their masks, but certainty is impossible.

This relationship between the living and the dead extends to the stage itself, although the connection between the dead, or the actor portraying the dead, onstage in a play during funeral *ludi* is more difficult to make. If plays commissioned by public figures were indeed performed during their funeral *ludi,* whether produced for the first time or in addition to an earlier production, then the semiotic implications are fascinating: did the mime actor imitating the deceased in the procession and in the audience at the oration leave the audience to appear onstage, or did a second actor imitating the deceased appear onstage before yet another actor in the audience[68]— either or both of whom were also in sight of the actual deceased? Either scenario is intriguing, especially if we consider the question of representation, and whether death masks were worn or modeled after portraits or whether generals were merely identified onstage by means of their senatorial robes.[69]

Whether the occasion of performance was a funeral, a triumph, a temple dedication, or votive games, the significance of these plays is that the *triumphator* would have been represented onstage with the honorand either alive and seated in the audience or deceased and within view of the stage. The representation of the deceased, whether onstage and/or in the audience, mirrors stage drama, in that the mourners/audience must accept "onstage reality" offstage; that is, theatrical allusion extends to the audience's reality: the audience must accept actors in their midst who are portraying real individuals who are, in fact, dead. The barrier between the stage and the audience is removed, thus presenting the audience with competing realities to interpret.

What if no dramatists were available or able to write a *praetexta*? How then, could one allude to offstage reality onstage in the dramatic text or within the dramatic reality of a nonhistorical play (illusory drama)? As chapter 4 explores, the opening program of Pompey's theatre illustrates that, unlike a *praetexta* celebrating contemporary aristocratic achievements, in which the honorand appears as a protagonist on the stage, a historical person was alluded to onstage within the dramatic context of a tragedy. If *praetextae* represent a *contaminatio* with reality, this appropriation of the audience's reality in a tragedy through visual referents onstage to encourage an allusion further points to the way in which a restaged production of a previously staged play could become topically relevant. Pompey's *exemplum* of incorporating the audience's reality into the dramatic action of the play as an allusion to contemporary political events produced tragedies that were theatricalized versions of the audience's reality. The honorand has replaced the dramatist. Furthermore, the attempted restaging of Accius' *Brutus* following the assassination of Julius Caesar and Augustus' choice of Varius Rufus' *Thyestes* for his triple triumph of 29 B.C.E. point to the extent to which tragedy could allude to the audience's reality without altering the dramatic text of a previously produced play.

# FOUR

# CREATING METATRAGEDY

*deerat hoc unum mihi,*
*spectator iste. nil adhuc facti reor:*
*quidquid sine insto fecimus sceleris perit.*

(SENECA *MEDEA* 992–994)[1]

I lacked this one thing,
Jason as spectator. Up to now, I have done nothing:
without him, whatever crime I committed is wasted.

After killing her children, Medea (Seneca *Medea* 982–994) considers
the effects of her anger and voices her one regret: that she did not turn
Jason into a spectator, since her crime does not exist without him as audience, despite the fact that a crime was committed—her children are
dead. In other words, Medea needs a stage audience to validate her stage
actions. Audience reaction onstage replaces stage action in a drama,
which makes the reaction of the actual audience irrelevant.

To examine the effects of this reciprocal relationship between the
stage and the audience, two questions inform this chapter, arising from
the semiotic reception of *praetextae:* How do dramatists or public figures advertise a historical event or their own status through mythological allusions on the tragic stage? How does the audience distinguish between actor, mythological character, and actual person being alluded to
onstage when the allusion challenges what it recognizes as real off the
stage? In other words, how does the audience interpret the simultaneous
referents arising from these competing realities when it is viewing its

own theatricalized reality onstage? From a semiotic perspective, culture informs theatre, theatre permeates society, and then theatricality is incorporated back into the theatre; but when the audience's own metatheatre is incorporated into stage reality, the metatragedy of Seneca results: theatricality replaces theatre, as characters become their own audience watching or commenting on their own stage actions. The audience seated in the theatre shifts roles from spectator to witness. Where is the "real" audience?

Allusions to mythological characters operate on many levels, those that are self-styled and those that are styled by others, often occurring concurrently with other allusions, which may themselves be either self-styled or styled by others. I focus on self-styled allusions to mythological characters arising from the production of a tragedy, and on any effect such an allusion had in making a corresponding allusion to another political figure, rather than on allusions that are styled by others in nondramatic contexts.[2]

The exact date when a dramatist or presenter first intended a mythological allusion arising from a production of a tragedy to be interpreted as political allusion is unknown. In support of a second-century B.C.E. date, Bilinski argues that Accius' plays reflect anti-Gracchan sentiment.[3] While we may suspect that some passages seem allusive, few details surrounding the production dates of any of Accius' plays survive; therefore it is difficult to interpret passages or plays as allusions to specific contemporary political events. However, in the case of Pompey's theatre opening, we do have evidence with which to interpret political allusions. The opening program of Pompey's theatre illustrates the effectiveness of alluding to a historical person onstage *within* the dramatic context of a tragedy, rather than having the actual person represented onstage, as in *praetextae,* therefore turning a nonillusory drama into an illusive one. As this chapter explores, Pompey's removal of the barrier between actor and audience through dramatic allusion influenced how tragedies could be at once fixed dramatic texts and allusive commentaries on contemporary political events in performance contexts. Versions of plays about Lucius Junius Brutus' expulsion of the Tarquins and Augustus' choice of Varius Rufus' *Thyestes* for his triple triumph point to the extent to which tragedy had become metatheatrical even before the stage appearances of Nero and the composition of Seneca's metatragedies.

## POMPEY'S THEATRE OPENING

When Pompey celebrated the gala opening of his theatre, which was the first permanent stone theatre at Rome, in 55 B.C.E., the lavish displays of the various *ludi* dazzled his audience with their extravagance.[4] In addition to scenic entertainment, there were numerous gladiatorial displays with many exotic animals.[5] This gala was carefully orchestrated by the dramatic censor, or more accurately manager, Spurius Maecius Tarpa, the first person ever to hold such a position in Rome. His appointment underlies the importance of the opening celebrations as a means of furthering Pompey's extraordinary prestige.[6] Aesopus, the most famous tragic actor then at Rome, was brought out of retirement to act in the opening production, but with disappointing results—at a key passage, his voice failed him.[7]

The theatre was part of a much larger complex that included the Temple of Venus Victrix, dedicated in 52 B.C.E., which was located directly across the stage, above the *cavea*.[8] At present, we know little about the form, appearance, or architecture of this temple.[9] There were also a *curia* or assembly hall, a Portico of Nations, gardens, a display gallery, and smaller shrines.[10] According to Pliny, the theatre could accommodate 40,000 spectators.[11] The luxuriousness of the theatre is demonstrated by its "air conditioning," effected by running water flowing in channels.[12] The theatre had a *scaena* three tiers high, and the entire stage area was lavishly decorated. Pompey's theatre was the sole permanent theatre at Rome for over forty years, until the construction of G. Cornelius Balbus' theatre in 13 B.C.E.[13] and the theatre of Marcellus, also dedicated in 13 B.C.E.[14] Due to its size, the theatre of Pompey continued to dominate the area after the construction of the later theatres, and its splendor ensured that it was one of the showplaces at Rome throughout its existence in a way that the other theatres were not.[15] These theatres were all built close to each other in the southern Campus Martius, thereby creating what would now be recognized as a theatre district, in an area readily accessible to, but technically outside the sacred line of, the *pomoerium*.[16]

Pompey's own description of his theatre at the dedication ceremony of the Temple of Venus Victrix in 52 B.C.E. is preserved by Tertullian, in a passage filled with Christian invective against pagan culture:

*cum illam arcem omnium turpitudinum extruxisset, veritus quandoque memoriae suae censoriam animadversionem Veneris aedem superposuit et ad dedicationem edicto populum vocans non theatrum sed Veneris templum nuncupavit, "cui subiecimus," inquit, "gradus spectaculorum."* [17]

Although he had built that monument of all things morally corrupt, in truth, even when he incorporated a censored temple of Venus as a memorial of himself, at the dedication ceremony, he called it, in an edict to the people, not a theatre but rather a temple of Venus, "to which I have added," he said, "the steps of a theatre."

Irony has been detected in Pompey's description of his theatre as a temple that could accommodate scenic productions; yet long before the construction of the theatre, Venus had been associated with theatrical or scenic productions. [18] With the dedication of the Temple of Venus Victrix, the relationship between theatre, politics, and religion becomes more complete than it had been in any of the previous temporary theatres. Up to that time, aediles were remembered for fabulous *ludi,* but they were not, except in the case of M. Aemilius Scaurus and his theatre, permanently associated with a particular structure for any of the games given. [19] Whereas plays were formerly produced on stages erected near temples *in conspectu dei,* they were now produced, in Pompey's theatre, both at and within the temple precinct of Venus Victrix. It is this architectural interplay between temple and theatre that leads to the construct: Venus' temple steps equal Pompey's theatre seats. According to Plutarch, Pompey later dreamed about Venus and his theatre on the eve of the Battle of Pharsalus and feared that through the family connection that he had cultivated with Venus, Caesar, who also claimed descent from Venus, would appropriate his glory. [20] Furthermore, it was a later irony that Augustus relocated the statue of Pompey, which had been erected in the theatre's *curia* and at the base of which Caesar was murdered, opposite the entrance of the theatre so that "Pompey" had to be passed in order for one to enter his theatre and the shrine of Venus. [21]

The importance of the theatre continued beyond Pompey's opening celebrations, most notably when Caesar celebrated his triumph over Pompey's African forces with spectacles in Pompey's own theatre in 46 B.C.E. [22] On a practical level, the theatre's seating capacity may have dictated the choice of venue, but on a symbolic level, Caesar seems to have taken hold of Venus' cult and her temple-theatre as a demonstration of his victory over Pompey and his own claims to Venus' cult. Julio-Claudian emperors continued to link their names with the theatre, most notably Claudius, who rededicated the Temple of Venus Victrix in a solemn ceremony:

*ludos dedicationis Pompeiani theatri, quod ambustum restituerat, e tribunali posito in orchestra commisit, cum prius apud superiores aedes supplicasset perque mediam caveam sedentibus ac silentibus cunctis descendisset.*[23]

[Claudius] opened the games at the [re]dedication of Pompey's theatre, which he had restored from fire damage, from a tribunal placed in the orchestra, after he had first offered sacrifice at the upper temples and had descended into the middle of the auditorium, before all the silently seated spectators.

Augustus restored some part of the complex in 32 B.C.E.[24] After a fire in 21 C.E., Tiberius again had the theatre restored, but the renovations were completed only under Caligula.[25] It was Claudius, however, who rededicated the temple, as Suetonius describes above, and who inscribed his name and that of Tiberius on the *scaena,* restoring once again, in the process, Pompey's name.[26] Nero put his stamp on the theatre for a visit by King Tiridates by having the interior gilded and adding purple awnings over the *cavea.*[27]

The theatre of M. Aemilius Scaurus, which preceded Pompey's theatre by only three years, had greater implications than any other temporary theatre for both its extravagance in theatre construction and its success in ensuring the immortality of its builder.[28] Although conceived of as a temporary theatre, it seems that no expense was spared in its construction. Pliny relates:

*in aedilitate hic sua fecit opus maximum omnium quae umquam fuere humana manu facta, non temporaria mora, verum etiam aeternitatis destinatione.*[29]

In his own aedileship he made the greatest of works ever made by human hand, not with temporary construction in mind, but rather made to last forever.

The *scaena* of the theatre was built in three tiers: the first of marble, the second of glass, and the top of gilded planks. Furthermore, it contained 360 Hymettus marble columns.[30] Between these columns stood 3,000 bronze statues.[31] The auditorium could accommodate 80,000 spectators, which is double the number of spectators Pompey's theatre could seat.[32] Pliny also mentions that the stage equipment, the gold cloth costumes, and the scene paintings were lavish to the extent that when

Scaurus reassembled all the theatre parts into his home on the Palatine, the lot was valued at 30,000,000 sesterces after being destroyed by fire.[33]

Pliny records that the theatre was intended to be used for a short period of time:

> CCCLX columnas M. Scauri aedilitate ad scaenam theatri temporari et vix mense uno futuri in usu viderunt portari silentio legum.[34]

> During the aedileship of M. Scaurus they saw 360 columns transferred to the stage of his theatre, which was temporary, and destined to be in use for scarcely a month, in silence of the laws.

Even though Pliny states that it was used "for scarcely a month," there is some evidence that the theatre actually stood for a number of years.[35] If this is true, then this theatre could be considered a prototype of the permanent stone theatre, since it stood longer than the festival for which it was built. One could also argue that the fact that this theatre became famous as Scaurus' own points in the direction of associating a theatre with a specific person rather than with the event being celebrated, and that Pompey's theatre represents the latest manifestation of a growing trend toward permanence.

Cicero provides us with rare information about Pompey's selection of plays for the opening program. Despite the lavish games given by Pompey on this occasion, Cicero reports in a letter to M. Marius that he was bored with the tragedies presented:

> quid enim delectationis habent sescenti muli in Clytaemestra aut in Equo Troiano creterrarum tria milia aut armatura varia peditatus et equitatus in aliqua pugna? quae popularem admirationem habuerunt, delectationem tibi nullam attulissent.[36]

> What pleasure, indeed, can 600 mules in the Clytemnestra or 3,000 bronze craters in the Trojan Horse or various armed battles of infantry or knights offer? What held the people captive would have brought no pleasure to you.

The Clytemnestra is that of Accius.[37] Two versions of the Equos Troianus were available to Pompey: that of Livius Andronicus and that of Naevius. While we can conjecture that the plot of each play centered on events surrounding the destruction of Troy, it is impossible to determine how these plays differed, if at all, or which of the two plays was performed. The third dramatic item listed by Cicero, *armatura varia peditatus et equitatus in aliqua pugna,* is difficult to qualify with any certainty. It is not clear whether he means that armed battles formed a part of the dramatic action within either of the two plays mentioned, in which case, of the two plays, the *Equos Troianus* seems the most likely, or that in addition to these plays an unnamed tragedy or *praetexta* was performed. If the reference is in fact to an unnamed *praetexta,* then the *praetexta* in question must have been a restaged version of an earlier play and not an original historical play; since we know of only a few *praetextae* produced in Rome by 55 B.C.E., one would have expected Cicero to record the name if a new play had been performed, especially given the importance of this occasion, rather than to treat the performance as something trite and uneventful. It is difficult to imagine that Pompey would have presented one of the known *praetextae* that glorify the ancestors of rival dynasties on an occasion where everything was carefully planned to promote his own prestige.

The plays presented were carefully selected for the occasion. The triumphant return of Agamemnon in the *Clytemnestra,* signaled by Cicero's reference to 600 mules, and the staging of a sacked city in the *Equos Troianus* not only recall, but actually recreate, Pompey's own triple triumph held only six years before the opening of his theatre. This triumph was celebrated for his victory over his third conquered continent—a feat unparalleled in Roman history, as were his first two triumphs, which were granted while he was still an *eques.*[38] Figures of fourteen nations served as a reminder of the nations and tribes subdued by Pompey.[39] It is not known how many statues were placed in or around the theatre, but it is interesting to note that even though the count may have fallen short of the number included by Scaurus at the opening of his temporary theatre, Pompey's statues had symbolic value, where Scaurus' had none. In effect, the inauguration of the theatre also became the inauguration of a monument that would serve as a permanent or perennial commemoration in Rome of Pompey's illustrious career, as the triumphal arch was to do later for triumphing generals.[40]

Despite the emphasis that Pompey placed on Agamemnon's triumphal entry into Mycenae, the surviving fragments from Accius' *Clytemnestra* do not give details of this scene.[41] The ten fragments that do survive reveal that Cassandra returns with Agamemnon and is murdered by Clytemnestra:

(1)

*. . . sed valvae resonunt regiae.*[42]

. . . but the palace doors resound.

(2)

*omnes gaudent facere recte, male pigrent.*

All men rejoice when they do the right thing, but regret it when they
do not.

The dramatic context of fragments 3–5 is unclear:

(3)

*deum regnator nocte caeca caelum e conspectu abstulit.*

The ruler of the gods removed the sky from sight with a blinding night.

(4)

*flucti inmisericordes iacere, taetra ad saxa adlidere.*

Merciless waves tossed and threw them against the foul rocks.

(5)

*pectore inchohatum fulmen flammam ostendabat Iovis.*

The just-begun lightning of Jupiter revealed a flame on his chest.

In fragment 6, Cassandra questions Clytemnestra's behavior toward her:

(6)

*cur me miseram inridet, magnis compotem et multis malis?*

Why does she mock pitiful me, who am a companion to great
hardships?

Cassandra correctly prophesized the day of her death in fragment 7:

(7)

*scibam hanc mihi supremam lucem et serviti finem dari.*

I knew that this day would be my last and an end to my slavery.

(8)

*. . . ut quae tum absentem rebus dubiis coniugem
tetinerit, nunc prodat ultorem?*

. . . as she who held him as husband in his absence
in uncertain times, now she betrays the avenger?

Is fragment 9 a description of the fate of Agamemnon and Cassandra?

(9)
. . . *seras potiuntur plagas.*

. . . they receive their late blows.

In fragment 10, Clytemnestra seems to be speaking to Electra:

(10)
*matrem ob iure factum incilas, genitorem iniustum adprobas.*

You blame your mother for a just act, you esteem your father for an
unjust one.

The emphasis on Agamemnon's triumphal entry in Pompey's production exaggerates the role of Agamemnon as a *triumphator* while down-
playing his imminent murder. Cicero's reference to 600 mules and the
gala events surrounding the theatre's opening make it clear that the audience was guided to interpret the triumph as Pompey's, rather than
as Agamemnon's. From a dramaturgical perspective, this creates a number of difficult problems. At what point, for example, did the audience
interpret the triumphal entry as Pompey's rather than Agamemnon's?
If the returning and soon-to-be-murdered Agamemnon is equated with
Pompey, does the audience need a selective response to know when Agamemnon ceases to be Pompey and when to return to the play proper
and cease reading topical allusions into it? These questions are difficult
to answer without knowing how the production "framed" the triumphal entry of Agamemnon and to what extent the audience was primed
through the various *ludi* and visual cues to interpret the stage productions in relation to Pompey's triple triumph.

The presence of Pompey in the audience further contributes to the
complex task of interpreting the effects of the opening program. A semiotic reading of Agamemnon's triumphal stage entrance produces the following dynamic: Pompey perceiving Agamemnon onstage as an allusion
to himself; the audience perceiving Pompey as Agamemnon onstage, but
also seeing him in the audience.

An audience would later face a similar interpretive dilemma at the
production of Cornelius Balbus' *praetexta, Iter,* discussed in chapter 3,

at which Balbus himself was in the audience. Whereas Pompey was alluding to himself onstage, Balbus was actually portrayed onstage, with the result that he could see himself onstage and the audience could see him onstage and in the audience. Balbus may have been consciously imitating Pompey at the opening of his theatre, but unfortunately for this discussion, we do not know whether Balbus was present at the opening of Pompey's theatre or whether he alluded to its opening celebrations at the opening of his own theatre.

It seems that the association between Pompey and Agamemnon on this occasion was so successful that it was later used as a term of reproach against him. In 48 B.C.E., seven years after the opening of the theatre and shortly before the Battle of Pharsalus, Domitius Ahenobarbus made Pompey odious, according to Plutarch, by calling him "Agamemnon" and the "King of Kings."[43] Complicating the allusion to Agamemnon, however, is Pompey's self-identification with Alexander the Great outside of the theatre. At the beginning of his political career, Pompey adopted Alexander's hairstyle, to the amusement of his detractors.[44] As mentioned above, Pompey again alluded to Alexander in his triple triumph of 61 B.C.E. by wearing, or at least claiming to be wearing, Alexander's purple cloak.[45] If Appian's account is accurate, then there is a possible double allusion at the restaged production of Accius' *Clytemnestra*: Pompey's self-styled allusion to Agamemnon would recall his earlier self-styled allusion to Alexander the Great in his triumphal procession. Did Pompey further connect the two allusions by having the actor portraying Agamemnon onstage wear Alexander's purple cloak?

The representation of a sacked city onstage in the *Equos Troianus* was another ingenious way for Pompey to allude to his recent triumph at his theatre's opening, thereby taking full advantage of the opportunity (and audience) for advertising his political prestige. We do not know how the sacking of the city was described or whether an enactment was inserted into either Livius' or Naevius' version, since only one fragment survives from each play, nor do we know whether one of the conquering Greek generals was intended as an allusion to Pompey in this production.[46] From Cicero's account, the sacking of Troy seems to have been represented by bronze bowls displayed onstage.[47] The emphasis on booty may have reflected Pompey's recent triumph, at which he advertised on signs the number of towns taken under his command.[48]

With the plays presented at his theatre's opening, Pompey removed the barrier between actor and audience through dramatic allusion, with the result that a fixed dramatic text was made topical, not by adapting the text onstage through actors' interpolations, thereby creating a new performance text, but by emphasizing scenes that the audience could understand both in the specific context of the play and in the more general context of the occasion of its restaging. The production alluded to a historical person or event onstage within the dramatic context of a tragedy, rather than having the person actually represented onstage, as in *praetextae*. The incorporation of offstage reality into the dramatic reality of the plays required the audience to have a selective response to the tragedies, resulting in changing perspectives: Are we watching Agamemnon's or Pompey's triumph? When does Agamemnon cease to allude to Pompey? Is this the destruction of Troy or some modern city? In essence we have the *contaminatio* of the play with allusions from the audience's reality, thereby turning ancient tragedy into a contemporary *praetexta*. Furthermore, whereas *praetextae* are dramatic recreations of historical events, here tragedy is understood *in relation to* a historical event.

## STAGING *BRUTUS*

The *contaminatio* of a tragedy with allusions from the audience's reality, whether or not these were physically incorporated into the drama onstage, finds frequent expression soon after Pompey's theatre opening. Of particular interest is the way in which a fixed dramatic text becomes a new performance text through allusion rather than through actors' interpolations. While the triumphing Agamemnon onstage in the *Clytemnestra* alluded to Pompey offstage, the dramatic allusion depended on the occasion of the theatre's opening rather than on its relation to a previous production. As allusive commentaries on contemporary political events in performance contexts, two plays emerge that show the intertextuality of themes and performances, the *Brutus* of Accius and the *Thyestes* of Varius Rufus. Not only do we have a character onstage alluding to a historical person in each, but we also have allusions to previously staged versions of these plays. In other words, the audience must interpret a play it is now watching in relation to how a previous version of the same play or a play on the same theme was understood as an allusion to a contemporary political figure.

Accius' *Brutus* recounted Sextus Tarquinius Superbus' rape of Lucretia and the expulsion of the Tarquins at the hands of Lucius Junius Brutus and (Lucius) Tarquinius Collatinus.[49] The original occasion for the performance of Accius' *Brutus* is unknown. Whatever the date, the play was commissioned by (D. Junius) Brutus Callaicus for an occasion designed to add his brilliant achievements to those of his homonymous ancestors. Although Callaicus could have commissioned a play based upon his own achievements, in the tradition of such contemporary historical plays as Naevius' *Clastidium,* Ennius' *Ambracia,* or Pacuvius' *Paullus,* his choice of a play about his homonymous ancestor's role in founding the Roman Republic proved especially effective. Not only did a play based upon the achievements of his "ancestor" advertise anew his family's early valor, but it also placed the achievements of Callaicus on a par with those of this illustrious ancestor.

Livy's account of the legend (1.56–60) may have been based upon Accius' play.[50] According to Livy, while beseiging Ardea, the prince Sextus Tarquinius, son of King Lucius Tarquinius Superbus, together with his brothers Titus and Arruns and his cousin Tarquinius Collatinus, decided to test the feminine virtues of their wives. The princes' wives were discovered at a banquet in the midst of young company, but Collatinus' wife, Lucretia, was home spinning wool in the midst of her slave women. Days later, Sextus returned to Ardea to rape Lucretia. Lucretia reported the crime to her husband Collatinus and to Brutus, whereupon she killed herself. Brutus, who had pretended to be dumb (hence his name) to survive the outrageous behavior of his uncle, King Tarquinius Superbus, revealed his true personality and gathered forces from Ardea to descend upon Rome. The king, who had usurped the throne from King Servius Tullius with his daughter Tullia's help, was expelled from Rome, with two of his sons, on account of his tyrannical behavior; he then settled in Caere (Etruria). His son Sextus, however, had assumed power at Gabii, where he was later killed. Brutus and Collatinus were elected the first consuls of the Roman Republic.

Four fragments from Accius' *Brutus* survive. It is not clear, however, at what point in the legend the dramatic action of the *Brutus* begins. We have speeches delivered by Tarquinius and a *vates,* but neither the names of any of the other characters nor the makeup of the chorus is recoverable, although one can assume that Brutus appeared in the play, as well as Lucretia, unless her rape was described in a messenger speech or a choral ode. The first two fragments, as previously cited in chapter 3, concern a dream of Tarquinius Superbus foretelling the rise of a Roman republic and its interpretation by a *vates,* or soothsayer.[51]

> TARQUINIUS: *quoniam quieti corpus nocturno impetu*
> *dedi sopore placans artus languidos,*

*visum est in somnis pastor ad me adpellere*
*pecus lanigerum eximia pulchritudine;*
*duos consanguineos arietes inde eligi*
*praeclarioremque alterum inmolare me.*
*deinde eius germanum cornibus conitier,*
*in me arietare, eoque ictu me ad casum dari:*
*exin prostratum terra, graviter saucium,*
*resupinum in caelo contueri maximum*
*mirificum facinus: dextrorsum orbem flammeum*
*radiatum solis liquier cursu novo.*

TARQUINIUS: Since then, at night's urging, I gave my body
to peaceful rest, soothing my tired limbs with sleep,
a shepherd, in a dream, seemed to drive toward me
a woolly flock of exceptional beauty;
two kindred rams were chosen,
and I slaughtered the nobler of the two.
Then the ram's brother butted with its horns
and rammed at me, and by that blow, I fell.
Then, lying on the ground on my back, seriously hurt,
I saw a great and marvelous deed in the sky:
the fiery radiating disk of the sun
melted to the righthand side on a new path.

This dream portends Tarquinius' overthrow by Brutus, who is still dis-
simulating his true intelligence at this point in the drama; but the *Vates*
offers an interpretation that assures the king of Rome's greatness without preserving Tarquinius' own fragile position:

VATES: *Rex, quae in vita usurpant homines, cogitant curant vident*
*quaeque agunt vigilantes agitantque, ea si cui in somno accidunt*
*minus mirum est, sed di in rem tantam haut temere inproviso offerunt.*
*proin vide ne quem tu esse hebetem deputes aeque ac pecus*
*is sapientia munitum pectus egregie gerat,*
*teque regno expellat; nam id quod de sole ostentum est tibi,*
*populo conmutationem rerum portendit fore*
*perpropinquam. haec bene verruncent populo! nam quod ad dexteram*
*cepit cursum ab laeva signum praepotens, pulcherrume*
*auguratum est rem Romanam publicam summam fore.*

SOOTHSAYER: Sire, what things men perform, ponder, worry over, and
    see in their lives

and what they do and busy themselves with when awake, if these things
    occur to one in a dream,
it is less a cause for wonder, but in such a great matter the gods offer
    you something unforeseen and not for nothing.
Be on guard lest the man whom you think is as dumb as a sheep bear
is a heart eminently fortified with wisdom,
and expels you from your kingdom; for that which was shown to you
    regarding the sun
portends a change of affairs for the people
in the near future. May these things turn out well for the people! For,
    since the powerful portent
took its course to the righthand side from the left, most wonderfully
did it foretell that the Roman state would be supreme.

These speeches are clearly modeled upon the speeches found in
Aeschylus' *Persians,* between Atossa and the chorus (159–225). By
modeling Tarquinius' dream upon that of Atossa, the mother of Xerxes,
Accius makes the connection between the Persian kings and the Tarquins as dynasties that inflicted the evils of monarchy upon their subjects and stood in the way of democracy in Athens and the future Republic in Rome. These speeches are also connected to Pseudo-Seneca's
*Octavia,* as discussed in chapter 3.

A reference to King Servius Tullius survives in the third fragment:[52]

*Tullius, qui libertatem civibus stabiliverat.*[53]

Tullius, who had established freedom for the citizens.

In the final surviving fragment, the office of the consuls is created:

*. . . qui recte consulat, consul siet.*[54]

. . . Let him who gives good counsel, be consul.

From a dramatic point of view, the creation of the consulship may not
seem exciting, but from a thematic point of view, the play's ending emphasizes the role played by Brutus in establishing the Republic—a role
that Brutus Callaicus was eager to promote in this play to add luster to
his own accomplishments.

The second known occasion on which Accius' *Brutus* played an important cultural role was in 57 B.C.E. at the *ludi Apollinares,* when the

actor Aesopus aggressively promoted the recall of Cicero from exile. In the *Pro Sestio* (56–58), Cicero claims that Aesopus made apposite interpolations and emphatic line readings to plead Cicero's cause from the stage. It is not clear from Cicero's account, however, what the exact theatre program was on this occasion, that is, whether the entire *Brutus* was performed in addition to another play, or whether a quote was simply inserted into Accius' *Eurysaces* or Ennius' *Andromache*, which were also performed, in whole or in part, at the games. Since Cicero quotes from both of these plays in his speech, it is impossible to determine which play was "contaminated" by quotes from the other. Cicero does make it clear that Aesopus was adding lines spontaneously in response to the enthusiasm of the audience. The line of the *Brutus* that Aesopus recited was the line on King Servius Tullius that I just quoted: *Tullius, qui libertatem civibus stabiliverat.*

Cicero, who in the *Pro Sestio* was defending his actions in connection with the Catilinarian conspiracy of 63 B.C.E., makes the incredible claim that he was mentioned by name in Accius' play: *nominatim sum appellatus in Bruto*, "In the *Brutus* I was mentioned by name." Clearly Cicero means that Accius' Tullius refers to himself in some way, but the most likely explanation is that Aesopus and the audience (re)interpreted Tullius to mean Cicero or understood that he is Accius' Tullius by metonymy.[55] In writing of the audience's activities on the same occasion but at the performance of a comedy, Cicero relates how the text and actor could make a play topical as an attack against Clodius, who was present at the theatre:

> *et quoniam facta mentio est ludorum, ne illud quidem praetermittam, in magna varietate sententiarum numquam ullum fuisse locum, in quo aliquid a poeta dictum cadere in tempus nostrum videretur, quod aut populum universum fugeret aut non exprimeret ipse actor.*
>
> (*PRO SESTIO* 55)

And since mention has been made of stage performances, I shall not omit to mention that never, in so great a variety of sentiments [in the comedy], was there a passage in which something written by the dramatist seemed relevant to our own time either that the entire audience failed to understand or that the actor himself failed to point out.

On another occasion when the actor emphasized lines that alluded to Pompey in a negative way, Cicero also understood the audience's interpretation of the allusion in relation to contemporary events rather than to the dramatist's foresight.[56]

By no stretch of historical revisionism could Cicero's claim be taken seriously by us today. Yet the fact that the claim *could* be made points to the extent to which descendants could lay claim to the accomplishments of ancestors, real or imagined, especially those made in service to the state. It furthermore illustrates the ability of Romans to accept such claims, thereby exchanging an interest in historical accuracy for the immediate benefits of historical instruction.

In the opening sentence of his *Pro Sestio,* Cicero claims that very few Romans have risked their lives for the sake of liberty and Rome's Republican constitution. That Cicero had his own services to the Roman people in mind is made clear by the later references to Aesopus' performance and his own recall from exile. By reminding his audience of the accomplishments of Servius Tullius, Cicero connects his own consulship to the achievements of the homonymous legendary figure.[57] Since Cicero was a *novus homo,* this connection provided a fictional royal pedigree for Cicero's family tree. Cicero had good reason to appeal to Roman legend to defend his infamous consulship, in which he executed leading conspirators without regard for proper legal precedents. As the self-appointed savior of Rome, in the dark hour of Catiline's conspiracy, Cicero was fashioning himself as another founder of the Roman Republic, although the title was never given, nor was it claimed by him. Since Romulus and Camillus were considered the previous founders of Rome, Cicero's posturing was extraordinary.[58] Assuming the glories of Roman legend also helped Cicero to exaggerate his own role in saving the Republic from Catiline's conspiracy.

If Cicero could position himself as a savior of the Republic, so, too, could Brutus in 44 B.C.E. As the putative descendant of the famous Brutus who expelled the Tarquins from Rome and helped establish the Roman Republic, Marcus Brutus, like Brutus Callaicus, tried to propagate a connection between himself and his "ancestor" using Accius' *Brutus* after the assassination of Julius Caesar.[59] Rome's legendary tradition already linked Marcus Junius Brutus' ancestors to the ideals of a Roman Republic, and his participation in Caesar's assassination in many ways echoed the heroism of his putative ancestor.

The perfect opportunity presented itself to Brutus at the *ludi Apollinares* in 44 B.C.E., four months after Caesar's death. During the *ludi,* Greek and Latin plays were staged, in addition to various other forms of scenic entertainment. As *praetor urbanus* for that year, Brutus was in charge of providing the games for this festival. But since Brutus was absent from Rome, Gaius Antonius, brother of Mark Antony, was instructed to have the *Brutus* produced.[60] Such a connection between the man who expelled Tarquinius and Caesar's assassin would have cast Brutus in the role of a present-day tyrannicide, freeing the Republic from a second monarchy. This association would not have been difficult for contemporaries to make, since Caesar had already been identified with Tarquinius following his attempted coronation at the Lupercalia in 44 B.C.E.[61] and in a popular verse that was attached to statues of Caesar and Lucius Brutus days before his assassination:

> *Brutus, quia reges eiecit, consul primus factus est:*
> hic, quia consules eiecit, rex postremus factus est.[62]

> Brutus, since he expelled the kings, was made the first consul:
> this man, since he expelled the consuls, was made the last king.

Brutus' immediate concern was his own safety and return to Rome by means of popular support expressed in the theatre. Clearly, he thought that his self-identification with his putative legendary ancestor would be the best means to gain it.[63] In invoking his "ancestor," Brutus would have been recording his services to the state with the very same *praetexta* that had been written for his more recent ancestor, Brutus Callaicus, and that celebrated the patriotic exploits of the even earlier Lucius Junius Brutus. Centuries of patriotism by the Bruti would be concentrated— and, more importantly, advertised—in a single play. Thus Accius' play written for Callaicus would also become Marcus Brutus' own *praetexta*. In one important respect, however, Marcus Junius Brutus surpassed his ancestor. Whereas Lucius Brutus simply expelled the Tarquins from Rome, Brutus actually committed tyrannicide.[64]

Despite Brutus' emulation of his putative ancestor, it should not surprise us that Cicero claimed that Brutus was imitating Cicero himself rather than his legendary ancestor when he killed Caesar. Immediately following his assassination of Caesar, Brutus, in a wonderful example of the invocation and perpetuation of historical precedent at Rome, apparently called upon Cicero to witness the deed, as Cicero himself relates in the *Second Philippic*, inveighing against Antony as follows (2.12.28):

> *at quem ad modum me coarguerit homo acutus, recordamini. "Caesare interfecto," inquit, "statim cruentum alte extollens Brutus pugionem Ci-*

*ceronem nominatim exclamavit atque ei recuperatam libertatem est grat-*
*ulatus." cur mihi potissimum? quia sciebam? vide, ne illa causa fuerit ad-*
*pellandi mei, quod, cum rem gessisset consimilem rebus iis, quas ipse ges-*
*seram, me potissimum testatus est se aemulum mearum laudium extitisse.*

But consider how this clever fellow [Antony] has convicted me. "After
Caesar had been slain," he said, "Brutus, at once raising up high his
bloody dagger, shouted for Cicero by name and congratulated him on
the recovery of freedom." Why me in particular? Because I was aware of
the plot? Consider whether the reason for Brutus' shouting of my name
wasn't for this reason, that, since he had done a deed exactly like the deeds
I had done, he called on me especially to witness that he had appeared as
a rival of my fame.

Cicero, in making this claim, actually lends contemporary political
relevance to his own earlier actions and provides for the posture that he
was even figuratively present at Caesar's assassination as a mentor to
Brutus. Brutus, of course, had good reason to connect his assassination
of Caesar with Cicero's execution of the Catilinarian conspirators. In
the framework of political precedents at Rome, Brutus was rivaling not
only the actions of his putative ancestor, but also, through his invocation of Cicero, the services rendered by Cicero to the state. Brutus, therefore, was at once appealing to his "ancestor" for a legendary precedent
for his own actions and to Cicero for contemporary political and legal
justification.[65]

Brutus' efforts as praetor to produce the *Brutus* in 44 B.C.E. were
thwarted, however, by Gaius Antony, who, fearing the audience's retaliation against the conspirators for Caesar's murder, substituted the
*Tereus* of Accius at the last minute.[66] This could have been the pretext
to obfuscate the real aim—to prevent what the tyrannicides intended to
create, namely, an enhancement of Brutus' image and status through his
association with the homonymous founder of the Republic. We know
from a letter he wrote to Cicero that Brutus, not knowing of the substitution, thought that the *Brutus* had been performed, and we can only
guess at his disappointment at the disappearance of such a politically apposite opportunity. Cicero, in a letter to Atticus, records that the *Tereus*
was nevertheless successful as political propaganda.[67] What was so topical about the *Tereus* that it was considered pertinent to Brutus' political situation at Rome?

The myth of Tereus' rape and mutilation of Philomela included the
circumstances surrounding the revenge of Procne, Tereus' wife and Phi-

lomela's sister, who, in retaliation for her husband's crime, murdered her son Itys and served him to Tereus; eventually all three were turned into birds.[68] Could the general theme of murder and vengeance for tyrannical behavior, even in a mythological and familial, not political, setting, have been enough to remind the audience of Caesar's murder? Or was the success of the play due more to audience expectation than to the dramatic plot? Cicero records that the audience actually expected the Latin play, on the occasion of the *ludi,* to be politically apposite, in proof of which very few people attended the presentation of the simultaneously produced Greek games.[69] In either case, one cannot rule out the possibility that there was an "organized reception" for the play—that support for Brutus would have been expressed by the audience regardless of the play performed, since Cicero claims that at least some pro-Republican supporters were planted in the audience, and further suggests that there was little in Accius' play worth cheering.[70] In essence, Cicero transforms the audience from spectators to jurors.

As Shakespeare realized, the assassination of Caesar was a perfect theme for a drama, yet it never made it onto the Roman stage. Although there is no direct evidence, one wonders whether there was a conscious effort on the part of Caesar's supporters to connect his assassination with the plot of a tragedy at his funeral. Suetonius reports that between the funeral *ludi* the following line was sung in order to arouse pity and resentment at his death:

> . . . *men servasse ut essent qui me perderent?*[71]

> . . . Did I save them so that they might destroy me?

This is a quote from the *Armorum iudicium* of Pacuvius, in which Ajax bemoans the treachery of his companions. Accius wrote a play by the same name, but it must be assumed that either Pacuvius' version or this particular line from his play was judged to be more apt for the occasion than Accius' *Armorum iudicium.* The line makes an association between Caesar and Ajax, who, according to the Greek myth, lost a contest against Odysseus unfairly, thus implying that the death of Caesar was undeserved.[72] Furthermore, it places the assassination itself in a sort of mythical light and would be an appropriate response to Brutus' sympathizers, who had used the staging of Accius' *Tereus* to express their support.

The second play written on the theme of Brutus' expulsion of the Tarquins, the *Brutus* of Cassius Parmensis, is a little-known play of enormous consequence for plays on the Brutus theme and the death of Caesar.[73] The author was an aristocrat who was also an enemy of Julius Caesar and Octavian/Augustus.[74] Although Cassius participated in Caesar's assassination, he should not be confused with Gaius Cassius Longinus, who, like Brutus, was the leader of the plot. The role played by Cassius Parmensis, however, was significant enough that he was killed following the Battle of Actium by Octavian's order.[75]

The evidence for attributing a *Brutus* to Cassius comes from Varro's *De lingua latina,* where he refers to the play by name:

> *inter vesperuginem et iubar dicta nox intempesta, ut in Bruto Cassii quod dicebat Lucretia: nocte intempesta nostram devenit domum.*[76]

> The period between dusk and dawn is called the dead of night, as Lucretia said in the *Brutus* of Cassius: "In the dead of night he came to our home."

The dramatic action of the play cannot be reconstructed from only one line, but it seems that if Lucretia is the speaker, the plot of Cassius' play centered upon her rape, and that the depiction of Brutus' expulsion of the Tarquins did not differ significantly in thematic content from either Accius' play or, indeed, Roman legend.

While a date in the 40's or 30's B.C.E. seems likely, it is not possible to determine the specific date of composition, nor even to know whether the play was ever performed. Of particular interest is the relation of this play to Accius' *Brutus.* A date of composition before Caesar's death is certainly possible, but it seems unlikely that Brutus would have selected Cassius' version over Accius' and failed to take advantage of the latter play's connection with his ancestors, real or imagined. A date following Caesar's assassination, however, would have had enormous consequences for Brutus' attempted restaging of Accius' play. Since Antony's brother substituted Accius' *Tereus* for his *Brutus,* an overt connection between the legendary and contemporary Brutus was not made. Did Cassius therefore write a new *Brutus,* either for stage production or for circulation, sometime after 43 B.C.E., to glorify all three Bruti—the legendary first consul and his homonymes, Callaicus and the contemporary tyrannicide—two of whom Accius' play had celebrated almost a century earlier? Certainty is impossible but, as in the earlier case of Brutus' attempted restaging of Accius' *Brutus,* the coincidence of legend and contemporary politics could not have been better planned.

Versions of plays on Lucius Junius Brutus' expulsion of the Tarquins illustrate the continuing removal of the barrier between actor and audience. Not only must the audience understand an allusion to a contemporary political figure effected through a character onstage, but it must also understand the relevance of this allusion to previously staged versions of the same play or theme. The (re)interpretation of stage reality in relation to the audience's reality results in the audience's growing theatricalized perception of its own reality: would Accius' play *Brutus* have alluded to Caesar's assassin, who himself imitated the actions of his putative ancestor Brutus? A similar dynamic is apparent with plays centering upon the Atreus-Thyestes myth, in particular the extent to which fixed dramatic texts continued to be understood as topical through allusions both to a contemporary political figure using a character portrayed onstage, and to previously staged versions.

## THYESTES ON THE ROMAN STAGE

The myth relating the rivalry between Atreus and Thyestes was popular on the Roman stage and involves three main episodes in dramatic versions, two of which take place in Mycenae and the third in Epirus. These episodes include Thyestes' adultery with Atreus' wife Aerope and his attempt to usurp the throne, Atreus' revenge at the infamous banquet in Mycenae, and Thyestes' exile to Epirus, where he rapes his daughter Pelopia and begets Aegisthus.[77] The myth was extremely popular on the Greek stage in the fifth and fourth centuries.[78] Roman versions include the *Thyestes* of Ennius, the *Atreus* of Accius, the *Thyestes* of Gracchus, the *Thyestes* of Cassius Parmensis, the *Thyestes* of Varius Rufus, the *Atreus* of P. Pomponius Secundus, the *Atreus* of Mamercus Aemilius Scaurus, the *Thyestes* of Seneca, and the *Thyestes* of Maternus.[79]

In recent studies, mythological tyrants on the Roman stage are treated as analogues to historical persons.[80] Separating drama from reality is difficult, however, when allusion is the means by which to distinguish the two. As a figurative device, allusion avoids direct analogy, thereby producing an "out" for dramatists undertaking dangerous themes, and for their perceived targets, of the "no offense intended, none taken" variety. When offense is actually taken, whether by the alleged target or by those pointing fingers (*animus nocendi*), only then does a generic description of a stage tyrant become a perceived insult. A ruler who is viewed as tyrannical differs from a self-styled tyrant who may choose to reciprocate the charges of tyranny, through mythological allusion, against those who make them. When an all-but-in-name king, like Augustus, presents a play that seems to draw attention to his precarious constitutional position, the intended meaning of the allusion becomes more complicated to interpret. What message(s) did Augustus intend to send by commissioning a seemingly anti-tyrannical play, the *Thyestes,* for his triumph in 29 B.C.E.? To consider this, one must place the play in the wider context of dramas either written or perceived to have been written as condemnations of Imperial power. A closer look at tragedies on the Thyestes theme at Rome and allusions to the mythological king on the political stage reveals that there was a strong interrelationship between theatrical and political allusion, but the exact nature of this relationship is often difficult to reconstruct.[81]

It seems that a myth depicting fraternal or civil strife was perennially apposite at Rome. From this observation, however, it cannot be argued that all references to tyranny and all plays on the Atreus-Thyestes myth were intended as specific attacks against contemporary figures, unless we have the cultural contexts surrounding original or restaged versions. Although we know that Ennius' *Thyestes* was presented at the *ludi Apollinares* in 169 B.C.E., for example, we do not know specific details surrounding the occasion of performance, and therefore it is impossible to place the play in its cultural context. The same is true of Accius' *Atreus* in the Gracchan era. As discussed at the beginning of this chapter, one may suspect anti-tyrannical sentiment and allusions to the political struggle at Rome between the Optimates and the Populares, yet without the original date of production, it is impossible to argue with any certainty the presence of contemporary allusions within the play. The plays presented at the opening of Pompey's theatre, therefore, remain the earliest surviving and most pivotal examples of the deliberate connection between the production of a tragedy and contemporary events.

The most important version of the Atreus-Thyestes myth for this study is Varius' *Thyestes,* whose production date is known, thereby allowing us an opportunity to consider its relation to earlier and later versions. My focus is on how plays on the Atreus-Thyestes myth may allude at once to contemporary political figures and previous versions and productions of plays on the same theme.

Varius' *Thyestes* was commissioned by Augustus and produced at the games presented after Actium in 29 B.C.E., celebrating his triple triumph.[82] The date and occasion of its production are established from two scholiast editions:

*Varius cognomento Rufus Thyesten tragoediam magna cura absolutam post Actiacam victoriam Augusto ludis euis in scaena edidit; pro qua fabula sestertium deciens accepit.*[83]

Varius Rufus produced the tragedy *Thyestes* onstage, which was composed with great care after Augustus' Actian victory, in his games; for this play, he accepted 1,000,000 sesterces.

Although there is no direct evidence in the form of an inscription to corroborate the date of Varius' play, there is no reason to doubt its accuracy.[84] Varius' *Thyestes* was well known in ancient Rome, and his connection with the Julian dynasty is supported by unflattering allusions to Antony in his epic poem *De morte*.[85] It is unknown why Varius was chosen for this important commission.[86] Was he the only poet in Maecenas' circle who wanted to try writing in this genre? After all, Propertius, Vergil, and Horace never attempted a dramatic work, and it is unlikely that Augustus would have approached the aristocratic Pollio, who did write tragedies, with this request.

Though commissioning a play on Aeneas would have seemed apt, Augustus could not look to a nonmythological ancestor, as the Bruti could, in the context of a *praetexta,* to frame an allusion to his own achievements. Had Julius Caesar commissioned a *praetexta* to record his military conquests, for example, Augustus could have restaged such a play to rival Brutus' attempted restaging of the play commissioned by Brutus Callaicus. Varius' *Thyestes* was perhaps one of the only plays written specifically for a triumph and produced in Rome since the triumph of Brutus Callaicus a century earlier.[87] If the scholiast's notice is accurate, then it is also the last recorded original production of a tragedy under the Republic.

The play is lost, and it seems to have been the only tragedy composed by Varius.[88] We know, however, that ancient literary criticism held Varius' play up as a model of excellence in tragic composition.[89] Only two lines survive, in a passage in which Quintilian compares Catiline's furious madness to Atreus' by quoting a speech by Atreus:

*iam fero infandissima,*
*iam facere cogor.*[90]

Now I bear most unspeakable crimes,
now I am forced to commit them.

Atreus' reference to the unspeakable deeds he is about to commit as a reaction to crimes committed against him points to a dramatic action centered in Mycenae preceding his revenge at the banquet scene.[91] Unfortunately, nothing is known of its actual performance and reception on this important occasion. The value of the performance as an allusion to Augustus, therefore, must be gauged by the popularity of the myth itself upon the Roman stage and, in particular, its relation to earlier dramatic versions at Rome.

Varius' play was preceded by three versions that established the dramatic tradition of the myth in Rome.[92] The first version to appear on the Roman stage was the *Thyestes* of Ennius. Although the point is controversial, Jocelyn convincingly argues that the events of Ennius' play take place in Thesprotus' court after the events in Mycenae, including Thyestes' adultery with Aerope and the banquet scene.[93] This implies that the myth was well known enough from Greek versions and literature for Ennius to treat a later aspect of the myth.

The plot of Accius' *Atreus,* on the other hand, does revolve around the infamous banquet scene. The surviving fragments reveal that Atreus has discovered Thyestes' adultery with Aerope, and they contain descriptions of the banquet and Thyestes' discovery of his crime.[94] In other plays on the Thyestes myth, Accius seems to have treated different events, such as the recognition of Aegisthus and the kidnapping of Chrysippus.[95]

In fragment 1, the family background of Atreus is given:

(1)

*Servius Dan. in Aen. VIII 130 "alii ita tradunt Steropes et Atlantis filios Oenomaum et Maiam fuisse, Oenomai Hippodamiam filiam, unde Atreus natus; at Maiae filius Mercurius, ex quo Arcades, de quibus Evander, quod Accius in Atreo plenius refert."*[96]

Servius Dan. on *Aen.* 8.130: "Others relate that Oenomaus and Maia were the children of Sterope and Atlas, that Hippodamia was the daughter of Oenomaus, of whom Atreus was born; also, Mercury was the son of Maia, from whom were the Arcadians, among whom was Evander, which Accius relates fully in the *Atreus.*"

Fragment 2 describes how Pelops won Hippodamia:

(2)
*simul et Pisaea praemia arrepta a socro*
*. . . possedit suo. . . .*

At the same time as he takes the Pisaean prize
... snatched from his father-in-law. ...

Atreus lists grievances he has with his brother and resolves to punish him in fragments 3–5:

(3)
ATREUS: *iterum Thyestes Atreum adtractatum advenit,*
*iterum iam adgreditur me et quietum exsuscitat:*
*maior mihi moles, maius miscendumst malum,*
*qui illius acerbum cor contundam et comprimam.*[97]

ATREUS: Again, Thyestes comes to annoy Atreus,
again, he approaches me and disturbs my peace:
greater the toil for me, a greater evil must be planned,
I, who, will crush and smother his bitter heart.

(4)
*⟨quae⟩ ego incipio conata exequar.*

What attempts that I begin, I will carry out.

(5)
ATREUS: *oderint,*
*dum metuant.*

ATREUS: Let them hate,
while they fear.[98]

In fragments 6–9a, Atreus describes how Thyestes committed adultery with his wife:

(6)
*qui non sat habuit coniugem inlexe in stuprum.*

He who did not think enough committed adultery with my wife.

(7)
*... quod re in summa summum esse arbitror*
*periclum, matres conquinari regias,*
*contaminari stirpem ac misceri genus.*

... Indeed, I consider it to be the highest danger
in high affairs of state, for mothers to have contaminated kingdoms,
to have fouled the stock and to have corrupted the tribe.

(8)
*adde huc quod mihi portento caelestum pater*
*prodigium misit, regni stabilimen mei,*
*agnum inter pecudes aurea clarum coma,*
*em clam Thyestem clepere ausum esse e regia,*
*qua in re adiutricem coniugem cepit sibi.*

Add, furthermore, the fact that the Father has sent to me a celestial sign,
through a portent, the foundation of my kingdom,
the golden fleece of a famous ram among the flocks,
which Thyestes dared to steal from my kingdom in secret;
in which deed, he took my wife as an accomplice to himself.

(9)
THYESTES: . . . *vigilandum est semper: multae insidiae sunt bonis.*[99]

THYESTES: . . . One must always be vigilant: for many ambushes are laid
for good men.

(9a)
*id quod multi invideant multique expetant inscitiast*
*postulare, nisi laborem summa cum cura ecferas.*

To seek that which many men envy and many seek
is foolish, unless you carry out the task with great care.

The description of the seating arrangement for the banquet is spoken by
an unknown character and includes the earliest extant use, in Latin, of
the term *tyrannus:*

(10)
*ne cum tyranno quisquam epulandi gratia*
*accumbat mensam aut eandem vescatur dapem.*

Neither let just anyone recline at the table for the sake of feasting
with a tyrant nor let him eat the same feast.[100]

Fragments 11 and 12 refer to Atreus' preparations for the banquet:

(11)
*epularum fictor, scelerum fratris delitor. . . .*

The maker of the feast, the destroyer of a brother's crimes. . . .

(12)
>                               *concoquit*
> *partem vapore flammae, veribus in foco*
> *lacerta tribuit.*

>                               He cooked
> part with the steam of the fire, over the hearth
> he separated the limbs onto spits.

Divine displeasure in the banquet is signaled by thunder in fragment 13:

(13)
> *sed quid tonitru turbida torvo*
> *concussa repente aequora caeli*
> *sensimus sonere?*

> But why did we hear
> the sky suddenly roar
> with the clash of thunder?

Fragment 14 describes Atreus' confirmation that Thyestes has eaten his children, but the fragment does not make clear whether Atreus is actually watching his brother as he delivers the line:

(14)
> ATREUS: *natis sepulchro ipse est parens.*

> ATREUS: A father himself is his children's tomb.

Thyestes realizes that he has been deceived by Atreus and reacts to the knowledge that he has eaten his own children and that he is now polluted:

(15)
> THYESTES: *fregisti fidem.*
> ATREUS: *neque dedi neque do infideli cuiquam. . . .*

> THYESTES: You broke your trust.
> ATREUS: Neither did I give, nor do I give, to one untrustworthy. . . .

(16)
> *ipsus hortatur me frater, ut meos malis miser*
> *manderem natos.*

My brother himself urged me, that I, poor wretch, through these evils,
would eat my children.

(17)
*egone Argivum imperium attingam aut Pelopia digner domo?*
*quoi me ostendam? quod templum adeam? quem ore funesto alloquar?*

Shall I attain Argive power or be deemed worthy of the House of
    Pelops?
Where shall I show myself? What temple shall I approach? Whom shall
    I address with my deathly lips?

It is not clear whether Atreus or Thyestes is the speaker of lines 18–19:

(18)
*ecquis hoc animadvortet? vincite!*

Is anyone paying attention? Subdue him!

(19)
*numquam istam imminuam curam infitiando tibi.*

Never will I weaken that care in denying to you.

The placement and context of the last fragment is unclear:

(20)
*probae etsi in segetem sunt deteriorem datae*
*fruges, tamen ipsae suapte natura enitent.*

Even if good grain is spread among a bad crop,
nevertheless, it shines through its innate nature.

Accius' Atreus possesses the typical features of a ruthless tyrant,
but his character may be tyrannical as a response to political pressures,
in particular the political ambitions, whether real or perceived, of his
brother Thyestes.[101] The fragments do not give an adequate picture of
the characterization of Thyestes that might justify, however tenuously,
Atreus' reasons for punishing him with such cruelty. Deception plays a
large role in the play, both Atreus' punishment of his brother and Thyestes' later knowledge of it, but the fragments do not reveal whether the
play contained an emphasis on deceit in the speeches.
    Evidence for a *Thyestes* by the same Cassius Parmensis who com-

posed a *Brutus* is controversial.[102] There are questions surrounding not only Cassius' composition of a *Thyestes* but also its possible stage production. The evidence is late and comes mainly from scholiasts: Apuleius the Grammarian, Porphyrion, and the Horatian scholiast Pseudo-Acro, who writes:

> . . . *multi crediderunt Thyestem Cassii Parmensis fuisse. scripserat enim multas alias tragoedias.*[103]

> . . . Many believed that there was a *Thyestes* by Cassius Parmensis. Indeed, he wrote many other tragedies.

No fragments survive from Cassius' play to corroborate the scholiasts' notices. The inherent anti-tyrannical sentiment of the Thyestes myth, while it fits into Cassius' known anti-Caesarian political stance, is not sufficient evidence for the play's existence.[104] The accumulated evidence, however, while sparse and somewhat contradictory, does point to the probability that Cassius wrote a *Thyestes*.[105] Depending on the date of Cassius' *Brutus*, we have the beginning of anti-tyrannical sentiment expressed in tragedies, at a date rarely, if ever, noticed.[106]

The importance of this play lies in its relation to Varius' *Thyestes*. The circulation or production of a *Thyestes* by a dramatist hostile to either Julius Caesar or Octavian/Augustus, depending upon the date of its composition, puts into perspective Augustus' commissioning a rival version of the *Thyestes* from Varius.[107] This response or challenge to Cassius would fit Augustus' style of literary discourse, since earlier he had responded to eulogies of Cato, written by various hands, with a treatise called *Anti Cato*. A number of important questions arise from the relationship between these two versions of the Thyestes myth: How does Varius' *Thyestes* allude to Augustus? What effect did this allusion, arising from the stage, have on the audience seeing Augustus seated in the audience? What is the relation of Augustus' triumphal celebrations to those of Pompey at the opening of his theatre?

The themes of fraternal strife and vengeance seem appropriate in a play that was produced for the festival celebrating the end of almost a century of civil strife at Rome and, most recently, Augustus' defeat of Antony and Cleopatra and the forces of Sextus Pompey. Even though both Atreus and Thyestes commit crimes against each other, Atreus seems to emerge as the successfully avenged party, however harsh his punishment against his brother.

The question of the timing of the play's production is also important in seeing either Atreus or Thyestes as an allusive referent to Antony or Augustus. An association between Thyestes and Augustus as the party "wronged" by the aggression of Atreus/Antony could have rallied support for Augustus' cause before Actium, but the play was produced after Antony's defeat, where the emphasis of the occasion was on victory and punishment rather than on any wrongs suffered.[108] Indeed, the sole surviving fragments present Atreus' justification for his punishment.[109] If this interpretation is correct, Augustus would have presented himself, to the extent that the audience understood and applied the allusion, as a modern Atreus, and his opponent, Antony, as a usurping Thyestes deserving punishment.[110] This correspondence would reflect the tradition of certain Republican *praetextae* that celebrated victories and were named after the "conquered." The plays *Clastidium* and *Ambracia,* for example, are named after captured cities, and the play *Sabinae* is named after the legendary Sabine women who were raped and afterward assimilated into Roman society. This would also reverse Cassius' earlier association of Caesar or Octavian as Thyestes.

Mythological plays, however, cannot be made wholly apposite to the occasion of their performance, since any allusion arising out of the performance depends upon the interpretive skills of the audience, however much it is guided by a dramatist or presenter. Interpreting the allusion of a historical figure to a contemporary one would have been easier in the attempted restaging of Accius' *Brutus* and in the production or circulation of Cassius' version, since Caesar's assassin shared the name of his putative ancestor and performed a similar act. In the case of Pompey's choice of plays at the opening of his theatre, the triumphal return of Agamemnon in the *Clytemnestra* obscured his subsequent murder within the play, and the sack of Troy portrayed in the *Equos Troianus* reflected Pompey's magnificent military conquests of a few years earlier, rather than elicited sympathy for the besieged. The presence of Augustus, seated in the audience, would certainly have been awkward at a play in which Atreus murders Thyestes' children and serves their flesh to him, but we cannot rule out the possibility that the audience had the same selective response to the play and its allusions as Pompey's audience did when viewing the murder of Agamemnon. Ultimately, any association that emerges between Atreus and Augustus and Antony and Thyestes must remain vague due to the ambiguous nature of mythological allusions.[111]

However one attributes the allusions, the importance of the play lies in its relation to Pompey's use of tragedies at his theatre's opening and to earlier versions on the Atreus and Thyestes theme more than in any direct analogy between Atreus and Augustus and Antony and Thyestes. We have fixed dramatic texts made topical through allusion, not only between contemporary political figures and mythological characters, but also between previous versions and productions of plays on the same theme. We do not know whether Augustus presented the *Thyestes* in Pompey's theatre, which would have provided a further allusion to both Pompey and the plays he presented at his theatre's opening.

Images of civil strife taken from mythology and other sources are common in Augustan poetry, yet the almost deliberate omission of the Thyestes myth following the production of Varius' play in the victory celebrations after Actium is noteworthy. There is no reference, for example, to the Thyestes myth in Vergil's poetry, and the only reference in Horace is in *Odes* 1.16.17–21, which roughly dates to the early to mid-twenties B.C.E., since *Odes* Books 1–3 were published in 23 B.C.E.:

> *irae Thyesten exitio gravi*
> *stravere et altis urbibus ultimae*
> *stetere causae, cur perirent*
> *funditus imprimeretque muris*
> *hostile aratrum exercitus insolens.*[112]

> Anger brought Thyestes to
> a tragic end, and for tall cities
> it is the first cause of destruction, why foundations
> tumble and a haughty enemy army
> ploughs under walls.

Ovid refers to the myth of the Thyestean banquet only once, at *Metamorphoses* 15.462. Did Augustus wish to downplay any associations between himself and the Atreus-Thyestes myth following his victory celebrations, to strike a note of reconciliation with Antony's former supporters?

The perception of Augustus as an avenger, whether for the Parthian victory over Roman forces, Caesar's assassination, or Mark Antony's political ambitions with Cleopatra, is persistent and finds expression outside of the theatre with evidence that connects Augustus to the House of Atreus and the theme of vengeance, in particular the mythological figure Orestes. The connection between Octavian/Augustus and Orestes the avenger of his father's murder would not have been difficult to make, but the support for any association depends on evidence gleaned from scattered literary and visual sources from various periods, before and after 29 B.C.E., and any role Octavian/Augustus played in encouraging the allusion remains unknown.[113] Complicating any figurative connection between Augustus and Orestes is the earlier allusion made by Pompey to Agamemnon at the games celebrating his own triple triumph. It is unclear how the audience could have been guided to make or avoid the connection, if it were intended, to such a complex allusion. Nero would later adopt the role of Orestes with frightening parallels for the audience.

Later versions of plays dealing with the Thyestes myth were also understood as allusive commentaries on contemporary politics, often with deleterious results for the dramatist. Dio records that Macro, who was intent on ruining M. Aemilius Scaurus, called Tiberius' attention to certain passages in Scaurus' *Atreus* that could have been construed as criticism of the emperor. Furthermore, Dio claims that this was the real cause of the downfall of Scaurus, who died the year of the play's production, in 34 C.E.[114] One must keep in mind that Scaurus' play was probably no more critical of the emperor than other versions then in vogue. Allusive generalizations on the nature of tyranny do not, in and of themselves, constitute direct attacks against emperors. Indeed, it was to an emperor's advantage not to identify with attacks by taking offense and risk being perceived as tyrannical in any response; he was better served to ignore them and thus advertise himself to be nontyrannical.[115] Scaurus was singled out because of the intercession of Macro, who interpreted the verses of Scaurus in the most damaging way.

Other productions of the Thyestes-Atreus theme are more difficult to date and therefore more difficult to place in a cultural context. While certainty is impossible, Quintilian may have seen the *Atreus* of Pomponius Secundus shortly before 60 C.E.[116] This was a period roughly contemporaneous with Agrippina's murder (in 59 C.E.), and a time in Nero's reign fraught with imperial intrigue. These events were later deemed the stuff of tragedy and were described in the *praetexta Octavia* of Pseudo-Seneca. The cultural context of Pomponius' play, however, is lost.

Although it is impossible to date Seneca's *Thyestes,* the play may reflect the troubled period that immediately preceded its composition, if not its performance.[117] Whatever the exact date of its composition, the play appeared immediately following many other versions and may even have been influenced by a revival of Accius' *Atreus,* if Seneca's familiarity with the dramatic text reflects a production rather than a reading of the play.[118]

Seneca's entire play survives, of course, but it yields no specific information concerning anti-tyrannical sentiment. Generalizations on the nature of tyranny and examples of the tyrannical behavior of kings certainly exist, but there is nothing that can be construed as a direct attack against a specific emperor.[119] Conversely, one could argue that allusion and innuendo need not be specific, but rather only "possible" in the vaguest terms, in order to have the widest possible number and range of applications. Macro, no doubt, used such generalizations against Scaurus, but one cannot argue from general references to tyranny in Seneca's play that he intended passages or the entire play as an attack against an emperor. The brief scene between Atreus and an attendant (*satelles*) in which Atreus displays tyrannical behavior (205–220) does more for character delineation within the play than for character defamation outside of it:

SATELLES:          *fama te populi nihil*
*adversa terret?* ATREUS: *maximum hoc regni bonum est,*
*quod facta domini cogitur populus sui*
*tam ferre quam laudare.* SAT.: *quos cogit metus*
*laudare, eosdem reddit inimicos metus.*
*at qui favoris gloriam veri petit,*
*animo magis quam voce laudari volet.*
AT.: *laus vera et humili saepe contingit viro,*
*non nisi potenti falsa. quod nolunt velint.*
SAT.: *rex velit honesta: nemo non eadem volet.*
AT.: *ubicumque tantum honesta dominanti licent,*
*precario regnatur.* SAT.: *ubi non est pudor*
*nec cura iuris sanctitas pietas fides,*
*instablile regnum est.* AT.: *sanctitas pietas fides*
*privata bona sunt; qua iuvat reges eant.*
SAT.: *nefas nocere vel malo fratri puta.*
AT.: *fas est in illo quidquid in fratre est nefas.*[120]

ATTENDANT:              Does the negative opinion of the people
not scare you at all? ATREUS: This is the greatest advantage of possessing
     a kingdom,
that the people are compelled to endure
rather than to praise the deeds of their master. ATT.: Those whom fear
     compels
to praise are the same whom fear causes to hate.
But let he who seeks the glory of true kindness
to be praised by the heart more than by the tongue.

ATR.: True praise often comes to a humble man,
but false praise comes unless he be powerful. Let them desire that which
     they dislike.
ATT.: Let the king desire what is right: for there is no one who does not
     want the same.
ATR.: Wherever what is right appeals to a king, he rules
on a tottering throne. ATT.: Where there is neither shame
nor a concern for the law, nor sanctity, piety and faith,
a throne is unstable. ATR.: Sanctity, piety, and faith
are for private life: Let whatever qualities that are beneficial to kings be
     prominent.
ATT.: It is wrong to harm even a destructive brother.
ATR.: It is right against him whatever is wrong to commit against a
     brother.

Are we missing the gist of this and other passages? Were contemporary audiences and readers more adept at identifying or understanding such sentiments? Did the reception of anti-tyrannical sentiment in tragedy, in the form of innuendo, depend solely upon the cultural context surrounding actual performances, whether in original or revived productions, as it did in mimes? By way of contrast to the unspecific anti-tyrannical sentiments found in Seneca's *Thyestes,* references to tyranny in the Pseudo-Senecan play *Octavia* are explicit and do more to criticize Nero specifically and tyranny in general, however rhetorically, especially in the exchange between Nero and Seneca. Here the youth and rashness of Nero are contrasted with the wisdom and experience of Seneca, with specific attacks expressed in political terms (440–461):

> SENECA: *nihil in propinquos temere constitui decet.*
> NERO: *iusto esse facile est cui vacat pectus metu.*
> SEN.: *magnum timoris remedium clementia est.*
> NERO: *extinguere hostem maxima est virtus ducis.*
> SEN.: *servare cives maior est partriae patri.*
> NERO: *praecipere mitem convenit pueris senem.*
> SEN.: *regenda magis est fervida adolescentia.*
> NERO: *aetate in hac satis esse consilii reor.*
> SEN.: *ut facta superi comprobent semper tua.*
> NERO: *stulte verebor, ipse cum faciam, deos.*
> SEN.: *hoc plus verere quod licet tantum tibi.*
> NERO: *fortuna nostra cuncta permittit mihi.*
> SEN.: *crede obsequenti parcius: levis est dea.*

NERO: *inertis est nescire quid liceat sibi.*
SEN.: *id facere laus est quod decet, non quod licet.*
NERO: *calcat iacentem vulgus.* SEN.: *invisum opprimit.*
NERO: *ferrum tuetur principem.* SEN.: *melius fides.*
NERO: *decet timeri Caesarem.* SEN.: *at plus diligi.*
NERO: *metuant necesse est—* SEN.: *quidquid exprimitur grave est.*
NERO: *iussisque nostris pareant.* SEN.: *iusta impera.*
NERO: *statuam ipse.* SEN.: *quae consensus efficiat rata.*
NERO: *destrictus ensis faciet.* SEN.: *hoc absit nefas.*[121]

SENECA: Is it right to treat relatives thoughtlessly?
NERO: It is easy for a man to be just whose heart knows no fear.
SEN.: Clemency is the best cure for fear.
NERO: To wipe out one's enemies is the greatest quality of a king.
SEN.: To preserve one's citizens is a greater quality for a *pater patriae*.
NERO: A soft old man should give instruction to children.
SEN.: Hot-headed youth ought to be controlled.
NERO: I think there is enough wisdom in youth.
SEN.: May the gods always approve your deeds.
NERO: I would be a fool to fear gods, when it is I who make them.
SEN.: You ought to fear the more power is yours.
NERO: My good luck allows all things to me.
SEN.: Trust in her favors less; she is a fickle goddess.
NERO: The man who does not know what is permitted to him is a fool.
SEN.: It is praiseworthy for a man to do what is right rather than what
he wants.
NERO: The mob always kicks a fallen man. SEN.: The mob crushes what
is hateful.
NERO: Weapons guard the *princeps*. SEN.: Trust is better.
NERO: It is right for Caesar to be feared. SEN.: Better for him to be
esteemed.
NERO: It is obligatory that they fear. SEN.: Whatever is serious is
expressed.
NERO: Let them obey my commands. SEN.: Command what is just.
NERO: I myself determine that. SEN.: What approval consensus
determines.
NERO: A drawn sword will effect that. SEN.: Let this crime be absent!

The author of the *Octavia* actually does more to attack tyranny and emperors by naming Nero specifically. However, the same passages without Nero mentioned by name would become generic complaints about power rather than specific attacks on an emperor.

Like the anonymous author of the *Octavia,* the tragedian Curiatius Maternus expressed political dissidence in his plays. Tacitus, in the *Dialogus de oratoribus,* states that Maternus intended the plot of his *Thyestes* together with apposite allusions to be received as condemnations of Imperial oppression.[122] It is Maternus' friend Julius Secundus who expresses the danger inherent in reading a text like Maternus' *Cato* in public:

> *tum Secundus "nihilne te" inquit, "Materne, fabulae malignorum terrent quo minus offensas Catonis tui ames? an ideo librum istum adprehendisti ut diligentius retractares et, sublatis si qua pravae interpretationi materiam dederunt, emitteres Cationem non quidem meliorem, sed tamen securiorem?"*[123]

> Then Secundus said, "Maternus, does the talk of malicious men not terrify you so that you love your offending Cato less? Or have you pulled that text with the intention of revising it more carefully, having removed anything that might provide substance for prejudiced interpretation, and then republishing your Cato, not quite better, but at least more safe?"

The ability of the audience to transform a passage into political "allusion" is stated clearly by Tacitus' expression *prava interpretatio.*[124] The use of tragedy as a tool for criticism, however, was not one-sided. If tragedy was the means by which dramatists and the audience could voice displeasure with an emperor, it was a means open to the emperor as well. The reciprocity of criticism or dissent through mythological allusion finds expression with emperors who quoted from tragedy to express displeasure with their subjects. However, rather than portray themselves as tragic victims of unmerited criticism, certain Julio-Claudian emperors after Augustus allied themselves with mythological aggressors found in tragic texts. The effect was to have the emperors speaking the same "tragic language" as their subjects in the reciprocal voicing of mutual displeasure.

Even a play like the *Atreus,* often thought to be anti-tyrannical, was used by emperors to portray themselves as Atreus and thereby reverse roles with dissenters and challenge the charges of "tyranny" and oppression by their subjects/critics. No official policy is suggested, but the frequency of quotation is noteworthy. Tiberius, for example, placed himself in the role of Atreus by quoting the famous line from Accius' *Atreus: oderint dum metuant* ("Let them hate while they fear"), which he changed to *oderint dum probent* ("Let them hate while they approve").[125] As discussed above, Tiberius also charged Aemilius Scaurus with slandering Agamemnon in a tragedy in a passage that was either exclusively about the mythical king or only ostensibly about Agamemnon and really about Tiberius.[126] The accusation suggests that Tiberius was sensitive to charges of tyranny and that he was encouraging an association between himself and Agamemnon. According to Dio, Tiberius, in turn, attacked Scaurus through mythological allusion by saying, "I will make him an Ajax," meaning he would force him to commit suicide.[127] Tiberius thus realized the value of mythological allusion to voice his own political views in a way that reversed his perceived detractor's use of an ambiguous allusion and depended on the *animus* of his audience to interpret.

Afterward, the same line from Accius' play, in its original form, *oderint dum metuant,* was bandied about by Gaius.[128] Gaius' quotation of the original line contrasts with Tiberius' earlier rewriting of the line. This line is usually quoted to demonstrate the cruelty of the emperor Gaius Caligula rather than to place it in the wider literary context of the tragic tradition. Cicero, for example, had used the line earlier to criticize Julius Caesar: *quem metuunt, oderunt; quem quisque odit, periisse expetit.*[129] Cicero, therefore, is able to allude to an Atreus in the late Republic and expect the reference to the play and the parallel drawn between Atreus and Julius Caesar to be understood. There is no evidence that Claudius quoted the line in any context.

The emperor Nero, however, unlike any of his Julio-Claudian precursors who encouraged the allusion, associated himself with Thyestes, instead of with Atreus. Rather than simply quote lines from plays in which Thyestes appeared, Nero actually performed the role onstage in pantomimic productions.[130] The effect of this mythological role-reversal was to have the emperor assume the identity of the usurping tyrant, possibly reversing Augustus' (self-)identification with Atreus, and definitely reversing Tiberius' and Gaius' self-identification with Atreus, thus confusing the roles of emperor and subject and blurring the distinction between theatre and reality.

## NERO: *IMPERATOR SCAENICUS*

Although Nero—dubbed *imperator scaenicus* by Pliny[131]—taxed the interpretive skills of his subjects more than had any of his Julio-Claudian precursors, his reign should be seen as the culmination and not the beginning of a reciprocal theatricality on and off the stage. Whereas

Gaius was only rumored to be preparing for a public pantomime performance on the day of his death, Nero actually performed onstage, thereby changing the relationship of emperor and subject to actor and audience, which was itself forced to act and dissimulate any disapproval of his performance/rule.[132]

Nowhere is this confusion more apparent than in Suetonius' report that Nero frequently acted the roles of gods and heroes and goddesses and heroines, wearing a mask in his own likeness or that of his current mistress:

> *tragoedias quoque cantavit personatus heroum deorumque, item heroidum ac dearum, personis effectis ad similtudinem oris sui et feminae, prout quamque diligeret. inter cetera cantavit Canacen parturientem, Oresten matricidam, Oedipodem excaecatum, Herculem insanum.*[133]

> Moreover, he sang the tragic roles of heroes and gods, and even of heroines and goddesses, with masks modeled upon his own features or upon whatever woman he was in love with. Among others, he sang the roles of Canace in labor, Orestes the matricide, Oedipus blinding himself, and Hercules insane.

Dio (63.9.5) also gives details concerning Nero's costumes and specifies that he wore a mask modeled upon Poppaea Sabina for the female roles so that even in her death she could still participate in the spectacle. The semiotic implications of Nero's role-playing are fascinating: Whereas the audience could view the actor portraying the honorand of a *praetexta* onstage with the actual honorand possibly in the audience (definitely in the audience in the case of Balbus' *Iter*), the audience now viewed Nero onstage as a mythological character represented as Nero himself, through his mask and costume. Therefore, two Neroes are onstage (the actual Nero and the character represented as Nero), with no Nero in the audience. The audience faced a similar interpretative challenge in the case of Nero performing the role of a heroine or goddess with a mask of the deceased Poppaea Sabina as he assumed, simultaneously, three different identities: his own as Poppaea, who is herself now a mythological character onstage.[134] Onstage representation competes with allusion as illusory drama becomes, at once, illusory and nonillusory.

When does Nero's behavior, on or off the stage, cease to be theatrical/theatricalized? In other words, how can one identify or keep track of his changing political and theatrical roles, physical appearance, or even sex? Apparently this was not easy. On one occasion, a soldier, upon seeing Nero in chains, rushed onto the stage in order to free him. On another, when Nero was onstage acting the role of Canace, a soldier replied to another who has asked what the emperor was doing: "He's in labor." [135] Intending to take advantage of access at one of Nero's stage appearances, one of Piso's fellow conspirators wanted to kill Nero while he was performing onstage, thereby transforming members of the audience into both spectators and witnesses. [136] As a symptom of the age, in which it was difficult to distinguish between theatre and theatricality, the conspirator himself seemed unaware that he would be transformed into an actor before his spectator/witness audience.

Nero's adoption of the role of Thyestes and his seemingly subversive self-identification with the tyrant raises important questions about his other roles—in particular, his association with the mythological hero Orestes. The association between Nero and Orestes as matricides was a popular one, as contemporary lampoons bear witness. [137] This association first took root in the popular imagination after Agrippina's murder, and at this time the act of matricide alone invited the parallel. It was only when Nero played the part of Orestes on the stage *after* the initial popular connection between the two had been made that the subversiveness of Nero's self-identification with the matricide became apparent. [138] Unfortunately we do not know whether he played the role wearing a mask of his own likeness to further confuse the audience. Nero's self-identification with the matricide was also evident in his refusal to take the stage in Athens because of the legendary Furies residing there. Nero himself pointed interpretation in this direction by claiming that he had nightmares and was haunted by his mother and the Furies. [139] Others may have followed Nero's lead of staging productions of the Orestes myth, since it seems that there were numerous revivals of earlier Latin versions of the Orestes myth on the Roman stage at this time, but whether these were encouraged by Nero or intended as criticism of Nero is unclear. Indeed, earlier versions of the myth were sufficiently popular for Seneca to incorporate elements into his *Agamemnon*. [140]

Our sources for the period are unanimous in criticizing Nero's stage performances. In the cases of Tacitus, Suetonius, and Pliny the Younger, themselves members of the Roman elite who were writing for the Roman elite, the outrage of these sources is not surprising. [141] In the case of Juvenal, the satirist's touch finds a ready target in so egregious a subject as Nero. Tacitus calls Nero's zeal for performing disgraceful (*foedum*), [142] and Suetonius traces Nero's gradual progression to the stage with disdain. [143] Juvenal criticizes Nero as a modern-day Orestes who, in addition to being a matricide, disgraces himself by performing on-stage.[144] Dio also criticizes Nero in speeches put in the mouths of Bou-dicca and Vindex, who ridicule him for being an actor and empress, rather than an imperator and emperor.[145]

The senatorial class had good cause to feel persecuted by Nero. In addition to the discomfort of watching and *seeming* to be enjoying Nero's acting, they were themselves forced to take the stage—an act that was humiliating and a cause of mirth for the lower classes.[146] The pressure to *seem* to be enjoying Nero's antics onstage was intensified by the position of the senators and knights in the first fourteen rows in the theatre, directly under Nero's gaze both when he was performing and, conversely, when he was in the audience watching them perform, and also by the presence of spies in the theatre audience watching the reac-tions of spectators for any signs of insincerity.[147]

Outside the theatre, theatricality played a role in the lives of those dis-simulating their true feelings toward Nero and members of his regime. Burrus and Seneca assisted Nero in his stage performances and pre-tended to approve of and enjoy his acting and singing.[148] Vespasian and Thrasea Paetus, however, refused to dissimulate their disapproval and boredom at Nero's performances.[149] Vespasian survived relatively unscathed, but Thrasea Paetus' behavior is cited as one of the reasons for his downfall.[150] In the *Annales* of Tacitus, Petronius emerges as the grand dissimulator. Under Petronius, who posed as the *arbiter elegen-tiae* of Nero's court while ridiculing the emperor privately, theatricality reaches new heights.[151]

Nero's bizarre and subversive behavior should not obscure the fact that for the most part he was extremely popular with the masses in Rome.[152] Nero's attacks against the sensibilities of traditional upper-class and upper-middle-class members, through participation in his own acting and their own forced appearances onstage, probably contributed to this popularity with the lower classes. Nero, furthermore, seems to have enjoyed the loyalty and goodwill of the soldiers, in addition to his own claque of *Augustiani*, and there is evidence that he was esteemed no less by them because of his stage appearances.[153] After Nero's death, nu-merous people claimed to be him in yet another, albeit late, example of metatheatrical role-playing associated with his reign.[154]

Even to an audience long accustomed to interpreting onstage charac-ters and actions in relation to historical personalities and events offstage, and offstage actions in relation to the theatre, the question of whether what one is viewing inside the theatre or witnessing outside of it is "real" was not easy to answer. Nero, like Pompey and Augustus, made a fixed dramatic text topical through allusion and physical representation: a known political figure is alluded to or recognized onstage; therefore, illusory drama becomes nonillusory drama—but ambiguity remains. When does Nero cease to be Nero? When does the theatre audience shift roles from spectator to witness? The result of this confusion is an audience—and indeed, even the stage characters themselves—searching for interpretive cues both inside and outside the theatre. In other words, theatricality replaces theatre as actors become their own audience watching or commenting on their own stage actions, leaving members of the stage audience wondering, once again, whether they are spectators or witnesses.

# METATRAGEDY

## SENECA'S ACTOR-AUDIENCE

When the audience's own theatricalized reality is incorporated into stage reality, the metatragedy of Seneca results: theatricality replaces theatre as characters become their own audience watching or commenting on their own theatricalized stage actions. The audience itself shifts roles from spectator to witness when the theatricalized stage actions of actors compete with their own perception of the world outside of the theatre, making the recognition of dramatic illusion on the stage and the interpretation of dramatic allusion off the stage difficult. Confusion replaces catharsis when the audience cannot distinguish between theatre and reality. Where is the "real" audience? The term "actor-audience" is coined by Boyle to describe how Senecan tragedy draws attention to its own theatricality:

> The recurrent dramatisation of role-playing in which characters become actors before other characters as audience: Phaedra before Theseus (*Phaedra* 864ff.), Medea before Jason (*Medea* 551ff.), Clytemnestra before Aegisthus (*Agamemnon* 239ff.), Atreus before Thyestes (*Thyestes* 491ff.)—underscores Senecan tragedy's own conventions and artifice. So too the related focus on characters as audience, on action as spectacle, on human behaviour as self-dramatisation; or the staging in *Medea* or *Thyestes* of a character's own staging as character, actor and dramaturge of the climactic evil itself.[1]

Seneca's actor-audience arrives onstage via the theatricalization of tragedy and contemporary rhetoric: Senecan tragedy is at once a product of its age, in which theatricality, on and off the stage, was endemic, and a product of the tragic tradition, from the theatricalization of tragedy under Pacuvius and Accius, and possibly the Augustan tragedians, to the reception of *praetextae,* in which the audience faced the task of interpreting competing realities.[2] Contemporary rhetoric—*declamatio* and *suasoria,* especially as adopted by Ovid—serves as a stylistic bridge between the plays of Accius and the plays of Seneca.[3] Seneca's plays, in turn, seem to have been influenced by the literary style of his nephew Lucan, which is similarly grounded in contemporary rhetoric. (For the dating of Seneca's plays, See Tarrant, 1985, 10.) Many factors went into creating the "rhetoricized mentality" of Seneca's contemporaries.[4]

Ten plays survive under the name of Seneca: *Hercules furens, Troades, Medea, Oedipus, Agamemnon, Thyestes, Hercules oetaeus, Phaedra,*[5] *Phoenissae,* and *Octavia.* It is generally agreed that Seneca wrote all of these plays except the *Hercules oetaeus* and the *Octavia.*[6] Seneca's confidence in his abilities as a tragic dramatist is reflected not only in the large number of plays he undertook, but also in the story that he disagreed with Pomponius Secundus over aspects of tragic diction and that he further enunciated his position in a published preface.[7]

The dating of Seneca's tragedies is unclear, and it is possible that some, if not all, were written before the reign of Nero.[8] As far as we know, the emperors Gaius, Claudius, and Nero did not "use" Seneca's plays for public entertainment and propaganda purposes on important occasions. In the case of Nero, there is no evidence that he even had earlier Latin tragedies restaged on important occasions of state, such as his reception of Tiridates at Pompey's theatre.[9] Yet Roman tragedies must have been staged in this period, in addition to pantomime, considering the tragic roles of Nero and the large number of scenic competitions. This distance between dramatist and ruler may be due to Nero's own literary compositions and performances, and his reluctance to let a literary rival write plays for his stage appearances. When we recall that Seneca coached Nero upon the stage, and Nero forced members of the aristocracy to perform, it becomes evident that the role reversal of emperor and dramatist also reversed the role of actor and audience.

The audience in the auditorium is irrelevant when characters onstage become their own audience. In addition to the examples cited by Boyle above, Medea's speech in which she needs Jason as witness to validate her actions (*Medea* 551ff.), cited at the beginning of chapter 4, shows Medea as dramatist plotting acts to be witnessed by Jason, while the actual audience watches a play seemingly unfold in a way that is scripted by her. Medea, as dramaturge, seems to allude to Seneca.[10]

Atreus performs the similar roles of audience and dramaturge in the *Thyestes*. As Atreus enters the stage for the first time, he chides himself for not yet having taken revenge on his brother (176–180):

> *ignave, iners, envervis et (quod maximum*
> *probrum tyranno rebus in summis reor)*
> *inulte, post tot scelera, post fratris dolos*
> *fasque omne ruptum questibus vanis agis*
> *iratus Atreus?*

> Cowardly, lazy, and impotent, and (what I think
> is the greatest fault to a king in affairs of state)
> unavenged, after so many crimes, after the plots of my brother
> and every violation to everything sacred, do you go on, angry Atreus,
> with useless complaints?

Atreus refers to himself with the Greek word for "king" (*tyranno*, 177) that has connotations of tyrannical behavior.[11] Atreus seems to typecast himself in this dual and conflicted role, as his punishment far exceeds any crime committed by Thyestes. Atreus also takes this duality of identity and roles further by assuming the role of actor and audience as he speaks and listens to himself. He continues to address himself and to debate whether he will take an active or passive role in his response to Thyestes' crimes, in a speech that echoes Atreus' speech in Accius' *Atreus* (192–204):[12]

> *age, anime, fac quod nulla posteritas probet,*
> *sed nulla taceat. aliquod audendum est nefas*
> *atrox, cruentum, tale quod frater meus*
> *suum esse mallet—scelera non ulcisceris,*
> *nisi vincis. et quid esse tam saevum potest*
> *quod superet illum? numquid abiectus iacet?*
> *numquid secundis patitur in rebus modum,*
> *fessis quietem? novi ego ingenium viri*
> *indocile: flecti non potest—frangi potest.*
> *proinde antequam se firmat aut vires parat,*
> *petatur ultro, ne quiescentem petat.*
> *aut perdet aut peribit: in medio est scelus*
> *positum occupanti.*

Come, my heart, do what no one will later approve,
nor keep silent about it. Some crime, vicious and cruel,
must be dared, such that my brother would have wished
to commit—you cannot avenge a crime
unless you surpass it. And what is so cruel
that can overcome him? Is he the sort that would lie resigned?
Would he exercise restraint in success,
or resignation in defeat? I know the fierce temper
of the man: he cannot be swayed—but he can be broken.
Therefore, before he strengthens himself or prepares his forces,
I will go for him, instead of him finding me unprepared.
Let him destroy or be destroyed: the crime is set in the middle
for the one who claims it first.

Atreus continues to serve as audience to his own drama as he sees
Thyestes enter the stage with his sons (491–495):

> *plagis tenetur clausa dispositis fera:*
> *et ipsum et una generis invisi indolem*
> *iunctam parenti cerno. iam tuto in loco*
> *versantur odia. venit in nostras manus*
> *tandem Thyestes, venit, et totus quidem.*

Let the prey be caught in the laid-out nets.
I see him together with his hateful sons
at his side. Now hatred can be unleashed
in a safe place. At last, Thyestes comes into my hands,
he comes with all besides.

Tarrant points out that Atreus' entrance speech, which begins with this
passage, is a combination of the entrance monologue and the eaves-
dropping aside that gives the impression that Atreus is in total control
of his brother's fate, which seems to be sealed as much as from Atreus'
plotting as from Thyestes' own inattention.[13] There is a voyeuristic quality to Atreus' perusal of his brother's unkempt features that seems to
foreshadow Thyestes' later appearance after feasting on the blood and
gore of his sons (505–507):

> *aspice, ut multo gravis*
> *squalore vultus obruat maestos coma,*
> *quam foeda iaceat barba.*

> Look, how his dirty hair
> hangs over his ruined face,
> how his beard lies filthy.

Atreus seems to address himself rather than the audience when he contemplates Thyestes' features. The voyeuristic unfolding of Atreus' plot reaches a climax after Thyestes has eaten his children. Atreus wishes he could drag the gods down from Olympus to witness his deed (894–895). We, as witness/audience, watch Atreus, as witness/audience, as he watches his brother's physical reactions to his cannibalistic meal (908–919):

> aperta multa tecta conlucent face.
> resupinus ipse purpurae atque auro incubat,
> vino gravatum fulciens laeva caput.
> eructat. o me caelitum excelssissimum,
> regumque regem! vota transcendi mea.
> satur est; capaci ducit argento merum —
> ne parce potu: restat etiamnunc cruor
> tot hostiarum; veteris hunc Bacchi color
> abscondet—hoc, hoc mensa cludatur scypho.
> mixtum suorum sanguinem genitor bibat:
> meum bibisset. ecce, iam cantus ciet
> festasque voces, nec satis menti imperat.

> The doors are opened and the room shines with light.
> He, himself, reclines on his back upon purple and gold,
> propping up, with his left hand, his head weighted with wine.
> He burps. O! I am the most blessed of gods,
> and king of kings! I have exceeded my prayers.
> He is stuffed; he is drinking from a large silver cup—
> don't sip it: there is still blood left
> from so many victims; the color of the vintage wine
> hides it—with another and another let the meal be ended.
> Let the father drink the mixed blood of his sons:
> he would have drunk mine. Look, now he is singing
> with a joyful voice, he is not in control of his mind.

Character as audience is also apparent in other plays. In the *Troades*, Polyxena watches Pyrrhus deliver the sword stroke that kills her (1148–1152):

> *ut primum ardui*
> *sublime montis tetigit, atque alte edito*
> *iuvenis paterni vertice in busti stetit,*
> *audax virago non tulit retro gradum;*
> *conversa ad ictum stat truci vultu ferox.*

> As soon as the youth
> reached the mountain's peak, and stood on
> the raised mound of his fathers tomb,
> the brave virgin did not take a step back;
> she, bold, stood facing the blow with a wild look.

The passage highlights Polyxena's bravery in facing death as it invites the audience to contemplate her reaction to her own death: we are watching her watching her killer.[14]

In the *Oedipus* we find a bizarre variation of the actor as audience—Oedipus' eyes watch and actually participate in the blinding (962–964):

> *at contra truces*
> *oculi steterunt et suam intenti manum*
> *ultro insecuntur, vulneri occurrunt suo.*

> But his wild eyes
> stood ready and, eagerly following his own hand,
> rushed from their own wound.

After Oedipus' eyes have been ripped out, even his eye sockets seek to see (971–973):

> *attollit caput*
> *cavisque lustrans orbibus caeli plagas*
> *noctem experitur.*

> He raised his head
> and tested the night, surveying the regions
> of the sky with empty sockets.

The grotesque details of Oedipus' self-mutilation highlight the potential for bathos in such a spectacle in that even his mutilated eye sockets seek to see the effect of their own mutilation.

In the *Phaedra*, Phaedra mourns over Hippolytus' body before all the parts have been collected and pieced together. Eyesight has become even more symbolic in this scene, since Phaedra witnesses the effects of her false denunciation of her stepson (1168–1169):

> *Hippolyte, tales intuor vultus tuos*
> *talesque feci?*

> Hippolytus, I look upon your face, such as it is,
> have I made them such?

The face she looks upon is no longer a face with recognizable features, able to see her own. Unlike the scene of Oedipus' blinding, which was reported in a messenger speech, this scene apparently features parts of Hippolytus' dismembered body onstage; thus Phaedra's own eyes look to the unresponsive body parts in search of an audience for her guilt and grief. Bathos mixes with pathos as the audience watches Phaedra's reaction upon viewing Hippolytus' corpse and her search for an interpretation of her actions.

These illustrative passages show the extent to which stage reaction has replaced stage action. Character reactions appear against a backdrop of spectacle, turning spectators into witnesses.[15] Spectacle itself plays a large role in the theatricalized reality of the characters onstage. Boyle refers to the dramatic action of Senecan tragedy as "action as spectacle," but one could also argue that it is as much "spectacle as theatricalized action."[16] Seneca, for example, calls attention to theatricalized actions in the *Agamemnon*. In the pivotal scene in which she murders Agamemnon, Clytemnestra is likened to a gladiator when Cassandra (quoting Clytemnestra?) refers to the murder with "*habet! peractum est!*" recalling the theatricality of Roman spectacle entertainment (900–905):[17]

> *sic huc et illuc impiam librat manum.*
> *habet. peractum est. pendet exigua male*
> *caput amputatum parte et hinc trunco cruor*
> *exundat, illinc ora cum fremitu iacent.*
> *nondum recedunt: ille iam exanimem petit*
> *laceratque corpus, illa fodientem adiuvat.*

> Here and there she swings her unholy hand.
> "He has it. The deed is done." His decapitated head barely hangs
> connected to his body from here and blood gushes out
> from his trunk, there, his moaning head lies.

> Not yet do they quit: he [Aegisthus] seeks and stabs
> the by-now lifeless corpse, she helps in the stabbing.

The shouting of "*habet. peractum est*" takes the reader/audience out of the play and into the arena. Since the text omits details of the actual murder, the spectator supplies his/her own visualization of the scene. The jarring effect of this interruption on the dramatic action and the breaking of the dramatic illusion would be the same as someone today alluding to a hockey game, in the act of murder, by shouting, "He shoots, he scores!" The inclusion of theatricalized violence and death onstage allows Seneca to control the reaction of the theatre audience in a way not possible in the arena.[18] The act of murder becomes an allusion to the Roman arena, but the image of a victor shouting over the vanquished suggests that Clytemnestra's victory was not fairly won, but rather was gained through treachery. The allusion to spectacle also transforms the theatre audience into an arena audience, from spectator to witness.

The descriptive gore found in Accius' plays finds ultimate expression in Senecan tragedy. Even though Seneca's plays may not (all) date to Nero's reign, the inherent theatrical and grotesque aspects of that emperor's rule found in the art and poetry of the period seem to be reflected in the plays.[19] If such a reflection is even remotely accurate, then offstage reality is just as bizarre and theatrical as anything seen in the theatre, especially if we consider the spectacle punishment of prisoners in the arena, which took on mythological allusions.[20] One could also argue that when it is incorporated onto the stage, allusions to the theatricalized violence of the audience might appear "normal" without even more hyperbolic or rhetorical emphasis added by the dramatist.

The *Phaedra* provides ready examples of Seneca's rhetorical debt to Ovid in using rhetoric to metatheatrical effect and in using "descriptive gore" for spectacle.[21] This play relates just one of the episodes associated with the larger Theseus cycle: Theseus' wife Phaedra, frustrated in her attempts to seduce her stepson Hippolytus, plots to accuse him of rape, which leads to Theseus' use of a curse, granted by Neptune, to kill his son. Seneca's version is modeled on the second *Hippolytus* of Euripides.[22] In Euripides' version, the play opens with a prologue by Aphrodite, who, having been scorned by Hippolytus, seeks his death. In Seneca's play, Hippolytus opens the play unaware of the chain of events to come. This change signals Seneca's focus on human freedom to plot and to commit errors rather than a divine agent exercising her wrath as the cause of Hippolytus' death.[23] With this freedom, Seneca's characters make optimum use of arguments (*controversia* and *suasoria*) to state and resolve their moral dilemmas.

Rhetorical figures are immediately apparent in the play. In Act I, Phaedra and her nurse debate the proper course for controlling passion in balanced speeches of similar length. Each character presents her arguments as though in rhetorical debate (*controversia*). Suddenly, the contemporary passion for rhetoric transforms a myth about sexual transgression into a debate on sexual transgression. Phaedra first argues that she has been conquered by passion and considers herself the latest victim of Venus (85–128). The Nurse counters with arguments of propriety and sin (129–176) and warns (140–144):

> *honesta primum est velle nec labi via,*
> *pudor est secundus nosse peccandi modum.*
> *quo, misera, pergis? quid domum infamem aggravas*
> *superasque matrem? maius est monstro nefas;*
> *nam monstra fato, moribus scelera imputes.*

> Best to desire respectability and not to veer off its path,
> second is shame that recognizes a measure of sinning.
> Where do you hasten, wretched woman? Why heap scandal upon your
>    house
> and outdo your mother? A sin is worse than an abhorrent passion;
> you may ascribe an abhorrent passion to fate, but a sin to character.

Once Phaedra has resolved to die, however, the Nurse becomes the model of expediency and urges the opposite advice to Phaedra, who takes it to advance the plot more than to admit defeat in argumentation (267–270):

> *solamen annis unicum fessis, era,*
> *si tam protervus incubat menti furor,*
> *contemne famam: fama vix vero favet,*
> *peius merenti melior et peior bono.*

> The one solace to my tired years, mistress,
> if such a shameless passion seduces your senses,
> despise your good reputation: reputation rarely favors the truth,
> it is better to the worse-deserving and worse to the better-deserving.

When the Nurse confronts Hippolytus with news of Phaedra's passion (435–482), she cleverly conceals her mission and tries to convince him to abandon his devotion to Diana through pursuasive arguments (*suasoria*); she urges him to enjoy the sexual pleasures of youth, consider the dangers of the world and advancing old age, and his duty to procreate. Hippolytus, however, has no intention of abandoning his carefree existence and remains "unseduced" by her arguments.

The play, moreover, is full of the *sententia,* or paradoxical epigrams, which were popular during the early Empire.[24] For example, the Nurse advises Phaedra, *fortem facit vicina libertas senem* ("Freedom nearby makes the aged brave," 139), and later adds, *quod non potest vult posse qui nimium potest* ("A man who is too powerful wishes for a power he is unable to possess," 215). After falsely accusing Hippolytus of rape, the Nurse advises the fainting Phaedra, *mens inpudicam facere, non casus solet* ("The mind causes impurity, not circumstance," 735).

Seneca's most obvious debt to Ovid is found in the Messenger's description of Hippolytus' death, which mirrors the description of Hippolytus' death in the *Metamorphoses.*[25] The Messenger in the *Phaedra* describes Hippolytus' death by the sea-bull and the mangling of his body in gory detail (1082–1104):

> tum vero pavida sonipedes mente exciti
> imperia solvunt seque luctantur iugo
> eripere rectique in pedes iactant onus.
> praeceps in ora fusus implicuit cadens
> laqueo tenaci corpus et quanto magis
> pugnat, sequaces hoc magis nodos ligat.
> sensere pecudes facinus—et curru levi,
> dominante nullo, qua timor iussit ruunt.
> talis per auras non suum agnoscens onus
> Solique falso creditum indignans diem
> Phaethonta currus devium excussit polo.
> Late cruentat arva et inlisum caput
> scopulis resultat; auferunt dumi comas,
> et ora durus pulcra populatur lapis
> peritque multo vulnere infelix decor.
> moribunda celeres membra pervoluunt rotae;
> tandemque raptum truncus ambusta sude
> medium per inguen stipite ingesto tenet;
> [paulumque domino currus affixo stetit]
> haesere biiuges vulnere—et pariter moram
> dominumque rumpunt. inde semianimem secant

*virgulta, acutis asperi vepres rubis*
*omnisque ruscus corporis partem tulit.*

Then, truth be told, the horses aroused by fear
escaped from control and struggled to snatch themselves from their
    yokes,
and having risen up, their burdensome yokes lie on the ground.
Falling headlong on his face, he tangled his body
in the entangling reins, and the more he struggled,
the tighter he drew those gripping knots.
The horses saw their crime—and the light chariot,
without a driver, rushed wherever fear gave command,
just as when, not recognizing their usual burden through the winds,
and upset that the day had been entrusted to an imposter sun,
Helios' horses flung transgressing Phaethon far from the sun's path.
Everywhere the fields bear blood and Hippolytus' head dashed against
    the rocks
knocks around; thornbushes rip out his hair,
and rough rocks mangle his pretty face
and an unlucky appearance destroys with many wounds.
Swift wheels run over his dying limbs;
and at last, a tree trunk, charred to a stake,
with pierced tip, stabs him in the groin;
[the chariot stands for a bit on its pierced master,]
the horses cling to a wound—and equally they break delay
and their master. Then shrubs and wild thornbushes
with razor-sharp thorns tear up his barely breathing body,
and every twig wears a part of his body.

Ovid described Hippolytus' death in similar terms, especially the description of Hippolytus' corpse as a living wound (*Met.* 15.521–529):

*nec tamen has vires rabies superasset equorum,*
*ni rota, perpetuum qua circumvertitur axem,*
*stipitis occursu fracta ac disiecta fuisset.*
*excutior curru, lorisque tenentibus artus*
*viscera viva trahi, nervos in stipe teneri,*
*membra rapi partim partimque reprensa relinqui,*
*ossa gravem dare fracta sonum fessamque videres*
*exhalari animam nullasque in corpore partes,*
*noscere quas posses: unumque erat omnia vulnus.*[26]

Nor would the rabid strength of the horses have surpassed my own,
except a wheel, where it is turned on the ever-turning axle,
had broken and shattered at the joint of the axle.
I was thrown from the chariot, and while the reins held my legs,
you would see a living wound dragged, sinews stuck to a stake,
my limbs partly ripped off and partly left caught,
my shattered bones cracked with a frightening sound,
and my exhausted life breathed in no part of my body,
which you would be able to recognize, all was one wound.

Seneca, of course, adds more detail, such as the impaling of Hippolytus' groin to stress his asexuality.

Another passage in Ovid that provides the same excessive gore and hyperbolic grotesqueness as the description of Hippolytus' death in the *Phaedra* is the narrative of the Lapiths' fight with the Centaurs. Theseus, for example, hurls an urn at the Centaur Eurytus' face (12.238–240):

> *sanguinis ille globos pariter cerebrumque merumque*
> *vulnere et ore vomens madida resupinus harena*
> *calcitrat.*

> [Eurytus] spewing chunks of brain and wine equally
> from his headwound and mouth, falling back, stepped
> on the drenched floor.

The Lapith Celadon's head is smashed past recognition (12.252–253):

> *exsilvere oculi, disiectisque ossibus oris*
> *acta retro naris medioque est fixa palato.*

> His eyes leaped out of their sockets, and with the bones of his face
>     shattered,
> his nose was pushed back and stuck to the middle of his throat.

Gryneus' eyes are pierced by antlers (12.268–270):

> *figitur hinc duplici Gryneus in lumina ramo*
> *erviturque oculos, quorum pars cornibus haeret,*
> *pars fluit in barbam concretaque sanquine pendet.*

> Grynaeus pierced his eyes against the two-branched horn
> and gouged his eyes out, part of which dangled from the horns,
> part seeped onto his beard and hung with chunkened blood.

Such gory detail is furthermore evident in the *Phaedra,* when Theseus tries to reassemble the bits of Hippolytus' body (1265–1268):

> *hoc quid est forma carens*
> *et turpe, multo vulnere abruptum undique?*
> *quae pars tui sit dubito; sed pars est tui.*
> *hic, hic repone, non suo, at vacuo loco.*

> What is this that lacks shape
> and is grotesque, and everywhere gaping with many wounds?
> What piece of you this is, I do not know; but it is a piece of you.
> Here, place it here, not the right spot, but an empty place.

Even though Seneca preserves the gory tone of such passages, one must keep in mind that he rejected passages of Ovid's more hyperbolic rhetoric as "childish," such as his description of the flood in the *Metamorphoses.*[27] Nevertheless, the self-conscious metatheatre of Ovid's narrative defines Seneca's tragedies.

Seneca's concentration on episodes, rather than on the dramatic action as a whole, may be due not only to the influence of epic, but also to the success of the episodic mime productions of Publius Syrus and to the influence of pantomime. Did rhetoric make tragedy less suited for stage production, while other performance genres, such as the pantomime and farce, flourished?[28] Pantomimic productions featured a sole mythological character in a specific scene or an episode of a myth, such as Thyestes or Kronos devouring his children, rather than a sequence of events that made up an entire drama. Music and gesticulation replaced dialogue as the hero/heroine communicated the myth and emotion involved. In the *Phaedra,* a certain unnaturalness in dialogue betrays composition for virtuoso performance roles—Phaedra and the Nurse are present onstage together in the same scene, but each character is given two long speeches before they speak to each other in a "natural" way, although dramatic reality should not be taken for granted.

The *Phoenissae,* a concise play of 664 lines, also presents a particular challenge since, even by the standards of Senecan tragedy, it is unique.[29] The play is divided into two halves: the blind Oedipus wandering with Antigone, and Jocasta's intercession with her sons Polynices and Eteocles. There is an abrupt transition after line 362 between the speeches of Oedipus and Jocasta (Oedipus then leaves the stage, but Antigone remains), but the two halves are well crafted with balanced scenes that contrast the exiles of Oedipus and Polynices, the *pietas* of Antigone and the power thirst of Eteocles. Jocasta is the figurative bridge between the two halves of the play and also between her two warring sons.

The most peculiar feature of the play is the absence of a chorus, and the name of the play need not imply that a chorus with speaking parts has dropped out of the manuscript tradition, or that it would have been included in a final draft, since that would imply an even more ornamental role for the traditional chorus on the Roman stage. The play does not end, therefore, with the customary closure by the chorus, but it could be argued that Seneca ends his plays most often with a single line of dialogue. The manuscript tradition preserves two alternate endings: a dialogue between Eteocles and Jocasta, and a dialogue between Polynices and Eteocles.[30] Other notable features of the *Phoenissae* include narration of events by the characters themselves, and extremely short messenger speeches that do more to advance the plot than to describe events that have taken place offstage.

Perhaps most surprising is the relative absence of "naturalistic dialogue."[31] Characters address each other at the end of speeches, but it is only at the very end of the play that Eteocles and Jocasta or Polynices actually seem to converse for thirteen lines (652–664), in a conversation about power. Except for this final dialogue, the reader/spectator is left with the impression that characters think out loud, but communicate with each other in a seeming vacuum.

The peculiarities of the play are a challenge if we look at it from the perspective of tragic conventions, but the play may actually be a combination of tragedy and pantomime. Pantomime depended on spectacle, rather than dialogue, to communicate mythological subjects to the audience. The absence of the chorus as a collective character in the *Phoenissae* may indicate that the audience was entertained by spectacle onstage. This would account for the possible stage appearance of the Phoenician women, described in the title, in pantomime dance spectacles. Perhaps only the "tragic" speaking parts of the dramatic text for the other characters were actually written, as a series of related monologues with only the barest of dialogue between characters.[32] It is possible that the physical depiction of spectacle replaces the allusion to it that defines the other plays, and this may account for the impression that the play is unfinished or incomplete.[33] Theatricality replaces dramatic realism and the traditional conventions of a staged tragedy. Perhaps the play is the best example of the metatheatricality of Senecan metatragedy.

Visualizing Seneca's tragedies onstage is sometimes difficult, and attempts to place Seneca's plays in a recital hall, in the theatre, or on no

stage at all are based on internal and external evidence that remains inconclusive. Perhaps visualization of dramatic performance is a matter of
perspective, Seneca's and the audience's.[34] What is significant is the fact
that the audience/reader is still searching for its own role in Senecan
drama. In other words, the audience feels left out of the theatre experience, causing some to question the extent to which the plays are actually connected to the theatre.

Commentators have expressed a variety of opinions, and their arguments illustrate the difficulty in assessing the potential for stage production. Recitation of the plays is argued on stylistic grounds and contemporary tastes.[35] Beare argues that in addition to internal evidence that
suggests that Seneca did not fully visualize the actions of the characters,
there exists the external "evidence" that Seneca would not have written
for the stage because he did not need to earn a living from it.[36] Beare
contends that the plays were modeled upon originals that had been
acted, but that the plays of Seneca were written to be declaimed.[37] Unfortunately, he does not explain how one declaims a play written for several speakers. If Beare means a "rhetorical recitation," then the exact
nature of delivery also remains obscure.[38] Herington finds the evidence
for the acting of the plays too inconclusive.[39] Yet he argues that at least
some of Seneca's plays were probably recited by several speakers rather
than mounted for stage production.[40] Elaine Fantham considers the
question of dramatic production in terms of the difficulties facing actors
who must communicate speakers' roles, which are sometimes uncertain,
to the audience. She argues that the plays were written to be read, and
that ultimately "only the readers would experience the plays as complete
works."[41] Fantham does concede, however, that reading would follow
some sort of recitation by Seneca himself or others.

Tarrant approaches the question of production from a figurative
standpoint.[42] In relation to Seneca's *Agamemnon,* however, Tarrant argues in favor of recitation.[43] Tarrant's observations of Seneca's stagecraft, such as creaking doors, a character looking around the stage, the
withdrawal of a character to plot future action, and the calling for water onstage, point to borrowings from Roman comedy and possibly to
a mounted production, but consistency of dramatic illusion remains a
problem.[44]

The question of whether the plays ever appeared onstage is related to
the dramaturgical question of whether the plays could be performed
successfully. Most recently, Boyle argues that even if there is no direct
evidence that the plays ever appeared onstage, the plays were and are
performable.[45] Sutton, too, argues, based on internal evidence, that the

plays could have been mounted successfully.[46] In addition to convincing arguments drawn from textual evidence, Sutton cites a graffito from Pompeii that suggests that the *Agamemnon* was sufficiently popular that performance of the play should at least be considered, if not produced by Seneca, then soon after his death.[47]

What seems clear from the texts themselves is that the theatre audience is irrelevant—Senecan tragedy is theatrical even without the theatre, or even an audience seated in an auditorium. When the audience's own metatheatre is incorporated into stage reality, the metatragedy of Seneca results: theatricality replaces theatre as characters become their own audience watching or commenting on their own rhetoricized stage actions. The audience seated in the theatre has effectively shifted roles from spectator to witness. Since Senecan drama undermined the very dramatic reality essential for theatre, the decline of tragedy after Seneca may be due to the inability of tragedy to compete with offstage theatricality, even if incorporated onstage, and to an audience in the auditorium, that felt alienated from the audience onstage. Perhaps pantomime engaged the audience's interpretative abilities without challenging their very notions of reality, as in opposed to tragedy's growing alienation from the audience in the auditorium in favor of the audience on the stage. The *Phoenissae* may point to the intrusion or fusion of pantomime into tragedy for spectacle, which would make distinctions between various genres of theatre performances irrelevant.

## FROM TRAGEDY TO METATRAGEDY

By looking forward from Livius rather than back from Seneca, this study has traced, in general, the development of theatre to theatricality that transformed tragedy to metatragedy. The fragments from the plays of Livius, Naevius, and Ennius illustrate that the stage was not the exclusive domain of actors unconnected with the reality of the audience. Ennius' rhetorical skill contributed to the perception of offstage theatricality in that only once actors say and do things appropriate to the theatre can they be quoted and imitated offstage and recognized as theatrical. The involvement of the audience or the inclusion of the audience's reality on the tragic stage points to the development of metatheatre concurrently with the development of the theatre itself: the recreation of the audience's reality onstage leads to a perception of theatre, whereas the recreation of stage reality or the framing of offstage reality in relation to the theatre leads to a perception of theatricality offstage.

Pacuvius' and Accius' plays point to their own theatricality. The seeming dialectic with rhetoric and Accius' exploitation of spectacle for pathos seems to reflect his audience's experience outside of the theatre, in particular the growing audience awareness and exploitation of a theatricalized reality off the stage. This reciprocal relationship between the theatre and the audience's perception of reality outside of the theatre, whether due to the plays of Accius, Varius' *Thyestes,* or Ovid's *Medea,* may have anticipated and shaped how Neronian Rome interacted with the theatre.

What happens, however, when the audience's reality, in the form of historical drama, enters the stage? The audience's theatricalized reality was reincorporated onto the stage, producing "competing realities." The dramatic recreation of historical events leads to a *contaminatio,* not with another play, but with reality. Since real or historic people assume stage roles in *praetextae,* the dramatizing of events alters both onstage and offstage reality and intentionally breaks down the separation between the stage and the audience. This is especially the case if, say, a celebrated general is depicted onstage by an actor watching "himself" in audience, and vice versa.

The opening program of Pompey's theatre, with visual referents to his own triumph, demonstrated to public figures exploiting the stage, through the restaging of previously produced plays and the inclusion of the audience's reality, that tragedy could be made topically relevant to produce a correspondence between real people and mythological characters, current events and mythological events, and the current stage production (dramatic text) and a previous stage production (dramatic text). Although the audience may have understood allusions to contemporary persons and events in stage productions before this date, Pompey's conscious self-association with a mythological character points to the manipulation of a theatre event to guide the audience's interpretation of that allusion. The attempted restaging of Accius' *Brutus* following the assassination of Julius Caesar and Augustus' choice of Varius Rufus' *Thyestes* point to the extent to which tragedy could allude to the audience's reality without altering the dramatic text of a previously produced play.

The theatricalization of the audience's world in the late Republic and early Empire competed with the dramatic illusion of reality onstage. The incorporation of the audience's theatricalized reality onto the stage led to the creation of Seneca's metatragedy. However, audience identification can also produce audience alienation: the spectators in the audience are irrelevant in a drama where characters have become their own audience. Seneca's "actor-audience" has transformed spectators into witnesses. Tragedy has come full circle as the audience's reality, which informed initial adaptations of Greek tragedy by Livius and Naevius, has usurped the stage in Senecan metatragedy, to produce a theatre undermined by its very theatricality.

# APPENDIX

Placing the tragedies of the Latin dramatists into a dramatic sequence creates an artificial line of development. Due to the silence of ancient sources concerning the dates of production for most plays, there is no way of knowing with any certainty the order of composition of plays by contemporary dramatists. Also, it is difficult to tell at times whether the titles of the plays listed are multiple listings of the same play. Therefore, the plays of each dramatist are listed in alphabetical order.

The word "precursor" here does not imply adaptation of the whole play or a deliberate imitation on the part of the Latin dramatist; rather, it means that Latin and Greek plays of the same title or similar themes were perhaps known to the dramatist and to the audience. Latin precursors are listed first, contrary to the customary practice of citing Greek models before Latin ones, since these were more recently seen on the Roman stage and thus perhaps were more familiar to the audience than the Greek plays of similar titles, which would have been either seen or read only by select members of the audience. For Greek models, I have consulted Brooks 1981, Ribbeck 1875, and Vahlen 1963.

## The Plays of the Roman Tragedians

| Author | Play | Latin Precursor | Greek Precursor | Date/Occasion |
|---|---|---|---|---|
| **Livius Andronicus**[a] | | | | |
| | *Achilles* | | Aeschylus? | |
| | *Aegisthus* | | | |
| | *Ajax Mastigophorus* | | Sophocles | |
| | *Andromeda* | | Euripides | |
| | *Danae* | Naevius? | Sophocles? | |
| | *Equos Troianus* | Naevius? | | |
| | *Hermiona* | | Sophocles? | |
| | *Ino?* | | | |
| | *Tereus* | | | |
| **Naevius**[a] | | | | |
| | *Danae* | | | |
| | *Equos Troianus* | Livius? | | |
| | *Hector proficiscens* | | Astydamas | |
| | *Hesione* | | | |
| | *Iphigenia* | | Euripides | |
| | *Lycurgus* | | | |
| | *Praetextae* | | | |
| | *Clastidium* | | | Restaged Oct. 55 B.C.E., ded. of Pompey's theatre |
| | *Romulus sive Lupus* | | | |

**Ennius** (acc. Vahlen/Brooks)

| Play | | Greek model | Notes |
|---|---|---|---|
| *Achilles* | Livius | Aristarchus | Before 184 B.C.E.? |
| *Ajax* | Livius? | Sophocles | Restaged often with Aesopus in title role? (Cic. *Off.* 1.114) |
| *Alcmeo* | | Euripides | |
| *Alexander* | | Euripides | c. 190 B.C.E. (Plaut. *Rud.* 86) |
| *Andromache (sive Andromache Aechmalotis)*[a] | | Eur. *Troades* | Did Cic. see play more than once? *De Or.* 3.217/ *Tusc* 1.85; Aesopus in title role before 57 B.C.E.? (Restaged 54 B.C.E. with Antiphon in title role, *Att.* 4.15.6) |
| *Andromeda* | Livius | Euripides | |
| *Athamas* | | | |
| *Chresphontes* | | Euripides? | |
| *Erectheus* | | Euripides | |
| *Eumenides* | | Aeschylus | |
| *Hectoris Lytra* | | | Restaged with Aesopus in title role |
| *Hecuba* | Naevius | Euripides | |
| *Iphigenia in Aulis* | | Euripides/ Aeschylus[a]/ Sophocles[a] | Restaged with Aesopus as Agamemnon and Cimber as Menelaos (Cic. *Ad Her.* 3.34) |

*(continued)*

APPENDIX TABLE (*continued*)
*The Plays of the Roman Tragedians*

| Author | Play | Latin Precursor | Greek Precursor | Date/Occasion |
|---|---|---|---|---|
| | Medea exul; Medea | | Euripides | Play was widely read (Cic. Fin. 1.2.4) |
| | Melanippa | | Euripides | |
| | Nemea | | | |
| | Phoenix | | Euripides | |
| | Telephus | | Euripides | |
| | Thyestes | | Sophocles/Euripides/ Apollodorus/ Tarsus/ Carcinus/ Chaeremon Cleophon/ Diogenes/ Agathon | 169 B.C.E. (E's last play; performed at first *ludi Apollinares*) |
| | *Praetextae* | | | |
| | Ambracia | | | |
| | Sabinae | | | |
| **Pacuvius**[a] | | | | |
| | Antiopa | | Euripides | Freq.? acted by Rupilius in Cic.'s youth (*Off.* 1.114) |
| | Armorum iudicium | | Aeschylus | Quoted at Caesar's funeral games with Attilius' *Electra* (Suet. *Iul.* 84) |

| Play | Greek model | Roman version | Notes |
|---|---|---|---|
| *Atalanta* | Sophocles | | |
| *Chryses* | Sophocles | | Produced vs. Accius in 140 B.C.E.? (Cic. *Amic.* 4; *Brut.* 64.229; Ribbeck 1875, 260) |
| *Dulorestes* | | Livius | |
| *Hermione* | Sophocles | | |
| *Iliona* | | | |
| *Medus* | | | |
| *Niptra* | | | |
| *Pentheus* | Homer/Soph. | [Naevius' *Lycurgus*?] | |
| *Periboea* | [Euripides] | | |
| *Teucer* | Sophocles | | Restaged 51 B.C.E., when Hortensius was hissed? (Cic. *Fam.* 8.2.1; Ribbeck 1875, 227 n. 9) |
| *Praetexta* | | | |
| *Paullus* | | | ?160 B.C.E. funeral games of L. Aemilius Paulus |
| **Accius**[a] | | | |
| *Achilles/Myrmidones* | Aeschylus | Livius/Ennius | |
| *Agamemnonidae/Erigona* | | | |
| *Alcmeo/Alphesiboea* | Euripides | Ennius | |
| *Amphitryo* | | | |
| *Andromeda* | Euripides | Livius/Ennius | |

*(continued)*

APPENDIX TABLE (*continued*)
*The Plays of the Roman Tragedians*

| Author | Play | Latin Precursor | Greek Precursor | Date/Occasion |
|---|---|---|---|---|
| | *Antenoridae* | | Sophocles? | |
| | *Antigona* | | Sophocles | |
| | *Armorum iudicium* | Pacuvius | Aesch.?/[Soph./ Eur.] | |
| | *Astyanax/Troades* | | | |
| | *Athamas* | Ennius | | |
| | *Atreus* | [Ennius' *Thyestes*] | Sophocles | Read to Pacuvius at Tarentum before 130 B.C.E.; restaged with Aesopus in title role (Plut. *Cic.* 6). Does Seneca refer to a contemporary restaging (*Ep.* 80)? |
| | *Bacchae* | [Pac.'s *Pentheus*?] [Naev.'s *Lycurgus*?] | Euripides | |
| | *Chrysippus*[b] | | Euripides | |
| | *Clytemnestra/or Aegisthus?* | Livius | | Restaged Oct. 55 B.C.E. ded. of Pompey's theatre |
| | *Deiphobus* | | Sophocles? | |
| | *Diomedes* | | | |
| | *Epigoni/Eriphyle?* | | Sophocles | |

| | Greek source | Roman predecessor | Notes |
|---|---|---|---|
| *Atalanta* | Sophocles | | Produced vs. Accius in 140 B.C.E.? (Cic. *Amic.* 4; *Brut.* 64.229; Ribbeck 1875, 260) |
| *Chryses* | Sophocles | | |
| *Dulorestes* | | | |
| *Hermione* | Sophocles | Livius | |
| *Iliona* | | | |
| *Medus* | | | |
| *Niptra* | | | |
| *Pentheus* | Homer/Soph. | [Naevius' *Lycurgus*?] | |
| *Periboea* | [Euripides] | | |
| *Teucer* | Sophocles | | Restaged 51 B.C.E., when Hortensius was hissed? (Cic. *Fam.* 8.2.1; Ribbeck 1875, 227 n. 9) |
| Praetexta | | | |
| *Paullus* | | | ?160 B.C.E. funeral games of L. Aemilius Paulus |
| **Accius**[a] | | | |
| *Achilles/Myrmidones* | Aeschylus | Livius/Ennius | |
| *Agamemnonidae/Erigona* | | | |
| *Alcmeo/Alphesiboea* | Euripides | Ennius | |
| *Amphitryo* | | | |
| *Andromeda* | | Livius/Ennius | |

*(continued)*

APPENDIX TABLE (*continued*)
The Plays of the Roman Tragedians

| Author | Play | Latin Precursor | Greek Precursor | Date/Occasion |
|---|---|---|---|---|
| | Antenoridae | | Sophocles? | |
| | Antigona | | Sophocles | |
| | Armorum iudicium | Pacuvius | Aesch.?/[Soph./Eur.] | |
| | Astyanax/Troades | | | |
| | Athamas | Ennius | | |
| | Atreus | [Ennius' Thyestes] | Sophocles | Read to Pacuvius at Tarentum before 130 B.C.E.; restaged with Aesopus in title role (Plut. Cic. 6). Does Seneca refer to a contemporary restaging (Ep. 80)? |
| | Bacchae | [Pac.'s Pentheus?] [Naev.'s Lycurgus?] | Euripides | |
| | Chrysippus^b | | Euripides | |
| | Clytemnestra/or Aegisthus? | Livius | Euripides | Restaged Oct. 55 B.C.E. ded. of Pompey's theatre |
| | Deiphobus | | Sophocles? | |
| | Diomedes | | | |
| | Epigoni/Eriphyle? | | Sophocles | |

| | | | |
|---|---|---|---|
| *Epinausimache* | | Homer | |
| *Eurysaces* | | Sophocles | 6–13 July, 57 B.C.E., at *ludi Apollinares.* Performed by Aesopus, with Afranius' *Simulans* |
| *Hecuba* | Ennius | | |
| *Hellenes?* | Cf. Naevius' *Lycurgus* | | |
| *Liberi* | Ennius | Apollodorus? | |
| *Medea/Argonautae* | | Sophocles? | |
| *Meleager* | | Euripides | |
| *Minos/Minotaurus* | | Euripides | |
| *Neoptolemus* | | Homer | |
| *Nyctegressia* | | Sophocles? | |
| *Oenomaus* | | | |
| *Pelopidae* | | Aesch./Soph./Eur. | |
| *Philoctetal* *Philocteta Lemnius* | | | |
| *Phinidae* | | | |
| *Phoenissae* | | Euripides | |
| *Prometheus?* | | Aeschylus | Restaged at *ludi Apollinares* in 59 B.C.E. with Diphilus? |
| *Stasiastae/Tropaeum* | [Naev.'s *Lycurgus?*] | | |

(*continued*)

APPENDIX TABLE (*continued*)
*The Plays of the Roman Tragedians*

| Author | Play | Latin Precursor | Greek Precursor | Date/Occasion |
|---|---|---|---|---|
| | *Telephus* | Ennius | Aesch.?/Eur.? | |
| | *Tereus* | Livius | Sophocles | 104 B.C.E. (Cic. *Phil.* 1.36 = 103?) Last known original production. Restaged 44 B.C.E. |
| | *Thebais?* | | | |
| | Praetextae | | | |
| | *Brutus* | | | Restaged 57 B.C.E. with Aesopus (Cic. *Sest.* 58) |
| | *Aeneadae sive Decius* | | | |
| | *Late Republican Tragedies*[a] | | | |
| **C. Julius Strabo** | *Adrastus* | | | (c. 100–90 B.C.E.) |
| | *Tecmessa* | | | |
| | *Teuthras* | | | |
| **C. Titius** | Titles unknown | | | Performed |
| **Pompilius** | Titles unknown | | | |
| **Atilius** | *Electra* | | Sophocles | Caesar's funeral games |

| | | | |
|---|---|---|---|
| **Quintus Cicero** | | | |
| | *Aeropa?* | | |
| | *Electra* | Sophocles | Cicero (Q *Fr.* 3.6.7) mentions this and 3 other plays |
| | *Erigona* | Sophocles | Cic. Q *Fr.* 3.1.13 |
| | *Sundeipnoi* | Sophocles | Cic. Q *Fr.* 2.15.3 |
| | *Troilus?* | Sophocles | |
| **Cornelius Balbus** | | | |
| | *Praetexta* | | |
| | *Iter or Journey to Gades* | | 43 B.C.E. at Gades |
| **Cassius Parmensis** | | | |
| | *Thyestes* | Ennius/Accius' *Atreus* | 40's–30's B.C.E. |
| | *Praetexta* | | |
| | *Brutus* | | |
| **Santra** (not the grammarian) | | | |
| | Titles unknown | | |
| | [*Nuptiae Bacchae?*] | | Cf. Ribbeck 1875, 685 |
| **Julius Caesar** | | | |
| | *Oedipus* | | |
| **Augustus** | | | |
| | *Ajax* | Livius/Ennius | Mocked and suppressed by Augustus |

(*continued*)

| Author | Play | Latin Precursor | Greek Precursor | Date/Occasion |
|---|---|---|---|---|
| **Asinius Pollio** | Titles unknown | | | |
| **Varius Rufus** | *Thyestes* | Ennius/Cassius/ cf. Accius' *Atreus* | | Performed at Augustus' Triumph, 29 B.C.E. |
| **Sempronius Gracchus** | | | | Little known of his life or work |
| | *Atalanta* | | | |
| | *Peliades* | | | |
| | *Thyestes* | Varius/Ennius/Cassius/ (cf. Accius' *Atreus*) | | |
| | | *Early Imperial Tragedies* | | |
| **Ovid** | *Medea* | Ennius/Accius | | Was there a contemporary production? |
| **Mam. Aemilius Scaurus** | *Atreus* | Accius/Pomponius (cf. Ennius/Cassius/ Varius/Gracchus for *Thyestes*) | | Dates to Tiberius' reign |

| Author | Play | Models/Comparisons | Notes |
|---|---|---|---|
| **P. Pomponius Secundus** | | | |
| | *Praetextae* | | |
| | *Aeneas* | | |
| | *Atreus* | Accius/Pomponius/ Scaurus/ (cf. Ennius/ Cassius/Varius/ Gracchus for *Thyestes*) | Dates to Claudius' reign; seen by Quintilian before 60 C.E. (10.1.98)? Dates to either Tiberius' or Claudius' reign. Seen by Quintilian before 60 C.E.? |
| **Seneca** | | | |
| | *Agamemnon* | cf. Accius' *Clytemnestra* | |
| | *Hercules furens* | | |
| | *Hippolytus* | | |
| | *Medea* | | |
| | *Oedipus* | | |
| | *Phoenissae* | | |
| | *Thyestes* | Ennius/Accius/Ovid Julius Caesar Accius Ennius/Gracchus Varius/ Cassius (cf. Accius/ Pomponius/Scaurus for *Atreus*) | |
| **Pseudo-Seneca** | | | |
| | *Troades* | | |
| | *Hercules oetaeus* | | |
| | *Praetexta* | | |
| | *Octavia* | | |

APPENDIX TABLE (continued)
The Plays of the Roman Tragedians

| Author | Play | Latin Precursor | Greek Precursor | Date/Occasion |
|---|---|---|---|---|
| **Cornutus** | Titles unknown | | | |
| **Lucan** | Medea | Ennius/Accius/ Ovid/Seneca | | Unfinished at Lucan's death (Vacca *Vit.* 63–68) |
| **Persius** | Titles unknown | | | |
| | *Praetexta* | | | |
| | Title unknown | | | |
| **M. Curiatius Maternus** | | | | Written in his youth; Plays date to Vespasian's reign |
| | Medea | Ennius/Accius/Ovid Seneca/Lucan | | |
| | Thyestes | Ennius/Gracchus Cassius/Varius/Seneca (cf. Accius/Pomponius/ Scaurus for *Atreus*) | | |
| | *Praetextae* | | | |
| | *Cato* | | | |
| | *Domitius* | | | |

[a] According to Ribbeck.
[b] Ribbeck attributed to Pacuvius.

# NOTES

## INTRODUCTION

1. We find *contaminatio,* the synthesis of Greek models to produce a "new" Latin play. See Gentili 1979, 33–49. Adaptation is also apparent in comedy. Aulus Gellius demonstrates that Caecilius' *Plocium* is no mere imitation of Menander's original, but rather a Roman adaptation (*NA* 2.23.4–20).

2. Concerning imitation, Quintilian (*Inst.* 10.2.15) makes the following plea: *atque utinam tam bona imitantes dicerent melius quam mala peius dicunt.* For an extended analysis, see Williams 1968, 250–357, and Gentili 1979, 89–105.

3. Changes to the logic of Greek prototypes are common: Ennius, in the opening lines of the *Medea,* adapts Euripides' play by altering the order in which the building of the Argo is described; Accius' *Philoctetes* has Lemnian shepherds who know where to find Philoctotes, rather than Sophocles' chorus of Greek warriors led by Odysseus, who remembers where he left him years earlier. Terence, in his prologues, frequently outlines changes that he made to his Greek and Latin sources.

4. For details of and sources for the process by which the archon eponymous selected three tragedians for the Great Dionysia at Athens, see Pickard-Cambridge 1988, 79; and, more recently, Rehm 1992, ch. 3: "Production as Participation."

5. The practice was, of course, more complex than my brief outline shows. The evidence suggests that a dramatist could sell his play to a stage manager (as Terence admits doing with Ambivius Turpio in his prologue to the *Eunuchus*), but this meant that the play became the buyer's property and he could restage it again whenever he liked; or the dramatist could sell it to an aedile for a specific occasion. If the aedile returned the play to the dramatist after the festival, it seems he was free to sell it again on a later occasion. If the dramatist was no longer alive, one must presume that an aedile was free to stage any of his plays. For a full discussion of this important aspect of Roman drama, see Lebek 1996, 29–48, which outlines the evidence and scholarship surrounding the selling and buying of plays in Republican Rome.

6. See Beacham 1999, 2–44, for an extensive discussion on the occasions of public entertainment in Rome.

7. Plutarch *Rom.* 8.7. See Turner 1982, ch. 4, for observations on acting in "real life" and "onstage" as components of a dynamic system of inter-dependence between social dramas and cultural performances.

8. Aiming for topicality and contemporary realism, for example, Jean Anouilh set his *Antigone* in German-occupied Paris, and Kenneth Branagh's film version of *Henry V* based the battle scenes on those found in films about the Vietnam War.

9. See Elam 1980, 98–134, for the boundaries and limitations of dramatic illusion. L. Abel's *Metatheatre* (1963) remains important.

10. For characters commonly alluding to themselves as characters in Plautus, see Duckworth 1994, 133–134; Moore 1998, 67–90. Metatheatrical self-references are rarer in the comedies of Terence—Chaerea's comment at *Eunuchus* 386 is among the exceptions: *an potius haec patri aequomst fieri ut a me ludatur dolis?*

11. Tragedy reflects the increased use of rhetoric in oratory in the second century B.C.E. Such a connection is natural, since both genres are constituted of speeches intended to sway the intellectual and emotional responses of the audience. This "rhetoricizing" of tragedy also occurred on the Greek stage, particularly in the case of Euripides. For a discussion on the "rhetorical" and "pathetic" traits of Roman tragedy, see Ribbeck 1875, 643–645 (which cites Horace *Ars poetica* 164–166), and La Penna 1979, 78–92, with references to earlier works.

12. Gentili (1979, 15) distinguishes his definition from that of M. Barchiesi, who defines metatheatre as "plays within plays." See Barchiesi 1969, 113ff.

13. Slater 1985, 14. Slater also elaborates on the relationship between metatheatre and nonillusory drama, in response to J. L. Styan's definition of nonillusory drama (ibid., 14, 15): "Not all non-illusory drama is metatheatrical, but all metatheatre is to some degree non-illusory. In so far as theatre becomes self-conscious and aware of its own processes, it ceases to be strictly illusory." See Styan 1975, 180–181, for Styan's discussion of nonillusory drama.

14. Cicero *Pro Sestio* 56. Earlier in ch. 55, Cicero mentions that the senators were applauded when they *resumed* their seats. Did the senate meet between various spectacles of the *ludi*? It seems that they met after an earlier event or dramatic performance, but before the tragic plays were to be produced; but nothing can be asserted with absolute certainty.

15. Cicero *Pro Sestio* 120. Quotations that follow also come from this speech, 121ff.

16. Elam 1980, 208–210.

17. See Hinds1998, 144, for the limitations of allusions: "The creative imagination is an endlessly mobile thing; and not even through the most apparently objectively verifiable allusion . . . can access ultimately be gained to what an alluding poet at any given moment *intended* by such an allusion."

18. Suetonius *Nero* 21.3. See further chapter 4 below.

19. Suetonius preserves a telling incident in which a spectator rushed onstage

during a dramatic production in order to free "Nero" from chains: *in qua fabula fama est tirunculum militem positum ad custodiam aditus, cum eum ornari ac vinciri catenis, sicut argumentum postulabat, videret, accurrisse ferendae opis gratia* (*Nero* 21.3). See further chapter 4 below.

20. Theatricality as the essence of Nero's reign is reflected in Tacitus, Dio Cassius, and Suetonius. See Rudich 1993, passim, and Bartsch 1994, passim.

## CHAPTER ONE

1. Cicero *Brutus* 72 secures the date of Livius' first production: *atqui hic Livius [qui] primus fabulam C. Claudio Caeci filio et M. Tuditano consulibus docuit anno ipso ante quam natus est Ennius, post Romam conditam autem quartodecimo et quingentensimo, ut hic ait, quem nos sequimur; est enim inter scriptores de numero annorum controversia.* Cicero's source was Varro. Ancient sources refer to the production of a *fabula*, the term normally used to denote a tragedy, rather than a comedy. See Cicero *Brut.* 72, *Sen.* 50, *Tusc.* 1.3; and Gell. 17.21.42. Unfortunately, the title of this play cannot be recovered from the known plays of Livius. Livy (7.2), in his brief sketch of the Etruscan origins of Roman drama, mentions that Livius was the first dramatist to compose a play with a plot, but he omits two important facts: that the dramatist was Greek-born, and that his tragedies were adaptations of Greek originals. See also Val. Max. 2.4.4. On Livy's claim that the first *ludi scaenici* in Rome took place in 364 B.C.E., see Wiseman 1995, 135.

2. In addition to writing the first Latin tragedy, comedy, and epic, Livius also composed the *Partheneion* in 207 B.C.E. In gratitude for his "services" to the state, the Temple of Minerva on the Aventine was dedicated as the seat of a *collegium poetarum,* or writers' guild. This temple provided a meeting place for writers involved in Rome's growing literary movement. On a more significant level, it symbolized the arrival and the importance of a Latin, and not a Greek, literature at Rome.

3. Before 240 B.C.E., less literary forms of scenic entertainment, consisting of Atellane farces and dance productions of the Etruscan *histriones,* appeared in Rome. Beare (1964, 17) points out that both native Italian and Greek actors were already in Rome by this date and that there is a strong possibility that they may have been experienced in the productions of Greek tragedies. Likewise, Jocelyn (1967, 14) suggests the possibility of more literary types of stage productions: "One can, however, leave open the possibility that forerunners and contemporaries of the 240 B.C., Latin-speaking *histriones* performed Etruscan adaptations of the Athenian classics." On the obscurity of ancient sources concerning the origins of Roman drama, see Kenney 1982, 78. Duckworth (1994, 4) argues that there must have been some form of dramatic activity before this date to account for a ready audience and the play's success. See, most recently, Beacham 1999, 2–4, for a discussion of the contexts of early dramatic presentations.

4. See Livy 7.2, where no mention is made of the nonleading roles.

5. Fragments from Caecilius' *Plocium* reveal extensive use of *cantica* to substitute for dialogue parts found in his Greek original, the *Plokion* of Menander. See Aulus Gellius *NA* 2.23 for his analysis of Caecilius' "translation" of Menander.

6. The orchestra area found in Greek theatres was not needed for Roman tragedies or comedies, and therefore it was diminished to a semi-circular area in the design of later Roman theatres.

7. Cicero *Brutus* 71: *nam et Odyssia Latina est sic tamquam opus aliquod Daedali et Livianae fabulae non satis dignae quae iterum legantur.* For an examination of Livius' dramatic style, see Mariotti 1986.

8. For Cicero's attitude toward the ancient poets and a tabulation of the frequency of citations of these poets in his works, see Zillinger 1911.

9. Suetonius *De poetis,* †Titus† *Livius tragoediarum scriptor clarus habetur . . .* , in Rostagni 1964.

10. The titles of the known plays by Livius are *Achilles, Aegisthus, Ajax Mastigophorus, Andromeda, Danae, Equos Troianus, Hermiona, Ino*(?), and the *Tereus.* The titles of at least six of these plays, first staged by Livius, appear in the works of later dramatists: the *Danae* and *Equos Troianus* of Naevius (throughout this study I assume both wrote a version of the *Equos Troianus*), the *Achilles, Ajax,* and *Andromeda* of Ennius, and the *Hermiona* of Pacuvius. By the time Accius was writing, three previous tragedians had presented plays, with the result that many of Accius' plays had received numerous earlier treatments, starting with Livius. Both Livius and Ennius, for example, wrote an *Achilles* and an *Andromeda* before Accius presented plays of the same names. The *Clytemnestra* and *Tereus* of Accius were preceded by Livius' *Aegisthus* and *Tereus,* respectively—plays that were popular in the late Republic.

11. "*Carmen*-style" refers to the highly alliterative features of archaic Latin verse. Examples from other plays include the description of the flood in the *Andromeda: confluges ubi conventu campum totum inumigant* (Ribbeck 1897, 3); and the following passage from the *Equos Troianus: da mihi hasce opes, / quas peto, quas precor: / porrige, opitula!* (ibid., 3). For a discussion of the features of this technique, see Lindsay 1968, and, most recently, Goldberg 1995, 58–82.

12. Quoted are the texts and fragment numbers as they appear in Ribbeck 1897, 1–2. The exact placement of the fragments within the play, in this and the other plays discussed in this chapter, must remain conjecture. In many instances, however, one can reconstruct the outlines of the dramatic action without the exact placement of speeches and episodes within the play.

13. For stereotypical traits of a tyrant onstage, see La Penna 1979, 66–68, and Leigh 1996, 171–197. In addition to references to tyrannical traits in Ennius' *Thyestes* and Accius' *Atreus,* which are discussed in chapter 4, we find references in Pacuvius' *Dulorestes: amplus, rubicundo colore et spectu protervo ferox* (Ribbeck 1897, frag. 147) and *heu, non tyrannum novi termeritudinem?* (ibid., frag. 149); and Accius' *Diomedes: ferre exanclavimus / Tyranni saevom ingenium atque execrabile* (ibid., frag. 269).

14. Alternate spellings of Clytemnestra's name are frequent. Ribbeck (1897, 1–2) spells her name "Clutemestra" in Accius' play of that name. For the sake

of consistency, I use the spelling "Clytemnestra" throughout, but note alternate spellings when found in cited texts.

15. Warmington's note to this fragment (1982, 7) suggests that the order is given to servants. Ribbeck (1875, 30) notes that *hanc* may refer to Cassandra rather than to Electra.

16. Eutropius 3.1–2: *ad ludos spectandos.*

17. Gell. 17.21.45. Was Naevius in the audience of Livius' first tragedy in 240 B.C.E.?

18. The *Andromache* is cited by Servius auctus ad Verg. *G.* 1.266, but the play may actually belong to Novius, a writer of Atellan farces.

19. As noted above, both Livius and Naevius are credited with the writing of an *Equos Troianus*. If this is correct, the play is the first repetition of a title and may have been written as a literary "challenge" to Livius' version. See chapter 4 for the importance of this play in the late Republic.

20. Terence *Andria* prologue 18 mentions that Naevius "contaminated" two Greek originals in the *Colax,* one of his comedies.

21. Cicero *Sen.* 50.

22. Suetonius *Poet.,* in Rostagni 1964: *Naevius comicus Uticae moritur; / pulsus Roma factione nobilum ac praecipue Metelli.*

23. Terence *Eunuchus* prologue 25 mentions that the characters of the parasite and the braggart soldier had previously appeared in the *Colax* of Naevius and the *Colax* of Plautus.

24. Aulus Gellius (3.3.15) claims that Naevius wrote two plays while in prison, but this may be a fictional response to meager evidence. See La Penna 1979, 50–51, and Goldberg 1995, 33–36.

25. See Cicero *Rep.* 4.11: *. . . sed Periclem . . . violari versibus et eos agi in scaena non plus decuit, quam si Plautus noster voluisset aut Naevius P. et Cn. Scipioni aut Caecilius M. Catoni maledicere.*

26. The title suggests alternative titles to a single play, but Ribbeck (1875, 63–72) and La Penna (1979, 50–51) argue for two separate plays.

27. Chapter 3 explores the historical and dramatic implications of the *praetextae* for the development of theatricality.

28. The fragments quoted follow the numbering given by Ribbeck 1897, 7–9.

29. Ribbeck (1897, 8) changes *contemplo* (found in all manuscripts) to *contempla.* With *contemplo,* the translation would be, "I examine quietly the shape and beauty of a virgin."

30. See La Penna 1979, 77–78, for an analysis of this line from the perspective of women in Roman tragedy as "ideal types."

31. Naevius himself was proud of his literary accomplishments and his promotion of Italian culture. According to Aulus Gellius (*NA* 1.24), he advertised this pride when he composed his own epitaph:

*immortales mortales flere si foret fas,*
*flerent divae Camenae Naeviom poetam:*
*itaque postquam est Orci traditus thesauro,*
*oblitei sunt Romai loquier lingua Latina.*

If it were right for gods to mourn for mortals,
the divine Camenae would weep for poet Naevius:
"And when he was surrendered to the vault of Orcus,
no more were Romans mindful to speak their Latin tongue."

See E. Fraenkel, *RE* suppl. 6.622–640, esp. p. 637, for a discussion of Naevius' epitaph, and, most recently, Goldberg 1995, 82.

32. *Brutus* 75–76. Whereas Cicero compares the style of Livius' *Odyssia* to a statue by Daedalus and, in the process, states that the plays were not worth a second reading, he likens the style of Naevius' *Bellum Punicum* to the art of Myron, suggesting in the comparison that it is a more polished literary achievement, yet one that falls short of the more sophisticated literary technique of Ennius. On Naevius' poetic style, see Mariotti 1955 and Barchiesi 1962.

33. Suetonius *De poetis*, in Rostagni 1964.

34. Gell. 171.17.1.

35. Silus Italicus *Pun.* 12.393ff.

36. Cornelius Nepos *Cato* 1.4; Jerome, anno 1777, 240.

37. See Jocelyn 1967, 44, for the possible connections between Ennius' tragedies and the political views of his patrons: "The political debates of 203–169 sometimes seem to make themselves heard in the scripts of the tragedies he adapted for the festivals managed by his aristocratic patrons." As examples, he offers fragment 84 from the *Hecuba* and fragment 105 from the *Medea*.

38. The titles of Ennius' known plays are *Achilles, Ajax, Alcmeo, Alexander, Andromache/Andromache Aechmalotis, Andromeda, Athamas, Chresphontes, Erectheus, Eumenides, Hectoris Lytra, Hecuba, Iphigenia in Aulis, Medea Exul/ Medea, Melanippa, Nemea, Phoenix, Telephus, Thyestes,* and the *praetextae Ambracia* and *Sabinae.* Of these plays, five may have been influenced by his contemporaries Livius and Naevius: he followed Livius' lead in writing an *Achilles,* an *Ajax,* and an *Andromeda,* and, like Naevius, he wrote an *Andromache* and an *Iphigenia in Aulis.* This is not to say that he necessarily followed the same part of the myth and plot development as the other two dramatists, but rather that the shared titles are indicative of an interest in the same plays, and furthermore that the audience would have been familiar with mythical details from these rival Latin versions. In his approach to Greek models for his plays, Ennius seems to have been mostly influenced by the plays of Euripides. On the relationship between Ennius' and Euripides' philosophies, see La Penna 1979, 71–78.

39. This passage is found in Jerome *Ep.* 60 and is cited by Warmington 1988, 304–305, but is not listed by Jocelyn (1967) among the fragments of the *Iphigenia.*

40. Elsewhere, Ennius again uses the image of a *plebs* to reflect Roman class distinctions on the stage: *palam muttire plebeio piaculum est* (Telephus): Jocelyn 1967, frag. 142.

41. On the political connotations of the terms *otium* and *negotium*, see André 1966.

42. Jocelyn 1967, frag. 99.

43. There is no evidence that the earliest tragedians at Rome were on per-

sonal terms with each other. Ennius arrived in Rome in 204 B.C.E. Livius was dead by 200 B.C.E., and Naevius was in exile about the time of Ennius' arrival. Ennius' relationship with Naevius, therefore, was strictly literary. Although the comic writer Plautus did live in Rome for at least twenty years after Ennius' arrival, there is no evidence that Ennius ever met him. Yet Plautus was familiar with Ennius' plays and was likely a member of Ennius' audience on more than one occasion. Plautus was also familiar with the events of Naevius' life (if not the dramatist himself), which are alluded to in the *Miles gloriosus* (210–214). For Plautus' familiarity with Ennius' plays, see Plautus *Poen.* prol., 54ff.

44. Cited are fragments from Book 7, \*\*i, \*\*ia, from the text of Skutsch 1986.

45. Cicero *Brutus* 75–76. Elsewhere, Cicero claims that Ennius frequently borrows from Homer (*Fin.* 1.3.7).

46. I quote the text of Jocelyn 1967, frag. 17, lines 32–40). I preserve his fragment order and number system of individual lines but not his arrangement of groups of fragments under one number. Jocelyn discusses the dramatic and linguistic context of these fragments fully in his pp. 202–234. For other texts of the fragments, see Ribbeck 1897, 19–22, and Warmington 1988, 234–245.

47. Jocelyn 1967, frag. 50.

48. Ibid., frag. 59.

49. Ibid., frag. 128.

50. Ibid., frag. 126.

51. Jocelyn (ibid., 343–350) examines fully the question of a second *Medea* set in Athens.

52. This is based on Cicero's quotation of the passage at *Nat. d.* 3.75. See further arguments in Jocelyn 1967, 350.

53. Cited is the text of Jocelyn (1967) with corresponding line numbers (208–216). I have changed the numbers of the fragments but not the order given by Jocelyn.

54. According to Jocelyn (1967, 347), "Similarity with the text of Euripides' *Medea* is a quite treacherous guide. Study of Nonius' quotations of the *Hecuba* shows that Ennius departed radically from the wording of his original even more than he adhered to it."

55. If the emphasis is not on the hill on which the women live, the reference to *arx* may signal the Capitoline Hill and allude to the epithet of Corinth as Akrokorinth. Ennius stresses Medea's wealth for a Roman audience even in his *Hecuba*. In a speech where Hecuba tries to persuade Ulysses to convince the Greeks not to slaughter Polyxena, Ennius changes his Euripidean model (*Hec.* 293–295) by emphasizing the effect of one's social class, rather than esteem as in Euripides, in obtaining one's wishes: *haec tu etsi perverse dices facile Achivos flexeris, / nam cum opulenti locuntur pariter atque ignobiles, / eadem dicta eademque oratio aequa non aeque valet,* Jocelyn 1967, 172–174.

56. So Duff's view, while somewhat dated and extreme, still stands as typical (1953, 168): "But two facts in the history of tragedy are significant. One is the persistence of the serious drama on the stage despite a popular preference for lighter performances. Beyond question comedy, satire, and epic were more in ac-

cord with the national genius. Yet tragedy lived on, encouraged chiefly by the Roman aristocracy."

57. Gruen 1992, 209–210: "The vast edifice, exhibiting solidarity and endurance, would enshrine the drama as an unshakeable institution, no longer dependent upon the resolve of magistrates and the verdict of the aristocracy. Resistance was inevitable. The stone theater crumbled under senatorial directive, and none other arose for a century thereafter. The nobility preferred the traditional system, which manifested their own cultural control."

58. Gorton 1972, 63.

59. See Gratwick 1988b, 60: "Allegory, though not yet literary allusion, was familiar to the public through tragedy."

60. Brooks 1981, 90: "There was more than a casual connection between Roman tragedy and comedy in the age of Plautus. The points on which his humor depends are sure to be more than vague hearsay to his audience, the plays of Ennius, therefore, seem to have appealed to the same public as the *servus currens* and the *avarus leno*." See also Anderson 1993, 140: "Plautus was popular because he appealed across the board to Romans of all classes and levels of culture."

61. Ribbeck (1897, 312) offers the following passages as comic parodies of tragic lines: *Bacch.* 1053; *Stich.* 365; *Men.* 102, 330, 350, 402ff.; *Rud.* 942; *Curc.* 86; *Persa* 3.1. Sedgwick (1927, 89) agrees with the first six.

62. See Sedgwick 1927, 88.

63. Fraenkel 1960, 55–62. Brooks (1981, 81), however, argues that the audience would have been familiar with a play previously produced on the Roman stage, "but if Plautus' mythological references are examined as a whole, it is clear that he elaborated the myths as for an audience already familiar with them, and that he deliberately chose these familiar myths from those that had already been presented on the tragic stage."

64. See Brooks 1981, 73: "About ⅔ and possibly ¾ of all these references [sc. heroic myths in Plautus] deal with themes which are found also in the tragedies of Livius, Naevius, and Ennius or in the *Odyssia*."

## CHAPTER TWO

1. The similarities also extend to the comic stage. In the prologue to Terence's *Hecyra* (1), Ambivius Turpio states, *orator ad vos venio ornatu prologi . . .* , illustrating the actor as orator paradigm, which also extends to the audience: *quare omnis vos oratos volo, / ne plus iniquom possit quam aequam oratio* (prologue to *Heauton Timorumenos*, 26–27). For recent studies on the connections between rhetoric and the theatre, see Goldberg 1997, 166–181; Hughes 1997, 182–197; and Conte 1994, 108. For the effect of *suasoria* on the perpetuation of theatricality under the early Empire, see chapter 4.

2. For the reciprocity of public and theatre spaces as performance and reception venues, see Wiseman 1995, 151–155; and Fantham 1997, 111–128. See Rawson 1985, 97–113, for performance contexts.

3. For the extension of theatre metaphors to the audience, from the reception of public figures in the theatre to self- and imposed identification of audience members with the theatre, see Parker 1999, 163–179. For the role of actors in encouraging allusions between characters onstage and members of the audience, see Beacham 1999, 56–61, discussing Aesopus' role in urging the recall of Cicero; and Purcell 1999, 181–193, for the social and political contexts of the theatre and for rivalries between actors themselves and their targets.

4. Cicero *Verr.* 5.35.

5. For the connection between drama and oratory, see the *Rhetorica ad Herennium,* passim, and Cicero *Brutus* 289ff.

6. For Cicero's self-identification with Accius' *Brutus,* see chapter 4 below.

7. Cicero *Mur.* 41.88, and *Att.* 10.12.1: quo me nunc vertam? In *Fam.* 12.29.1, Cicero claims that he displayed his friendship for L. Lamia on a worldwide stage (*magno theatro*).

8. For unflattering allusions to actors and the stage, see Corbeill 1996, passim, and 167–168 for the orator Hortensius' comparison to the mime actress Dionysia.

9. Horace (*Ep.* 2.1.197–198) imagines the Greek philosopher Democritus' reaction to scenic entertainment both on the stage and in the audience: *spectaret populum ludis attentius ipsis, ut sibi praebentem nimio spectacula plura,* "He would watch the crowd more carefully than the games themselves since the crowd offers far more spectacles."

10. See Parker 1999, 173–174, for the importance of an "audience" to aristocrats in gauging public opinion, and 175–176 for the "semiotics of failure"; and see Richlin 1997, 99ff., for the dangers to an orator's reputation of being compared to an actor. See also Graf 1992, 36–58; Dupont 1985, 31–34; and Von Hessberg 1999, 65–75, for the reciprocity of theatricality between the stage and the political sphere of Hellenistic rulers offstage.

11. Boyle 1997, 114.

12. Pliny *HN* 35.19.

13. See the *Vita,* lines 3–4, in Rostagni 1964, 47–48. Beacham (1992, 121) argues from the innovative nature of Pacuvius' plays that Pacuvius did not depend on the theatre for his livelihood: "That he could afford to take risks may be reflected in his choice of unusual subject matter, dealing with mythic material which was relatively unfamiliar to his audience and therefore might not have readily won its approval. Few of his works handled the stories commonly used by his Roman predecessors, who, as noted, mutually recycled their subjects."

14. See the *Vita,* line 1, in Rostagni 1964, 47. Fulgentius' testimony that Pacuvius also wrote a comedy, the *Seudon,* is unreliable. Did his tragedies inform his paintings and vice versa? The titles of some thirteen plays survive: *Antiopa, Armorum iudicium, Atalanta, Chryses, Dulorestes, Hermione, Iliona, Medus, Niptra, Pentheus, Periboea, Teucer,* and the *fabula praetexta Paullus.*

15. This is arguing against the Aristotleian concept of an effective tragedy, but even in the use of spectacle, Roman tragedians demonstrated independence from Aristotle's precepts. For the Roman tragedian's use of spectacle to arouse pity and fear contra Aristotle *Poetics* 1453b1ff., see Boyle 1997, 231 n. 18.

16. Ribbeck 1897, frag. 7, p. 104. I separate the speeches since they may not come from the same passage or be spoken by the same character.

17. Beacham (1992, 121) argues: "The audience presumably was equal to the challenge of Pacuvius' works, despite somewhat obscure subjects and elevated style, because he joined these with a deft understanding of dramaturgical technique. Suspense, pathos, startling revelations, moments of spirited rhetoric; Pacuvius evidently had a particular talent for forming and moulding such elements to create compelling theatre." La Penna (1979, 73) questions the audience's ability to follow a complex philosophical excursus or debate.

18. For Bronislaw Bilinski's argument that Pacuvius sympathized with the plebs, see Bilinski 1957, 8–9. For the influence of the *Dulorestes* and the *Chryses* on the Sicilian slave revolt, see ibid., 26.

19. See La Penna 1979, 72–78, for a discussion of Ennius' influence on Pacuvius and Accius in including and questioning the validity of Greek philosophic passages in their plays; and Conte 1994, 107: "When these poets [Pacuvius and Accius] deal with religious, political, moral, or philosophical themes, they use the tragic myths freely and touch upon themes and problems felt in contemporary society."

20. See Ribbeck 1875, 218, for an Aeschylean model for Pacuvius' play.

21. Teucer expresses his rage in a *canticum*, indicating that this scene was central to the play's action (Ribbeck 1897, 12, p. 136):

TELAMON: *segregare abs te ausu's aut sine illo Salaminem ingredi,*
*neque paternum aspectum es veritus, quom aetate exacta indigem*
*liberum lacerasti orbasti exstinxti, neque fratris necis*
*neque eius gnati parui, qui tibi in tutelam est traditus . . . ?*

TELAMON: You dared to separate yourself, even went to Salamis without
   him,
nor did you fear your father's sight; whom, spent in years, bereft of sons
you have wounded, made childless, and wiped out, nor [did you think]
   of a brother's death,
nor of his infant son, who was entrusted to your safe-keeping . . . ?

22. Ribbeck 1897, 17, p. 122.

23. Ribbeck (1897, 44, p. 152) lists this fragment under *Ex Incertis Fabulis* but offers: "*Vix dubium quin ad Teucrum pertineant.*" Pacuvius' line bears some similarity to Livius' *Aegisthus* fragment 2: *tum autem lascivum Nerei simum pecus / ludens ad cantum classem lustratur vias.*

24. Marx 1963, frag. 875 of *Satire* 29.4, p. 59.

25. Cicero *De Or.* 2.46.193.

26. Cicero, who preserves this passage (*Tusc.* 1.44.106 = Ribbeck 1897, 4, p. 114), writes of the sympathy elicited by this speech by Umbra for the dead: *haec cum pressis et flebilis modis, qui totis theatris maestitiam inferant, concinuntur, difficile est non eos qui inhumati sint miseros iudicare. . . .*

27. Cf. Horace *Sat.* 2.3.60.

28. Ribbeck 1897, *Ex Incertis Fabulis*, 14, p. 144.

29. See La Penna 1979, 72–73, for an analysis of the relationship between Pacuvius' and Ennius' philosophical thought, which, like Euripides', is critical of both philosophy and rhetoric.

30. In Propertius' version of the myth (3.15), Antiopa escapes from Dirce and discovers her sons, but finds Amphion the more sympathetic of the two. The later rivalry between the sons during the construction of the walls of Thebes is also described.

31. For a discussion of the relationship between Euripides' and Pacuvius' plays, see Ribbeck 1875, 281–301.

32. Cited is the text of Ribbeck 1897, 86–90.

33. Warmington (1982, 160–161) ascribes this line to Amphion, together with the following line, which Ribbeck ascribes to unassigned fragments: *tu cornifrontes pascere armentas soles*. See Ribbeck 1875, 286, for possible literary meanings of *horrida*.

34. The digression annoyed the author of *Rhetorica ad Herennium* (2.27.43): *item verendum est ne de alia re dicatur cum alia de re controversia sit . . . uti apud Pacuvium Zethus cum Amphione, quorum controversia de musica inducta est, disputationem in sapientiae rationem et virtutis utilitatem consumit.* Ribbeck (1897) cites this notice as fragment 2.

35. Following this fragment, Warmington (1982, 164–165) gives the following line to Zethus: *odi ego homines ignava opera et philosopha sententia.*

36. Or are these lines spoken by Dirce on her stage entrance? Warmington (1982, 166–167) adds the following fragment found in the unassigned fragments of Pacuvius after fragment 10:

> *agite ite evolvite rapite, coma*
> *tractate per aspera saxa et humum;*
> *scindite vestem ocius!*

> (M. Victorinus, *Grammatici Latini* 7.77.2)

37. Marx 1963, Book 5, 211, p. 16. Other passages ridiculed by Lucilius include Book 26, *Sat.* 3, 665; Book 26, *Sat.* 6, 720–721, 722, 723, 724–725, 726, 727–728, 729–730, and 731; Book 29, *Sat.* 2, 879, 880, 881; and unassigned frag. 1261, Warmington 1982, 413.

38. *itaque licet dicere et Ennium summum epicum poetam et Pacuvium tragicum et Caecilium fortasse comicum,* Cicero *Opt. Gen.* 1. Velleius (1.17), however, accorded the highest place to Accius.

39. Cicero *Tusc.* 2.21.

40. Quintilian *Inst.* 10.1.97; Horace *Epist.* 2.1.53–56:

> *Naevius in manibus non est et mentibus haeret*
> *paene recens? adeo sanctum est vetus omne poema.*
> *ambigitur quotiens, uter utro sit prior, aufert*
> *Pacuvius docti famam senis, Accius alti. . . .*

41. Persius *Satirae* 1.77.

42. Lucilius challenged many of Accius' grammatical rules: Book 9, *Sat.* 2.366–367, 368.

43. Bilinski 1957, 49: "Come sappiamo, è appunto in una atellana del poeta comico Novio che comparvero sulla scena Phoenissae e Andromache e nell' atellana di Pomponio Armorum iudicium, tratte entrambe dal repertorio di Accio."

44. One should recall, however, that at *Dial.* 20, Marcus Aper is the speaker, and his opinions should not be taken as those of Tacitus. Tacitus' own potential as a tragic dramatist was remarked upon by Syme (1958, 363): "Roman history gave scope for poetry and for high politics, notably the catastrophe of the Republic. Hence the 'Cato' composed by Curiatius Maternus (senator, orator, and poet) whom the young Tacitus knew and admired. And, if Cato or Brutus were exhausted, did not the tragedy of the Caesars embody a sequence of dramatic themes, with ambition, power, and crime recalling the House of Atreus? The aptitude disclosed in the *Annales* might have found expression and renown with a 'Sejanus' or an 'Agrippina.'" See also Walker 1952; Mellor 1993; Luce and Woodman 1993; and Bartsch 1994, 22–24, 35, 55–56.

45. A large number of fragments from the titles of Accius' tragedies survive. In many instances, however, little more than a few fragments can be assigned to each play. Known titles are *Achilles sive Myrmidones, Agamemnonidae sive Erigona, Alcmeo sive Alphesiboea, Amphitryo, Andromeda, Antenoridae, Antigona, Armorum iudicium, Astyanax sive Troades, Athamas, Atreus, Bacchae, Chrysippus, Clytemnestra sive Aegisthus* (which may actually be one play), *Deiphobus, Epigoni sive Eriphyle, Epinausimache, Eurysaces, Hecuba, Hellenes, Liberi, Medea sive Argonautae, Meleager, Minos sive Minotaurus, Neoptolemus, Nyctegressia, Oenomaus, Pelopidae, Philocteta sive Philocteta Lemnius, Phinidae, Phoenissae, Prometheus, Stasiastae sive Tropaeum, Telephus, Tereus, Thebais,* and the *fabulae praetextae Brutus* and *Aeneadae sive Decius.*

46. More of Accius' plays are titled after the chorus than any of his predecessors'. See Conte 1994, 107; and Leo 1910, 18: *inter Acci tragoedias magnus numerus est titulorum ipsum chorum significantium: Bacchae Hellenes Myrmidones Phoenissae Stasiastae Troades; cuius generis inter Enni tragoedias esse diximus Eumenides et Sabinas, inter Pacuvianas nulla est.*

47. Bilinski (1957, 38–44) argues that Accius was sympathetic to the aristocracy and hostile to the plebs, and that the social upheavals surrounding Tiberius Gracchus' reforms in 133 B.C.E. are reflected in his *Atreus.* While some themes seem suggestive of this period, we do not know the original production date for this play. La Penna (1979, 49–104) examines passages and recent scholarship on the complex issue of political views expressed in the plays of Pacuvius and Accius. See chapter 4 for various later cultural contexts of Accius' *Atreus.*

48. See La Penna 1979, 63–71.

49. Ribbeck 1897, 4, p. 182.

50. Ibid. 2, p. 163.

51. Ibid. 5, p. 177.

52. See Beacham 1992, 124: "Accius' plays were admired for their flamboyance and energy; they also contained much verbal violence and descriptive gore:

Thyestes dining upon his sons; Philomela raped by Tereus who cuts out her tongue to avoid detection; Medea's murder of her children. Accius probed mythical material to bring forth its most intense pathos and horror."

53. See Tarrant 1978, 257ff.; and Dangel 1990, 107–122.

54. Only two lines survive from apparently two different points in the play: Medea's *servare potui: perdere an possim, rogas?* and *feror huc illuc, vae, plena deo.* Quoted are the lines from Ribbeck 1897, 267. The rhetorical connections between the *Metamorphoses* and Seneca's tragedies are analyzed in chapter 4.

55. Quintilian *Inst.* 10.1.98: *Ovidii Medea videtur mihi ostendere, quantam ille vir praestare potuerit, si ingenio suo imperare quam indulgere maluisset.*

56. Warmington 1982, 456, following Ribbeck 1875, 528–536, suggests a play by Sophocles as the possible model, but the closest play of Sophocles on the Medea myth is the *Scythians,* in which Apsyrtus appears as a boy. See Hugh Lloyd Jones, *Sophocles,* vol. 3, *Fragments,* Loeb ed. (Cambridge, Mass., 1996), 274–277.

57. Cited is the text of Ribbeck 1897, 216–220.

58. Ribbeck (1875, 533) conjectures Jason speaking to himself, while Warmington (1982, 463) assigns the line to Medea as a threat to Jason. Dangel (1995, 351) assigns the line to Medea to express the hope that he will share the same fate as herself. In my *Archaic Latin Verse* (Erasmo 2001a, 104), I assigned the line to Medea, but I am now less confident about the designation.

59. Ribbeck (1875, 533) conjectures a king or priest of Diana as the speaker of this line. I assigned the line to Apsyrtus (2001a, 57), but the fragment may actually come from another play, in particular, Accius' *Diomedes.*

60. Ribbeck (1875) lists the names of some 36 poets and 150 tragedies after Accius, but much of this information is inconclusive.

61. Paratore (1957, 57) divides the age of the Republican theatre into two eras: 1) Livius to Plautus, and 2) Ennius to the age of Sulla.

62. Pollio, using Pacuvius and Accius as literary models, was accused of having a harsh and dry style by Tacitus (*Dial.* 21.7: *Pacuvium certe Accium non solum tragoediis sed etiam orationibus suis expressit; adeo durus et siccus est*). I list Ovid here, but as stated in the introduction, it is not clear whether the *Medea* appeared on the stage. Cornelius Balbus wrote and produced in Gades a *praetexta* entitled *Iter,* but it was never produced in Rome. For more details concerning this play, see chapter 3. Too little is known of the dramatic activities of other tragedians, such as C. Titius, Pompilius, and Atilius. See the appendix for the known titles of their plays.

63. According to Jory (1986, 149–150 n. 2): "Presentation of complete Roman dramas in the Empire is rarely recorded but may not have been as exceptional as generally assumed, at least in the first century." Further, Jory argues that the increased number of festivals throughout the Republic and Empire points to a robust dramatic tradition that is not reflected in the surviving dramatic notices and ancient sources (144): "It [the number of days on which scenic entertainment was featured] rose from eleven in the time of Plautus through about fifty-five at the death of Julius Caesar to one hundred and one in the mid-fourth century A.D., and the frequency of the *instaurationes* as well as of funeral

and votive games meant that these figures represent only the minimum number of days in each year on which scenic performances were staged. Thus the evidence of literary texts is misleading. The heyday of the Roman theatre was not in the Republic but in the Empire." On the decline of tragic productions under the Empire, see Goldberg 1996, 265–286.

## CHAPTER THREE

1. T. P. Wiseman's *Roman Drama and Roman History* (1998) provides valuable analyses of ancient sources for the production contexts of nonliterary forms of drama in the third and second centuries B.C.E. My focus on the semiotic and dramaturgical implications of staging historical plays and the shared theatricality of drama and historiographic sources complements Wiseman's examination of the historic contexts for the production of *praetextae.* Other recent important studies on *praetextae* include Pedroli 1953; Zorzetti 1980; Flower 1995, 170–190; and Manuwald 2001.

2. On the close connection between historiography and drama in the Hellenistic world, in particular the framing of events by historiographic sources in the context of a drama, see Wiseman 1994, 1–22, which is discussed by Flower (1995, 173–174), who disagrees with Wiseman's analysis of *praetextae* as a form of popular drama. In addition to the name *praetextae,* ancient sources also preserve the form *praetextatae.*

3. On the literary connections between tragedy and *praetextae,* see La Penna 1979, 51–56; Flower (1995, 172), however, cautions against defining all *praetextae* as belonging to a subcategory of tragedy.

4. See Manuwald 2001, 29–52, for an extensive analysis of ancient conceptions of *praetextae.*

5. Flower (1995, 178–179, 180–181) weighs the evidence for the production of *praetextae* at various events, favoring votive games as the most likely occasion of performance, as does Nicholas Purcell (1999, 184). See, most recently, the extensive discussion in Manuwald 2001, 110–130.

6. The view of David Raven stands as typical (1969, 290): "A striking indication of the [Republican] tragedians' unoriginality lies in the relative failure of the *fabula praetexta.*" Most recently, Flower (1995, 190) argues: "Their meaning and importance was inextricably connected to the spectacle itself in the context of the immediate political climate, and this helps to explain their ephemeral interest and the few fragments quoted by later authors."

7. See La Penna 1979, 63–71, for general remarks on the relation of *praetextae* and tragedy to Roman politics at large.

8. For discussions on the existence of preliterary forms of historical drama, see Zorzetti 1980, 11–52; Horsfall 1994, 50–75, in particular for his analysis of the Varronian origin of our knowledge of preliterary forms of drama; and Wiseman 1998, 1–16.

9. For the *Gyges* fragments, see *TGF* adesp. p. 664, with bibliography. The text is reprinted in Diggle 1998, 182. The date of this play may be Hellenistic.

10. La Penna 1979, 51–56. Zorzetti (1980, 53–73) describes *praetextae* as "celebrations of *imperium.*" Flower (1995, 171), however, defines a *fabula praetexta* as "a play about Roman aristocrats and their status." Possible additions to the list of known Republican *praetextae* include an anonymous *Claudia*, mentioned by Ovid (*Fasti* 4.326), which was probably performed at the *ludi Magalenses* (but the actual performance date[s] and author cannot be recovered), and a play of unknown title and authorship that celebrated the *Nonae Caprotinae*, a festival with connections to the *ludi Apollinares*. For further details surrounding this play, see Zorzetti 1980, 39–40; Bremmer 1987, 76–88; and Wiseman 1998, 8–11.

11. The title suggests alternative titles for a single play, but Ribbeck (1875, 63–72) and La Penna (1979, 50–51) argue for two separate plays.

12. See chapter 4 for details of the plays of Cassius Parmensis.

13. The didascalia for Terence's *Adelphoe* does not mention this play. Flower (1995, 186–187) argues against the performance of this play at Paullus' funeral games in favor of its performance at earlier votive games.

14. Text from Keil 1857, bk. 3, 487–488: *prima species est togatarum, quae praetextatae dicuntur, in quibus imperatorum negotia aguntur et publica[,] et reges Romani vel duces inducuntur, personarum dignitate et sublimitate tragoediis similes . . . togata praetextata a tragoedia differt, quod in tragoedia heroes inducuntur, ut Pacuvius tragoedias nominibus heroicis inscripsit, Orestem, Chrysen, et his similia, item Accius; in praetextata autem reges Romani vel duces, ut quae inscribitur Brutus vel Decius item Marcellus* (1.487). This notice is somewhat late but, at least in theory, Diomedes had access to many, if not all, of the *praetextae* upon which to base his observations. See Manuwald 2001, 30–36, for a discussion of Diomedes' definition.

15. In relation to the plays of Ennius, Ribbeck (1875, 212) observes: "Kriegerischen Charakter haben die Dramen der Ilias gemeinsam mit den beiden Prätextaten: neben ausfürlichen Schlacht berichten mag dem Zuschauer auf der Bühne selbst ein bewegtes Kriegs-und Lagerleben vorgeführt sein." This observation seems more applicable to Ennius' description of Ambracia's fall in his *Annales,* Book 15, than to the extant fragments of the *Ambracia*. It is unclear how any descriptions of battles and camp life relate to Ennius' other *praetexta,* the *Sabinae*.

16. Zorzetti (1980, 93–103) analyzes Imperial *praetextae* from the point of view of aristocratic opposition. For an analysis of the arguments in favor of viewing the *Octavia* in the context of Republican *praetextae*, see Coffey 1957, 113–186.

17. A recent biography of former U.S. president Ronald Reagan, *Dutch: A Memoir of Ronald Reagan* (2000), in which the author, Edmund Morris, inserts himself as a bystander to the historical events recounted, has generated much controversy concerning historical accuracy and objectivity in research: if the narrator is a fictional witness, how accurate are his observations of the biographical subject?

18. Cf. Ribbeck 1875, 207–211, for Ennius' *praetextae*.

19. Ribbeck 1897, frag. 3, p. 325: *nivit sagittis, plumbo et saxis grandinat.*

20. See Skutsch 1985, 104–105, for fragments.

21. See most recently the extensive discussion in Manuwald 2001, 259–339, in particular 305ff. for an analysis of contemporary references in the play.

22. This consistency of historical fact is noted by Herington (1961, 22): "Yet in spite of this highly artificial design, the author has been very successful in building-in the scattered events which he has chosen for his play; there is internal consistency and smooth progression as one reads it, and at the same time little violence has been done to historical fact, apart from the compression of the time-element." In terms of actual historical inconsistencies, one can point to the appearance of Seneca at the court, since he was already in Imperial disfavor at the time of Nero's marriage to Poppaea.

23. This is not to say that the play does not share historical information with Suetonius and Dio. For example, R. Helm (1934, 283–347) has pointed out that there is a reference to Tiridates, who was vassal in Rome in 66 C.E., at lines 627ff. Both Dio (63.5) and Suetonius (Nero 13) also mention his coronation in Rome. Coffey (1957) argues that the author of the Octavia does not intend a reference to Vindex in the use of the adjective at line 255. In Dio (63.22.1–6) and Suetonius (Nero 40–44), however, Vindex plays a narrative role in signaling Nero's imminent fall, and indeed, his name appears as a pun for an "avenger."

24. Nero had Octavia killed in 62 C.E., only months before the birth of Poppaea's child, in January 63 C.E. The Octavia mentions the pregnancy twice: at lines 181ff. and 591ff. Tacitus (14.1) only hints at Poppaea's pregnancy. This omission in the literary sources was noted by J.P.V.D. Balsdon, quoted by Herington (1961, 29 n. 3).

25. Vasily Rudich reminded me in conversation that Tigellinus is not mentioned by name, only by position, perhaps signaling that Tigellinus was still alive when the play was written.

26. The monument is confirmed by an inscription. See CIL 10.6599.

27. See Pantzerhielm Thomas 1945, 65. Nero's acceptance of the title early in his reign is confirmed by inscriptions.

28. Herington (1961, 28) argues that Seneca later alludes to the De clementia in conversation with Nero.

29. See Jocelyn 1971, 87–88. The influence of Greek tragedy is also evident in the Octavia. There are stylistic parallels and verbal echoes between the first 262 lines of the Octavia and the Electra of Sophocles. See Herington 1961, 20: "I have no doubt that the Octavia is influenced by the Electra. The influence is clearest in the Octavia's prologue: the empress's anapaestic song, which opens the play, and her dialogue with the Nurse (partly in anapaests and partly in iambics) remind one very strongly of Electra's entrance-song and her exchanges with the Chorus. And it is in this part also that the verbal echoes of the Electra come thickest."

30. Cited is the text of Denys Page, Aeschyli Septem Quae Supersunt Tragoedias (Oxford, 1972, reprinted 1989), 8–10.

31. Cicero Div. 1.22.44 preserves both passages. Cited is the text of Diehl

1967, frags. 212–214. A more detailed analysis of this passage in relation to the *Brutus* appears in chapter 4.

32. The parallel is noted by Pedroli (1953, 219). However, Coffey (1957, 175), in his review of Mickwitz 1928, doubts that the parallels between the two plays are anything more than a similarity of a shared tragic trope.

33. Cited is the text of Zwierlein 1988.

34. See chapter 4, "Staging Brutus," for the cultural contexts surrounding Accius' *Brutus* under the late Republic, and Cassius' version as a vehicle for criticism of Imperial oppression.

35. See Tarrant 1978, 238–239, for an analysis of this parallel and for additional related scenes in Plautus, such as *Merc.* 864, *nescioquoia vox ad auris mi advolavit*, and *Rud.* 233, *certo vox muliebris auris tetigit meas*.

36. Quoted is the Oxford Classical Text of W. M. Lindsay (1989).

37. Although the text of the *Domitius* does not survive, one can assume from Maternus' comments about his *Cato* and *Thyestes* that the play was written not as an encomium but rather as criticism of Imperial power. It is not clear which Domitius is described in the play. The play may have been written about either Lucius or Gnaeus Domitius Ahenobarbus, both of whom were ancestors of Nero. The date of the play, therefore, may be further removed in time from the date of composition than is suggested above. Tenney Frank (1937, 225–229) argues that the play was about Lucius Domitius Ahenobarbus and that it was composed about 67 C.E. to break the power of Nero's courtier Vatinius (cf. Tacitus *Dial.* 11). In the same article (229), Frank speculates that Maternus' *Medea* may have been written as a criticism of Nero for choosing Poppaea over Octavia—a situation analogous to Jason's leaving of Medea for Creusa. See chapter 4 for further discussion of Maternus and *interpretatio prava* (prejudiced interpretation).

38. Pseudo-Seneca *Octavia* 166–173:

> *tu quoque extinctus iaces,*
> *deflende nobis semper, infelix puer,*
> *modo sidus orbis, columen augustae domus,*
> *Britannice, heu me, nunc levis tantum cinis*
> *et tristis umbra; saeva cui lacrimas dedit*
> *etiam noverca, cum rogis artus tuos*
> *dedit cremandos membraque et vultus deo*
> *similes volanti saeviens flamma abstulit.*

Quoted is the Oxford Classical Text of Otto Zwierlein (1988).

39. Although Maternus probably advertised his own *animus nocendi* against Vespasian's court, Tacitus suggests that it was also the way Maternus read his play, that is, his passionate undertaking of the role of Cato, in addition to the sentiments expressed, that made his recitation dangerous: *nam postero die quam Curiatius Maternus Catonem recitaverat, cum offendisse potentium animos diceretur, tamquam in eo tragoediae argumento sui oblitus tantum Catonem cogitasset . . . (Dial.* 2).

40. Was this at the expense of artistic value? The *Octavia* is considered an artistic failure by critics who do not consider its theme in the context of *praetextae,* but who hold it up against the idealized traits of Greek tragedy. David Raven (1969, 292) argues: "It [*Octavia*] is omitted from separate discussion here, owing to its colourlessness and lack of individuality in nearly all respects save that of its theme—Octavia's tragic death at Nero's orders." Herington (1961, 29) praises the "tragic experience" of contemporary events that the play contains rather than the play itself: "And if I have found the *Octavia,* in its own modest way, a moving experience, it is not through any of its rather inept rhetorical and tragical adornments. It is because somehow, in spite of them, the fumbling author does convey something of the tragic experience of that time which we cannot gather from any other quarter."

41. Ronald Syme (1958, 363) suggests that Tacitus would have written good *praetextae:* "Roman history gave scope for poetry and for high politics, notably the catastrophe of the Republic. Hence the *Cato* composed by Curiatius Maternus (senator, orator, and poet) whom the young Tacitus knew and admired. And, if Cato or Brutus were exhausted, did not the tragedy of the Caesars embody a sequence of dramatic themes, with ambition, power, and crime recalling the House of Atreus? The aptitude disclosed in the *Annales* might have found expression and renown with a 'Sejanus' or an 'Agrippina'."

42. I cite the text and fragment numbers of Ribbeck 1897, 326–328.

43. See Pedroli 1953, 115, on the identification of the *Caleti.*

44. Timpanaro would add the line *Martis manubias Musis consecrare* from Cicero's *Pro Archia* (27) to the fragments of the *Ambracia.* This line was first noticed by W. Zillinger (1911, 145). See Timpanaro 1949, 186–204.

45. I cite the fragments and sequence of Ribbeck 1897, 323–324.

46. Warmington 1988, 358–360.

47. For an extensive analysis of the cultural contexts of Greek historical dramas, see Hall 1989, in particular 64–65 for Themistocles' involvement with the *Sack of Miletus* and the *Phoenissae.*

48. See Zehnacker 1981, 40.

49. Warmington 1988, 359.

50. Flower (1995, 189) includes a chart with possible performance dates and occasions for the production of *praetextae.*

51. For arguments against the appearance of contemporary Romans onstage (besides Cornelius Balbus), see, most recently, Zorzetti 1980, 55; and see the discussion in the text below.

52. *De re publica* 4.10.12: *veteribus displicuisse Romanis vel laudari quemquam in scaena vivum hominem vel vituperari.* For a more detailed discussion of this passage and bibliography, see Flower 1995, 177–179, and Manuwald 2001, 122–123.

53. See Lana 1958–59, 371–376, for an analysis of the historical context of this play and for questions regarding the title, *Iter.*

54. Cicero *Fam.* 10.32.3–5. Cited is the text of Shackelton Bailey 2001, 358. See Manuwald 2001, 54–62, for an analysis of this passage and for a discussion

of recent criticism on Balbus' play and his composition of it. Pollio also informs Cicero that he may obtain a copy of the play from Cornelius Gallus.

55. See Purcell 1999, 184–185, for the displacement of the honorand into the role of dramatic representation: "The *praetexta* seems to me to gain meaning and to acquire extra importance—rather than losing significance—from the apparent fact that its central function was magnifying the hero by abstracting him from the domain of ordinary, unrepresented existence and relocating him in the select company of those who are represented—gods and heroes all."

56. Pollio reports that, in addition to throwing wild animals to beasts, Balbus ordered the soldier to be buried and burned, but he fills his narrative with details that depict Balbus as a tyrant: he was pacing leisurely after a meal while the soldier was being tortured, he was dressed leisurely (barefoot with loosened tunic), and even mocked the soldier by calling out that he should report this illegal punishment: *deinde abstractum defodit in ludo et vivum combussit, cum quidem pransus nudis pedibus, tunica soluta, manibus ad tergum reiectis inambularet et illi misero quiritanti "c.R. natus sum" responderet "abi nunc, populi fidem implora"; bestiis vero civis Romanos . . . (Fam.* 10.32.3, text of Shackelton Bailey 2001, 360).

57. Dupont 1985, 219ff.

58. Flower (1995, 177–179) argues that there is no evidence connecting the production of *praetextae* exclusively with funerals. The evidence, however, does not rule it out either.

59. See Flower 1996, 91–127, for a more detailed discussion of all aspects of funerals and the participation of ancestors. I take a semiotic approach in my analysis of the same evidence.

60. Polybius *Histories* 6.53.1–10. Translation from the text of Paton 1972, 388–391.

61. The evidence for *ludi scaenici* in the forum comes from Livy 31.50.4: *et ludi funebres eo anno per quadriduum in foro mortis causa M. Valeri Laevini a Publio et Marco filiis eius facti, et munus gladiatorium datum ab iis; paria quinque et viginti pugnarunt.* In favor of the forum as the site of funeral games, see Saunders 1913, 93–94; Hanson 1959, 17; and Richardson 1992, 380, contra.

62. Hanson (1959, 29–39) discusses the somewhat controversial evidence for the location of early stages and spectator seats at Rome.

63. See Purcell 1999, 182–184, for the role played by an actor *lusor* in the imitation of a deceased emperor during the funeral ceremony, in particular the link between the actor and the divine.

64. The *Amphitryon* contains a pun based on the *imagines* masks and the comic and tragic masks worn by actors. Sosias, looking at Mercury, who is wearing a mask resembling Sosias' own face, exclaims (458–459): *nam hicquidem omnem imaginem meam, quae antehac fuerat, possidet. / vivo fit quod numquam quisquam mortuo faciet mihi* ("This man has got hold of my total image, which used to be my own! / My image is carried around now that I am alive, more than anyone will do so when I'm dead"). Thus in the play, we have an actor imitating a god, who in turn is seen to be imitating a dead actor.

65. Diodorus Siculus *World History (Bibliotheca)* 31.25, from the text and translation of Walton 1968, 376–377.

66. See Flower 1996, 104–106, for an analysis of this passage.

67. A further connection between the theatre audience and the dead is made figuratively by Seneca, who in the *Hercules furens* compares the crowds of the dead in the Underworld to the excited *populus* of Rome at the premiere performance of a play in a new theatre (838–839): *quantus incedit populus per urbes / ad novi ludos avidus theatri* ("As much as the populace hastens through cities / anxious for the plays of a new theatre").

68. Flower (1995, 179) poses three similar questions: "Would the ancestors watch too? Would the actors on stage wear the same or similar masks in the play? If actors had been hired to impersonate the ancestors or even the dead man himself in the procession, would these same people perform in the play?"

69. The question of whether theatre masks differed from *imagines* is complex. See Wiles 1991, 130, who argues that they were probably not similar so as not to offend a noble family, and see the extensive discussion on the possible similarities between theatre masks and *imagines* in Flower 1996, 91–127, in particular 114–115, where she argues, contra Wiles, that it is possible that both masks were similar. See also the discussion in Slater 1996, 38–39.

## CHAPTER FOUR

1. This and subsequent citations from Seneca's plays come from the text of Zwierlein 1988.

2. Pro-Antony propaganda, for example, associated Octavian with Apollo, and pro-Octavian propaganda associated Antony with Dionysus and Sextus Pompey with Neptune. See Taylor 1931, 102–103, 120–121; and Gowling 1995, 309–310. For audience fondness for tragic texts as allusions to contemporary personalities and events, see Nicolet 1980, 366–373.

3. Bilinski 1957. Bilinski (43) offers a date for Accius' *Atreus* of sometime between 140 and 130 B.C.E., a little before or a little after 133 B.C.E. D'Antò (1980, 282–283) questions Bilinski's thesis due to the imprecise dating of Accius' plays. See also Lana 1958–59, 348–351, for the dating of Accius' *Atreus*.

4. See Gruen 1992, 183–222, and Richardson 1992, 380, for a discussion of the ancient (Livy *Epit.* 48; Val. Max. 2.4.1–2; Tacitus *Ann.* 14.20) and modern controversy concerning the opposition at Rome to the construction of a permanent theatre; and more recently, see Beacham 1999, 61–71.

5. Pliny records the variety of gladiatorial shows and the animals imported into Rome (*HN* 8.53, 64, 70, 72, 84). In addition to animals, both Plutarch (*Pompey* 52) and Cassius Dio (39.38) list music and gymnastic contests, but Cassius Dio also refers to a horse race in the Circus.

6. Pompey may have also wished to erase from popular memory the successful games given by Sulla—the *ludi Victoriae Sullanae*. The success on this occasion of courting popular favor obscures the fact that Pompey had been jeered at a short while earlier in the theatre; see Cicero *Att.* 2.19.

7. Cicero *Fam.* 7.1.2.

8. For the construction and architectural details of Pompey's theatre complex, see Platner and Ashby 1965, 428–429 and 515–517; Richardson 1992, 318–319 and 383–385; Gros 1998, 148–149 ("Porticus Pompei"), and 1999a, 35–38 ("Theatrum Pompeii"); and Beacham 1999, 61–71.

9. For the various reconstructions of the temple and *cavea* suggested to date, see Hill 1944, 360–365; Hanson 1959, 44–52; L. Richardson, Jr., "A Note on the Architecture of the Theatrum Pompeii in Rome," *AJA* 91 (1987): 123–126; Richardson 1992, 411; Gros 1999b, 120–121.

10. Shrines to Honos, Virtus, Felicitas, and a fourth deity preserved in an inscription only as V[. . .]. See Hanson 1959, 52–53, for a discussion of the inscriptions found on the *Fasti Amiterni* and *Alliterni*.

11. *HN* 36.115. Platner and Ashby (1965, 517), however, put the number at around 10,000, and Richardson (1992, 385) at around 11,000.

12. Cf. Val. Max. 11.6.4.

13. The "Younger" Balbus dedicated his theatre in 13 B.C.E. (Suetonius *Aug.* 29.5; Cass. Dio. 54.25.2) with lavish games and with the *scaena* ornamented with four onyx columns (Pliny *HN* 36.60). The theatre could accommodate 7,700 spectators, making it the smallest of Rome's three permanent theatres. See Platner and Ashby 1965, 513, and Richardson 1992, 381–382; Manacorda 1999, 30–31 ("Theatrum Balbi").

14. Cassius Dio associates Julius Caesar with the theatre's site: "[Caesar] announced his intention to build a theatre after the model of Pompey's, but he did not fulfill his wish. Augustus, however, did, and after the theatre was built, he named it after Marcellus" (43.49.3). It is not clear, however, whether this theatre would have been connected symbolically to the Temple of Apollo Sosianus in the same configuration and with the same significance as the Temple of Venus Genetrix to Pompey's theatre.

The still-uncompleted theatre was used during the *ludi Saeculares* in 17 B.C.E. (*CIL* 6.32323.157) but was dedicated in 13 B.C.E. (Cassius Dio 54.26.1). See Platner and Ashby 1965, 513–515; Hanson 1959, 22–23; and Richardson 1992, 382–383.

15. Cassius Dio (39.38.1) claims that the Theatre of Pompey is still a source of pride.

16. For the urban contexts of the theatres, see Anderson 1997, 285–287, and Gros 1987.

17. Tert. *De spect.* 10.

18. Hanson 1959, 55: "Architecturally, despite Pompey's assertion that he was dedicating principally a temple, the theater was now the dominant element, as it was to be to an even greater extent in the later examples of the same combination." Livy (30.38.10) mentions that in 202 B.C.E., due to flooding, the *ludi Apollinares* had to be transferred from their usual performance location to the Temple of Venus Erycina. See Hanson 1959, 52, for a Spanish inscription from Castulo (*CIL* 2.3270) connecting Venus to the theatre: *signa Veneris Genetricis et Cupidinis ad theatrum.*

19. Gruen (1992, 183ff.) argues, contra popular scholarly view, that there is

no proof of the relation between *ludi* and future career advancement and political success. The theatre of C. Scribonius Curio, which was built in 53 B.C.E.
for his father's funeral games and consisted of two wooden theatres that could
revolve on pivots to create an amphitheatre, postdates the construction of Pompey's theatre. See Pliny *HN* 36.117–120. This theatre was still standing in
51 B.C.E. (Cicero *Fam.* 8.2.1).

20. Cf. *Pompey* 68.2.

21. Suetonius *Aug.* 31: *Pompei quoque statuam contra theatri eius regiam
marmoreo Iano superposuit translatam e curia, in qua C. Caesar fuerat occisus.*

22. The theatre is not named specifically in the ancient sources, but its use on
this occasion may be inferred: Suetonius (*Iul.* 39.1–2) states that Caesar presented plays (*ludos*) in every ward all over the city, and that the actor Decimus
Laberius was made a knight following his performance in a farce and that he
passed from the stage through the orchestra and took his place in the first fourteen rows. Plutarch (*Caes.* 55.4) only mentions that Caesar gave spectacles
(*theai*).

23. Suetonius *Claud.* 21.1.

24. *Res gestae* 20.

25. For Tiberius' restorations, see Tacitus *Ann.* 3.72, and Velleius Paterculus
2.130.1. Suetonius (*Tib.* 47) records that his renovation of the theatre was incomplete. For Caligula's completion of the theatre, see Suetonius *Calig.* 21.

26. For Claudius' rededication and the inscription of names, see Cassius Dio
60.6.8.

27. For Nero's costly renovations, see Pliny *HN* 33.54, and Cassius Dio
62.6.1–2. The *scaena* was burned in the great fire at Rome in 80 C.E. See Richardson 1992, 385, for later renovations of the theatre.

28. Pliny (*HN* 36.108) relates that the theatre built by Libo in 63 B.C.E. was
completely covered by a roof. Previously, theatres had been adorned with mate-
rials thought to be inappropriate to a temporary structure. Sometime before
100 B.C.E., when L. Licinius Crassus was aedile, for example, the Hymettus
marble used to decorate either the *scaena* or the theatre itself caused a scandal,
no doubt arising out of the expenditure involved for such a temporary stucture.
See Richardson 1992, 380, for the growing extravagance and expense of temporary theatres.

29. Pliny *HN* 36.114. The location of this theatre is unknown, but the
Campus Martius is the most likely site. See Pollard 1999, 38–39 ("Theatrum
Scauri").

30. Pliny *HN* 36.114.

31. Ibid. 36.115.

32. Ibid. Richardson (1992, 385) puts the actual number at 20,000 based on
the seating capacity of Pompey's theatre.

33. Pliny *HN* 36.115.

34. Ibid. 36.114.

35. Cf. Richardson 1992, 380.

36. Cf. *Fam.* 7.1.2 (text of Watt 1982, 198). For Pompey's selection of plays,
see Beacham 1999, 65. Careful planning, however, was no guarantee for a suc-

cessful opening, as Balbus and Augustus were to learn: the Tiber flooded Balbus' theatre at its opening, causing guests to arrive by boat (Cassius Dio 54.25.2), and at the opening ceremony of the theatre of Marcellus, Augustus' chair collapsed (Suetonius *Aug.* 43.5).

37. Nonius cites two distinct plays by Accius—the *Aegisthus* and the *Clytaemnestra*—but the fragments may actually come from the same play. Ribbeck (1897, 138–141) cites fragments under separate titles (but using the spelling *Clutemestra*), as do Warmington (1982: *Aegisthus* 328–331; *Clytaemnestra* 406–411), Franchella (1968, 239–260), and Dangel (1995, 165–168).

38. Plutarch *Pompey* 45.1–4. Appian (*Mith.* 116–117) provides an account of the triumphal procession to the Capitol, including the detail that Pompey wore, or claimed to be wearing, Alexander the Great's purple cloak.

39. See Suetonius *Nero* 46.1; Pliny *HN* 36. Richardson (1992, 384) suggests that these statues were placed against the piers of the exterior arcade rather than installed as a crown on the *cavea*. A similar portico was later imitated by Augustus. For Augustus' *porticus ad nationes,* see Pliny *HN* 36.39.

40. See Beacham 1992, 158, for a discussion of the theatre as a permanent memorial to Pompey's triumph. See also Coarelli 1971–72, 99–122.

41. See Ribbeck 1875, 460–464, for possible Greek models. Warmington (1982, 406 ff.) argues that Accius followed the story of Agamemnon's return found in Hyginus *Fabulae* 117: upon learning from Oeax that Cassandra was returning to Mycenae as Agamemnon's captive and concubine, Clytemnestra plotted to kill both while Agamemnon was sacrificing. Whatever Clytemnestra's motivation, we have a victorious Agamemnon returning to Mycenae and his subsequent murder with Cassandra by Clytemnestra in either plot scenario.

42. Cited is the text of Ribbeck 1897, 161–163.

43. Plutarch *Pompey* 67.3.

44. Ibid. 2.2; see Corbeill 1996, 176–178, for an analysis of the political implications of this allusion.

45. Appian *Mith.* 117, where he questions the credibility of Alexander's connection with the cloak.

46. The sole surviving fragment from Livius' play comes from a speech appealing for help: *da mihi hasce opes, / quas peto, quas precor; / porrige, opitula!* (text from Ribbeck 1897, 3). The speaker of the sole surviving fragment from Livius' play is unknown: *numquam hodie effugies quin mea moriaris manu* (text from Ribbeck 1897, 9).

47. See Slater 1985, 111, for the reception of Plautus' *Bacchides*, in particular his analysis (contra Jocelyn) of the audience's interpretation of seeing Troy being sacked on stage.

48. The number is extraordinary. Plutarch reports that just under 900 towns were captured. In the procession were also captives from numerous nations that had been subdued: Pontus, Armenia, Cappadocia, Paphlagonia, Media, Colchis, Iberia, Albania, Syria, Cilicia, Mesopotamia, Phoenicia, and Palestine. Cf. Plutarch *Pompey* passim.

49. For recent analyses of this play, see Flower 1996, 88–89, and Manuwald 2001, 62ff.

50. In Book 1, Livy's interest in the parallels between Roman history and the tragic stage is apparent when he compares the crimes of the Tarquins to those of the Theban and Mycenaean kings on the Greek stage: *tulit enim et Romana regia sceleris tragici exemplum, ut taedio regum maturior veniret libertas ultimumque regnum esset quod scelere partum foret* (1.46.3). On the play of Accius as a historical source for Livy, see Coulton 1940, 465–466.

51. Cicero *Div.* 1.22.44 preserves both passages. Cited is the text of Diehl 1967, frags. 212–214.

52. Warmington 1982, 563, citing the error of a scribe, assigns a speech by Lucretia as the third fragment of Accius' play, but as Varro's passage (*Ling.* 7.42) states, it actually comes from Cassius Parmensis' *Brutus.*

53. Cicero *Sest.* 58, 123.

54. Varro *Ling.* 5.80.

55. The scholiast's gloss of this line casts doubt on Cicero's literal interpretation of the allusion: *haec etiam tragoedia praetextata Brutus inscribitur, in qua nominatus quidem Tullius videtur, sed non idem ipse Cicero, quantum pertineat ad Accium poetam: quantum ad actorem tamen, sine dubio per qualitatem nominis utique significatio passionis eius eluxit (Schol. Bob.* ad 1.1).

56. Cicero (*Att.* 2.19) states that the actor Diphilus attacked Pompey with the lines *nostra miseria tu es magnus—; eandem virtutem istam veniet tempus cum graviter gemes;* and *si neque leges neque mores cogunt—*, but it is not clear whether Diphilus inserted or emphasized these lines. Cicero's remark on the relevance of the lines: *nam et eius modi sunt ii versus, uti in tempus ab inimico Pompei scripti esse videantur. . . .*

57. Lana (1958–59, 354–356), however, argues that Cicero was equating his actions with those of Lucius Junius Brutus.

58. For a discussion of the *conditores* of Rome, see Edwards 1996, 44–52.

59. The fact that Marcus Junius Brutus was not related by blood to the legendary Lucius Junius Brutus, who had killed his two sons and heirs, did not bother him since he constructed a family tree of the Junius family anyway, as though his relationship with the legendary Brutus were based on genealogy. Atticus compiled this family tree for Brutus, as Cicero makes clear: *ubi igitur philotechnema illud tuum, quod vidi in Parthenone, Ahalam et Brutum?* (*Att.* 13.40). See also Nepos *Att.* 18.

60. Cicero records that Brutus sought to produce the play in absentia: *Att.* 16.1.11, 16.41; and *Phil.* 10.8.

61. According to Plutarch (*Caesar* 61.8), the tribunes Flavius and Marullus removed crowns that had been placed on Caesar's statues after the failed coronation attempt and were called "Brutus" by the populace. Plutarch further records (61.10) that Caesar, unhappy with the allusion, removed Marullus from office and turned the reference against the tribunes and populace by exploiting the pun in Brutus' name, calling them "Brutes" and "Cumaeans." "Cumaeans" refers to the legend that Tarquin had received from Cumae the original Sibylline Books, which stated that only under a king would Rome conquer Parthia. Thus, according to Corbeill (1996, 201), "Marullus and Flavius become stupid regicides who have arrived from Cumae spreading unbelievable prophecies."

62. Suetonius *Julius* 80.3; Plutarch *Brutus* 9.5–7; Appian *B Civ.* 2.112; and Dio 44.12.3. Only if Caesar had been viewed as a king or as aspiring to kingship could such a connection between Caesar and Tarquinius have been sustained. The actual constitutional and religious position of Caesar immediately preceding his death is controversial. See Weinstock 1971 and Fishwick 1987 with their extensive bibliographies.

63. Appian *B Civ.* 3.23–24.

64. Seneca in the *De beneficiis* (2.20.2) condemns Brutus' actions and defends Caesar by claiming that a good king is the best form of government for the Roman state.

65. Perhaps mirroring the report of Brutus' appeal to Cicero, Plutarch claims that Cassius himself appealed to Pompey prior to the assassination by invoking his statue. In the *Life of Caesar* (66.1–2), Plutarch places great symbolic importance on the location of the assassination: "So far, perhaps these things [portents and coincidences] may have happened on their own accord; the place however, which was the scene of that struggle and murder, and in which the senate was then assembled, since it contained a statue of Pompey and had been dedicated by Pompey as an additional ornament to his theatre, made it wholly clear that it was the work of some heavenly power that was calling and guiding the action thither. Indeed, it is also said that Cassius, turning his eyes toward the statue of Pompey before the attack began, invoked it silently, although he was much addicted to the doctrines of Epicurus." Plutarch (66.13), furthermore, places the statue in the role of witness to the murder: "And the pedestal was drenched with his blood, so that one might have thought that Pompey himself was presiding over this vengeance upon his enemy, who now lay prostrate at his feet, quivering from a multitude of wounds." (Translations from Perrin 1968, 594–598.) Though Plutarch's narrative contains theatrical elements, the conspirators themselves did not "frame" the assassination in theatrical terms.

66. For a detailed analysis of events surrounding the attempted restaging of Accius' *Brutus,* see Lana 1958–59, 356–359; and, more recently, Nicolet 1980, 371–373.

67. Cic. *Att.* 16.5.1: *tuas iam litteras Brutus exspectabat. cui quidem ego novum attuleram de Tereo Acci. ille Brutum putabat.* See Lana 1958–59, 356–357 n. 3, for a discussion of tyranny in the Tereus myth and for an analysis of Bilinski 1957, 44, which posits an anti-L. Appuleius Saturninus context to Accius' original production of the *Tereus.* See Parker 1999, 172, for the audience's ability to reinterpret the dramatic text on this occasion.

68. See Warmington 1982, 542ff., for fragments of the *Tereus* and a reconstruction of the plot based on Sophocles. Livius Andronicus had also written a *Tereus.*

69. Cicero *Att.* 16.5.1.

70. Cf. *Att.* 16.2.3; *Phil.* 1.15.36–37, where Cicero downplays the importance of the *Tereus,* stating that the audience passed judgment on Brutus' cause rather than give applause for the play; *Phil.* 2.13.31, for honors granted to Brutus and Cassius following the *ludi Apollinares.* Appian (*B Civ.* 3.24), however, suggests that hired supporters were planted in the audience on this occasion to

foster only the impression of popular support for Brutus and Caesar's assassination. Cicero (*Att.* 16.2.3) also takes the opportunity to chide the audience for
cheering actors in support of Republican sentiments but not defending the Republic with deeds in its hour of need. Ribbeck (1875, 669–670) summarizes
other references to audiences whose favorable or hostile reception to a play was
organized, notably the prologues to Plautus' *Amphitruo* and Terence's *Eunuchus*. See Parker 1999, 172, for Brutus' hiring of supporters before Gaius Antony substituted plays.

71. Suetonius *Iul.* 84: *inter ludos cantata sunt quaedam ad miserationem et
invidiam caedis eius accommodata ex Pacuvi Armorum iudicio.* . . . Suetonius
also reports that similar sentiments were sung from the *Electra* of Atilius.

72. According to Ribbeck (1875, 218), the model for Pacuvius' play was the
play of the same theme by Aeschylus. Earlier Latin versions of the Ajax myth include the *Ajax Mastigophorus* of Livius and the *Ajax* of Ennius. See the appendix for the conjectured models of these plays.

73. Since A. Weichert's *De L. Varii et Cassii Parmensis vita et carminibus*
(1836), there have been few studies on Cassius and his composition of a *Brutus*:
Nicolas 1851; Ribbeck *1897, 363,* which lists Cassius as the probable author of
a *praetexta* and includes the play in his list of *praetextae,* p. 365; F. Skutsch
1899, 1743–1744; Pedroli 1953, 74, which lists the speech by Lucretia among
the fragments of Accius' *Brutus;* Helm 1954, 1571 (Helm gives further notice of
two anonymous *praetextae,* pp. 1571–1572); Jona 1962–63, 68–104,
esp. 95–98; La Penna 1979, 143–151, on the likelihood that Cassius composed
a *Brutus;* Flower 1995, 172; and Manuwald 2001, 237–243.

74. Suetonius records that Cassius sneered at Augustus' low birth in political
pamphlets, and preserves his actual words: *materna tibi farina est ex crudissimo
Ariciae pistrino; hanc finxit manibus collybo decoloratis Nerulonensis mensar-
ius (Augustus* 4).

75. Vell. 2.87.3; Val. Max. 1.7 preserves the story that Cassius' execution
came soon after being visited by apparitions at night.

76. Varro *Ling.* 6.7. The passage is quoted again at 7.72: *nunc de temporibus
dicam. quod est apud Cassium: "nocte intempesta nostram devenit domum."
nox intempesta dicta ab tempestate, tempestas ab tempore, nox intempesta quo
tempore nihil agitur!* For a discussion of the manuscript tradition that replaces
*Accii* and *Accium* with *Cassii* and *Cassium,* see Kent 1967, 178–179. Ribbeck
(1897, frag. 5, p. 331) lists the fragment among those of Accius' *Brutus* but lists
Cassius as the probable author. Warmington (1982, 563) assigns this fragment
to Accius' *Brutus,* attributing the references to *Casii* and *Cassium* in Varro *Ling.*
6.7 and 7.72 to a scribal error. La Penna (1979, 143–145) argues that Varro
may have included a rare contemporary reference due to his friendship with Cassius and their political affinities to the Pompeians.

77. Hyginus *Fabulae* 86–88 conflates many details of the Atreus-Thyestes
myth.

78. There seem to have been at least eight plays in Greek with the name *Thyestes:* by Sophocles, Euripides, Apollodorus of Tarsus, Carcinus, Chaeremon,
Cleophon, Diogenes of Sinope, and Agathon. See Jocelyn 1967, 418. R. J. Tar-

rant (1985, 40) cites other plays: "Sophocles wrote at least two plays on the subject [House of Tantalus], an *Atreus* and the play usually called *Thyestes in Sicyon;* Euripides wrote a *Thyestes,* a *Plisthenes* (dealing with Thyestes' efforts to avenge the loss of his children), and a third play, *The Cretan Women,* in which both Thyestes and Aerope appeared; plays with the title *Thyestes* or *Aerope* are recorded for several other Greek tragedians (Agathon, Chaeremon, Carcinus, Cleophon, Diogenes, Apollodorus of Tarsus)." This list of Greek plays illustrates that one need not consider the plays of Aeschylus, Sophocles, or Euripides as the sole possible models for dramatists writing centuries later and within the Hellenistic literary tradition in both tragedy and comedy. See Tarrant 1976, 6ff., for a discussion of the relatively small effect fifth-century B.C.E. Athenian tragedy had on Augustan and later Imperial tragedy.

79. Ennius' *Thyestes,* the last play written by Ennius, was performed at the first *ludi Apollinares* in 169 B.C.E. (Cic. *Brut.* 78). Accius read his *Atreus* to Pacuvius in Tarentum before 130 B.C.E. (Aul. Gell. *NA* 13.2.2). The *Thyestes* of Cassius of Parma dates to the 40's/30's B.C.E. Varius Rufus produced his *Thyestes* in 29 B.C.E. for Augustus' triple triumph. The dates of Sempronius Gracchus' plays, including his *Thyestes,* are insecure but seem to date to the teens B.C.E. The *Atreus* of Mamercus Aemilius Scaurus dates to before 34 C.E. (the year of his death). Pomponius Secundus' *Atreus* dates to before 60 C.E. (the year of his death). The exact date of Seneca's *Thyestes,* in addition to the dates of his other plays, is unknown. The *Thyestes* of Curiatius Maternus dates to Vespasian's reign. Fulgentius (*Serm. Ant.* 57) ascribes a *Thyestes* to Pacuvius, but his testimony is unreliable. On this attribution, see Valsa 1957, 56.

80. See Lana 1958–59, 326–327: "Si può supporre, nella tragedia variana, un riferimento, più o meno aperto, ad Antonio, presentato come un tiranno," and, most recently, Leigh 1996, 171–197, which equates Antony with Atreus. J. D. Bishop (1985) has sought to apply allusive language to contemporary figures and events. See esp. 16–23, where he attempts to attribute mythological tyrants' names to historical personalities.

81. Scholarship on the significance of this myth at Rome is extensive. In addition to Bilinski 1957, see in particular Ribbeck 1875, 199–204 (Ennius' *Thyestes*), 447–457 (Accius' *Atreus*); La Penna's important study (1979, 127–141), which argues for less emphasis on the inherent theme of tyranny in favor of more analysis of the philosophical implications of the myth, citing in particular Accius' *Atreus* and Seneca's *Thyestes;* Lana 1958–59, 292–358; Jocelyn 1967, 412–419; D'Antò 1980, 277–290; Dangel 1995, 275–283; Lefèvre 1971; Tarrant 1978, 213–263; Calder 1983, 184–198; Tarrant 1985; Cova 1989; and the review of Cova by H. D. Jocelyn (1990, 596–600). Unfortunately, Schiesaro 2003 appeared too late to be included in this study.

82. Varius' dates are approximately 74 to 14 B.C.E. Cova (1989, 15–27) argues for a production date prior to Augustus' triple triumph. See Jocelyn 1980, 399–400, however, for counterarguments.

83. Didasc. in cod. Paris, 7530 S. VIII and Rome, Bibl. Casanatense 1086; see Beare 1964, 233. Ribbeck (1897, 229) cites the scholiast edition of Julius Quiceratus, *Bibliothèque de l'école des chartes* (Paris, 1839), 1:52. A copy of

the manuscript page is also printed in *CLA* 5.569. For a historical analysis of these scholiasts, see Jocelyn 1980, 387–400.

84. The *Res gestae* (22) includes many references to the *ludi* given by Augustus under his own name or the names of others, yet the only specific reference to *ludi scaenici* appears in a summary of other games that he sponsored: *impensa praestita in spectacula scaenica et munera gladiatorum atque athletas et venationes et naumachiam et donata pecunia . . .* (Summary, 19.4). Cited is the text of Diehl 1925, 46. The relative brevity of this reference to scenic entertainment when compared to the details of athletic, gladiatorial, and hunting spectacles found on the inscription seems odd, since Augustus thought it important enough to record his renovation of Pompey's theatre (20) and the construction of the theatre of Marcellus.

85. See Courtney 1993, 272, for analysis of frag. 2 as an allusion to Antony: *incubet ut Tyriis atque ex solido bibat auro.* On unflattering allusions to Antony, see Gordon Williams, "Varius," in *OCD*, 2d ed. (Hammond and Scullard 1970, 1107); and Edward Courtney, "Varius," in *OCD*, 3d ed. (Hornblower and Spawforth 1996, 1581), with recent bibliography.

86. Varius seems to have taken this commission quite seriously, according to the scholiast notice that stresses the care taken in its composition: *tragoediam magna cura absolutam.* Augustus must have been pleased with the result, as the amount of his payment bears witness.

87. As discussed in chapter 3, the *Iter* of Cornelius Balbus was also composed for a triumph, but it was never performed in Rome.

88. Ribbeck (1897, 265), however, lists further passages from unknown plays.

89. Tacitus, in the *Dialogus de oratoribus* (12), praises the play, and Quintilian claims that Varius' *Thyestes* rivaled Greek plays (10.1.98). Since the *Thyestes* of Varius predates Horace's *Ars poetica*, did the play serve as Horace's model? See Boissier 1897.

90. Cited is the text of Ribbeck 1897, 265. Quintilian 3.8.45: *neque enim quisquam est tam malus ut videri velit. sic Catilina apud Sallustium loquitur, ut rem scelestissimam non malitia, sed indignatione videatur audere: sic Atreus apud Varium iam fero, inquit, infandissima, iam facere cogor.*

91. See Tarrant 1985, 41, for the dramatic action of Varius' play and alternative plot reconstructions. With regard to the later dramatic tradition of the play, Tarrant cautions against viewing Varius' play as the model for Seneca's due to a lack of secure evidence. In particular, there is no basis for assuming that the banquet scene in Varius' play was the dénouement, as it is in Seneca's play (and indeed Accius'). See Morford 2000, 173–174, for an analysis of Manilius *Astronomica* 5.458–463 as a possible summary of the banquet scene from Varius' play.

92. I omit Livius Andronicus' *Aegisthus* from this list since the events from this play center on Agamemnon's return from Troy and not the feud between Atreus and Thyestes. See Ribbeck 1875, 28–31. Accius' version was still popular and Ennius' version was current enough to be quoted several times by Cicero in his philosophical and forensic works: *Tusc.* 1.106–107, 3.25; *Orat.* 103;

*Brut.* 78; and *Pis.* 43. The tragedian Gracchus' plays date to the teens B.C.E.; therefore I do not list his play *Thyestes* as a dramatic precursor to Varius' version. Many references to Atreus and Thyestes appear in the unassigned fragments of tragic plays, but unfortunately these cannot be identified with any one version.

93. Jocelyn 1967, 413: "I propose that the events [Thyestes' adultery with Aerope, wife of Atreus; Thyestes' banishment, subsequent recall, and infamous banquet] took place before the action of the *Thyestes* and that Ennius' tragedy was set at the court of Thesprotus in Epirus." Warmington (1988, 346ff.) divided the action of the play between two scenes, Atreus' court in Mycenae and Thesprotus' in Epirus.

94. See Ribbeck 1897, 161–163; Warmington 1982, 381–393; D'Antò 1980, 280–281; Dangel 1995, 275–276.

95. Accius wrote the *Pelopidae* and the *Chrysippus* about other episodes surrounding this myth. According to Jocelyn (1967, 414), "The *Atreus* quite certainly dealt with the feast while the meagre remains of the *Pelopidae* can be very plausibly interpreted as dealing with the recognition of Aegisthus. If Thyestes had any role in Accius' *Chrysippus* it could only have been a minor one."

96. Cited is the text and fragment order of Ribbeck 1897, 186–192.

97. La Penna (1979, 128) emphasizes the ruthlessness and cruel sarcasm of Atreus.

98. See below for the quotation of this line by certain Julio-Claudian emperors. La Penna (1979, 66–67) notes a similarity between this line and Ennius', *quem metuunt oderunt; quem quisque odit perisse expetit* (Jocelyn 1967, 348), which comes from an unknown play.

99. La Penna (1979, 130–131) discusses the possibility (based on Cicero *Sest.* 102) that these lines belong to Atreus.

100. Leigh (1996, 185) argues that these lines cast Atreus in an ideological tyrannical light: "What is perhaps most characteristic of this quotation and most worthy of note is the manner in which it casts Atreus not just as the villain of the piece but as a representative of an ideological category, the tyrant." However, from a different perspective, it is Thyestes' tyranny (i.e., his usurpation attempt by sleeping with Atreus' wife) that Atreus is punishing. On the difficulty of assessing Thyestes' character in this play, see La Penna 1979, 129–132.

101. See La Penna 1979, 66–71, for an analysis of the philosophical political contexts of generic tyrannical sentiments found in Accius' *Atreus* and Pacuvius' *Dulorestes*.

102. For Cassius' composition of a *Thyestes*, see Nicolas 1851, 42–49; Ribbeck, in his index to 1897, 335, places a question mark next to Cassius' name as the author of a *Thyestes*; F. Skutsch 1899, 1743–1744; La Penna (1979, 148–149), however, argues that the evidence is inconclusive.

103. Pseudo-Acro at Horace *Epist.* 1.4.3. Jona (1962–63, 83–98) analyzes the realiability of ancient sources concerning Cassius and reviews scholarship on the question of Cassius' composition of tragedies. La Penna (1979, 146–147), however, questions the reliability of Acro as a source. The Cruqii scholiasts record the same notice as Acro, which is also found in Porphyrion at Horace

*Epist.* 1.4.3. In addition, at Horace *Sat.* 1.10.61, Porphyrion glosses: *Cassii fab-ulam Thyestem sua tempestate exstitisse confitetur.* Even the title of the play is called into question by La Penna (1979, 147–148 n. 2), who discusses the appearance in a manuscript of the title *Orestes* in place of *Thyestes.*

104. In addition to Nicolas 1851, see F. Skutsch 1899, 1743. Helm 1954 only mentions the *Brutus* in connection with Cassius.

105. La Penna (1979, 148) argues that the evidence does not support this conclusion.

106. Cf. Zorzetti 1980, 93–103; Flower 1995, 172.

107. La Penna (1979, 149) argues that Varius' *Thyestes* may be a response to Cassius' *Brutus,* but this argument is based on his rejection of a *Thyestes* by Cassius.

108. Augustus emphasized his victory over Cleopatra by displaying her children Alexander (Helios) and Cleopatra (Selene) as trophies in his triumph, together with an effigy of Cleopatra. See Plutarch *Ant.* 86.2; Dio Cassius 51.21.8.

109. A point emphasized by Lana (1958–59, 326).

110. My reading of the allusion differs from that of Leigh (1996, 171–197), who argues in favor of an identification of Antony with Atreus. The fact that we come to different conclusions about the same evidence illustrates how difficult it is for a dramatist to control audience interpretation. Suetonius (*Aug.* 7.2) and Dio Cassius (53.16.7) report that Augustus considered adopting the name Romulus, which demonstrates that he understood the value of political allusion to a mythological/legendary figure but perhaps not all of its consequences, since this name would have placed Augustus' defeat of Mark Antony (Remus, by analogy) in the context of a civil war. See Wiseman 1995b, 144–150, for the significance of the allusion in Augustan Rome.

111. See Della Corta 1981, 234–235: "Ni la servilité vis-à-vis du pouvoir, compte tenu de ton libertoire du sujet, ni son actualité ne semblent avoir dirigé le choix de Varius. . . . Nous prévient qu'il ne faut pas voir Antoine en Atrée et moins encore Octavien en Thyeste." Lana (1958–59, 326–327), while recognizing an allusion to Antony in the play, cautions against assigning historical identities to these allusions.

112. Text of Wickham 1959.

113. Michael Dewar (1988, 563–565) argues that in addition to *Georgics* 1.511–514, another metaphor connecting Augustus with Orestes occurs at *Aeneid* 4.471–473, where an allusion to a stage production of a tragedy in which Orestes appears is used, among other mythological figures, to describe Dido in her madness: *aut Agamemnonius scaenis agitatus Orestes, / armatam facibus matrem et serpentibus atris, / cum fugit ultricesque sedent in limine Dirae. agitatus* has the general sense of "aroused" or the technical sense, stemming from the theatre, of "acted." For visual evidence connecting Augustus with Orestes, see Pausanias 2.17.3, and Cecioni 1993, 506, which reviews the evidence for the renaming of Greek statues with the names of Romans.

114. Dio Cassius 58.24.3–5. The ostensible reason given for Scaurus' prosecution was that he had committed adultery with Livilla. Tiberius seems to have

identified himself not only with Atreus, but also with Agamemnon, since he prosecuted a dramatist for having slandered the mythical king. See Suetonius *Tib*. 61.3. Tiberius' own identification with Agamemnon may have been in response to Agrippina's initial comparison of him with the two kings. See also Tacitus *Ann*. 6.29.3.

115. Suetonius (*Nero* 39) is surprised by Nero's tolerance of criticism and his ignoring of insults and lampoons aimed at his matricide, his singing ability, and his golden house. In fact, when presented with a list of names of detractors, Nero chose to let the offenders off lightly, thereby advertising his clemency. At Tacitus *Ann*. 13.15, however, Nero interprets a song sung by Britannicus as being an attack on him for having usurped the throne.

116. Of Pomponius' two known plays, the *Atreus* and the *Aeneas,* it is not clear in Quintilian *Inst*. 10.1.98 whether Quintilian has seen either play. As a literary connoisseur and a defender of Pomponius' style, it would be difficult to argue that he saw only one of his plays rather than both: *eorum quos viderim longe princeps Pomponius Secundus, quem senes quidem parum tragicum putabant, eruditione ac nitore praestare confitebantur.*

117. Michael Coffey (1986) argues that this play was written after Seneca became a magistrate (praetor in 50 C.E.): "It may therefore be suggested that A.D. 49 is the *terminus post quem* for the composition of Seneca's *Thyestes,* which must have been written either before the accession of Nero in A.D. 54 or in the early years of his reign when Seneca and his master were engaged in writing poetry" (48).

118. Seneca *Ad Lucilium epistulae morales* 80. See also Tarrant 1985, 43: "From this brief survey it appears that the disposition of scenes and some of the elements of character-depiction in Seneca's *Thyestes* follow an outline used at least by Accius (if not by Varius as well), and possibly worked out as early as Sophocles or Euripides." For similarities between Accius' *Atreus* and Seneca's *Thyestes,* see Ribbeck 1875, 448ff.; Lana 1958–59, 316ff.; La Penna 1979, 135.

119. Tarrant (1985, 10) argues that no such sentiments are present: "The plays do not overtly mention contemporary persons or events; veiled topical allusions have often been suggested, but no dating on them has won general acceptance." Beare (1964, 236) argues that the presence of absolute rulers depicted in an odious light is sufficient evidence that Seneca's plays were not presented on the Roman stage, but this theory does not account for the role of interpretation in understanding allusions arising from the stage.

120. Text of Zwierlein 1988, 302.

121. Text of Zwierlein 1988, 432–433.

122. See *Dialogus* 1–3. The likelihood that Maternus is simply a fictional creation and not a historical personality seems remote. See Barnes 1981, 382–384, which reviews the relevant theories and bibliography, including Syme 1958, 798–799, and Lana 1958–59, 336–340.

123. *Dialogus* 3.2.

124. See Bartsch 1994, 89–90, which translates "misguided interpretation" as the argument of Secundus, but the point is that the audience has been guided

by Maternus as to the gist and force of his allusions. See Rudich 1993, 10–13; 1997, 8–16, for an extensive analysis of Tacitus' use of the expression *prava interpretatio*.

125. Suetonius *Tib.* 59.

126. Ibid. 61.3. Suetonius states that Tiberius took offense at Scaurus' play and at a history glorifying Cassius and Brutus that had not offended Augustus when he heard the work sometime earlier. Did Augustus understand the unflattering allusions to himself but choose not to take offense?

127. Dio Cassius 58.24.4

128. Suetonius *Gaius* 30.1; Dio Cassius 59.13.6.

129. Cicero *De officiis* 2.7.23.

130. Thyestes was among Nero's most frequently acted roles. See Dio Cassius 62.9.4, 63.22.6. Suetonius reports that Nero planned to act the role of Turnus onstage in the games he would hold if he were to survive Galba's revolt (*Nero* 54). Identification with Turnus, rather than with Aeneas, would have signaled further Nero's conflicting "roles" and his own precarious political position.

131. The title *imperator scaenicus* was given to Nero by Pliny in his *Panegyric to Trajan* (46.4), where he contrasts the sober tastes of Trajan and his subjects with the excesses of Nero and his contemporaries.

132. See the extensive analysis of this role-playing in Bartsch 1994, 46–50; Rudich 1993, passim; and, most recently, Beacham 1999, 197ff.

133. Suetonius *Nero* 21.3. See Bartsch 1994, 50 and 227 n. 21, for a bibliography for the alternate reading of *Oresten*. Varner (2000, 131–132, and 136 n. 62) discusses the connections between Neronian art and the theatricality of Nero's stage roles.

134. The fact that Poppaea was already deceased further complicates any interpretation of Nero onstage. See Slater 1996, 39, which argues that the appearance of Nero onstage wearing a mask in the likeness of Poppaea would have reminded the audience of his responsibility for her death. Also, it is possible that members of the audience might question her death, since she was embalmed, rather than cremated as was the Roman custom, thus making her "appearance" onstage even more bizarre. Varner (2000, 136 n. 63) discusses two cameo portraits of Poppaea that may give us some idea how Poppaea's features were reproduced on theatre masks.

135. Both anecdotes are preserved in Dio Cassius 63.10.2. Suetonius *Nero* 21.3 gives more details surrounding the story of the soldier rushing to Nero's aid: *in qua fabula fama est tirunculum militem positum ad custodiam aditus, cum eum ornari ac vinciri catenis, sicut argumentum postulabat, videret, accurrisse ferendae opis gratia.* For the undermining of theatrical representation, see the excellent discussions of these passages in Bartsch 1994, 47–49 and Slater 1996, 33–35. Slater raises the important question of whether Nero's mask was more like a portrait or an exaggerated stage mask as a factor in examining the tension between realism and theatricality of this passage.

136. Tacitus (*Ann.* 15.50) attributes this idea to Subrius Flavus. Unfortunately we do not know whether Flavus considered assassinating Nero onstage to

exploit a connection between Nero and the role he would have been singing/acting at the time.

137. Rumors and rhymes (*carmen*) in 59 C.E., after Agrippina's murder, compared Nero to Orestes (Suetonius *Nero* 39.2). Placards were set up in Rome that compared Nero to the matricides Alcmaeon and Orestes (Dio Cassius 62.16.2; Suetonius *Nero* 39). Other indications that the urban mob in Rome thought Nero a matricide include the placement of a leather bag on one of his statues to show that he should be punished as a parricide (Dio Cassius 61.16.1); the exposure of a baby in the forum with a tag that read, "I will not raise you lest you slaughter your mother" (Dio Cassius 16.16.2); and gossip circulated all over the city that Nero had killed Agrippina (Dio Cassius 16.16.3). For Nero's role in the murder of Agrippina, see Tacitus *Ann.* 14.1–10; Suetonius *Nero* 34.

138. For the tragedy-like structure of Tacitus' narrative that contributes to the identification of Nero with Orestes, see Walker 1952; Dawson 1968, 253–267.

139. Suetonius *Nero* 34: *saepe confessus, exagitari se materna specie, verberibus Furiarum, ac taedis ardentibus.* See also Dio Cassius 61.14.4. Pseudo-Seneca, in the *Octavia*, makes several allusions to Agrippina as a Fury (lines 23ff., 161, 263). At lines 593–645, Agrippina's ghost appears as an avenging Fury.

140. See Tarrant 1976, 3ff., for parallels between Seneca's *Agamemnon*, Livius Andronicus' *Aegisthus*, and Accius' *Clytemnestra.*

141. See the extensive discussion on historiographic sources hostile to Nero's reign in Bartsch 1994, passim.

142. Tacitus expresses his disapproval in *Ann.* 14.14–16; for *foedum*, see *Ann.* 14.14: *vetus illi cupido erat curriculo quadigarum insistere nec minus foedum studium cithara ludicrum in modum canere.*

143. *Nero* 20–25.

144. In *Satire* 8.220–221, Juvenal alludes to Nero's killing of his mother by referring to his adoption of the role of Orestes: . . . *in scaena numquam cantavit Orestes, / Troica non scripsit.* Both matricides committed a crime, but Juvenal's implication is that Nero's was worse since, in addition to actually killing his mother, he also enacted the role of matricide upon the stage.

145. Dio creates vituperative speeches for them aimed at the paradox of having an effeminate actor as ruler of the world. For example, Boudicca, in her speech to her troops, emphasizes Nero's effeminacy. Whereas Britons are led by a real woman, she argues, Rome is being ruled by a man who acts and looks like a woman, in the company of the empresses Messalina and Agrippina (62.6.2). At the end of her speech, she actually calls Nero a "queen" (62.6.5). Vindex, however, stresses Nero's stage performances and denies to such an acting emperor any relation to the "real emperors" Augustus and Claudius (63.22.1–6). It is interesting to note that Nero's detractors Boudicca and Vindex came from Britain and Gaul respectively.

146. Dio Cassius 61.19.1 relates that Nero forced members of the noblest families to perform onstage, such as the 80-year-old Aelia Catella, who had to dance in a pantomime; furthermore, he would not allow them to wear masks.

For other instances, see Suetonius *Nero* 11; Tacitus *Ann.* 14.14–15; and Juvenal *Sat.* 8.193. See Rudich 1993, 41: "It was Nero's 'artistic tyranny,' not only in regard to his personal conduct but to his impositions on public taste and behaviour, that was highly offensive to traditional Roman feelings. In addition to their disgust at observing Nero's own histrionic feats, most senators hated the whole idea since he repeatedly and relentlessly pressured them to participate."

147. Dio Cassius 63.15.2–3; see Bartsch 1994, 4–6.

148. Burrus was famous for his moral rectitude (Tac. *Ann.* 13.2). See Tacitus *Ann.* 14.15, for Burrus' reluctant participation in Nero's stage performance: *maerens Burrus ac laudans*. Dio Cassius (62.20) writes that Burrus and Seneca coached Nero on the stage.

149. Suetonius (*Vesp.* 4.4) writes that Vespasian toured with Nero on his Greek tour and that he angered the emperor by leaving the recital room or by falling asleep. Suetonius also claims that as a result of this, Vespasian was dismissed from Nero's court and hid in a town until called to be governor. Tacitus (*Ann.* 16.5.3) claims that Vespasian was caught sleeping by Phoebus while Nero was onstage at the continuation of the Second Neronia in 65 C.E., and that only "a higher destiny saved him." See also Dio Cassius 66.11.2, where Vespasian is caught frowning and not sleeping. Likewise, Thrasea Paetus did not dissimulate his disapproval of Nero, and he did not encourage or participate in Nero's stage performances. See Dio Cassius 62.20.

150. Dio Cassius (62.26.3–4) gives the following reasons for Thrasea's death: his irregular attendance at the Senate; his refusal to listen to Nero while he was performing; his lack of public exhibitions; and his having acted in a tragedy in his hometown that was of ancient tradition. But this last reason is certainly no cause for shame, since an appearance on the stage by a noble at this festival was sanctioned by ancient tradition.

151. See Tacitus *Ann.* 16.18–19. Rudich (1993, 153–158) examines the role of Petronius as an "aesthetic dissident."

152. See Tacitus *Hist.* 1.78.2; Suetonius *Otho* 7.1, *Vit.* 11.2. See Griffin 1985, 160–163, for a discussion of the emperor on the stage. Griffin presents Nero's theatrical interests in the context of Nero's manic desire to obtain popularity. See also Manning 1975, 164–175, esp. p. 169: "It is more than plausible to suggest that Nero's productions and his stage appearances were the result of a certain amount of political calculation. Moreover there is every indication that Nero's calculations were realistic and that he won the genuine popularity he desired." Rudich (1993, 40) argues that Nero succeeded where Agrippina failed: "But he proved more successful than his mother; there was a strong 'populist' component in his self-image as the 'artistic tyrant' craving his audience's applause. By contrast, Agrippina's peculiar persona as an arrogant female autocrat was universally detested." Nero's popularity on the stage, however, did not prevent the populace from staging several riots over the availability of grain.

153. See Tacitus *Hist.* 1.5.2, 1.8.2, 1.25.2. An important exception is the praetorian Subrius Flavus, who claimed to hate Nero but was nevertheless loyal as a soldier—in Flavus' opinion, Nero deserved to be hated for killing his

mother and wife and for being a charioteer, actor, and incendiary. See Tacitus *Ann.* 15.67.

154. See Tacitus *Hist.* 2.8.1; and Suetonius *Nero* 57.2.


## CHAPTER FIVE

1. Boyle 1997, 114. Since Boyle examines, with numerous examples, passages that define Seneca's actor-audience, my discussion will complement his by focusing on the effects of this theatricalization of tragedy on audience reception, on and off the stage. Given the scope of this study, it is impossible to analyze examples from every play; therefore, I offer illustrative examples.

2. For the possible influence of Augustan tragedians on Seneca, see Tarrant 1978, 261: "All that is known or that can be plausibly conjectured, however, suggests that the tragedy of the Augustans resembled that of Seneca in several important respects, and that the synthesis of fifth-century subject matter, post-Euripidean form and technique, stylistic and metrical refinement, sporadic archaisms of language, and abstraction from the physical realities of the stage which is generally associated with Seneca was in fact an Augustan achievement"; and Boyle 1997, 85–111, for Seneca's rewriting of earlier texts, especially those of the Athenenian tragedians, Vergil, and Ovid.

3. For the influence of Ovid and contemporary rhetoric, see Coffey and Mayer 1990, 18: "No previous writer had a greater influence on Seneca the tragedian than Ovid both as poet and as dramatist"; and Costa 1973, 5: "The first essential for the appreciation of these tragedies is to come to terms with the rhetoric that informs them through and through. They illustrate all the declamatory elements outlined above, in particular the use of epigram and the 'sententia'; and because of the static nature of their plots, their unsubtle characterization, their profusion of set-piece speeches, and their preoccupation with horror and blood, they have long since lost the wide appeal they once enjoyed." See Conte 1994, 405–407, for *declamatio* and *recitatio* under the early Empire; and Boyle 1997, 15–31, for an analysis of Seneca's declamatory style, and 116, for the role played by rhetorical training (*declamatio* and *suasoria*) in creating *persona*: "Indeed it is arguable that in early Imperial Rome's confounding culture personal identity began to be constructed from the performance of a plurality of politically and socially determined roles, thus collapsing the distinction between persona and person. Certainly the distinction between 'reality' and 'theatre' dissolves conspicuously within the theatre-amphitheatre itself, where buildings burn, actors bleed, spectators are thrust into the arena, human and animal bodies dismembered, and pain, suffering, death become objects of the theatrical gaze and of theatrical pleasure." Goldberg (1996, 283) argues that Seneca's rhetoric produced successful dramatic results: "The success of this new formula had a profound effect on tragedy because rhetoric had given Seneca not just a technical skill—the choice of 'colores' and dexterity in manipulating the language that creates them—but confidence in the power of that manipulation. Action became

secondary when the dramatist could describe effectively what might then, perhaps mercifully, remain unseen."

4. See Rudich 1997, 1–16, for an extensive discussion of the "rhetoricized mentality" of Neronian Rome, in particular 10–12, for the events in Seneca's life that contributed to his own rhetorical response to his age.

5. The alternate title of *Hippolytus* is occasionally given to this play.

6. See the discussions and bibliographies found in Herington 1966, 422ff.; Tarrant 1976, which discusses the manuscript tradition of the Senecan plays; and, more recently, Tarrant 1985, 9–11, and Fitch 2002, 10–14.

7. Quintilian recalls this controversy from his youth and states further that Pomponius also published his views on proper tragic diction: *nam memini iuvenis admodum inter Pomponium ac Senecam etiam praefationibus esse tractatum, an gradus eliminat in tragoedia dici oportuisset (Inst. 8.3.31).*

8. Seneca's plays cannot be connected with a single emperor, let alone more than one. According to Tarrant (1976, 7): "What should be clear, however, is that the fashionable interpretation of these works as 'Neronian' has no secure basis in fact; they could with equal justification be regarded as Claudian, Gaian, or even Tiberian." On the dating of the plays see Tarrant, 1985, 10–13, and Fitch, 1981, 289–307.

9. Dio Cassius 63.5.

10. See Boyle 1997, 114, for the character as dramaturge in the *Medea* and the *Thyestes*.

11. See Tarrant 1985, 117: "Atreus makes no apology for being a dictator, and appeals several times to the 'rules' of tyrannical behavior, cf. 205–218, 247–48, 312–13."

12. See Lana 1958–59, 316–321, for similarities between the two plays, in particular 317, where he compares Atreus' speech to a similar one spoken by Atreus in Accius' *Atreus,* cited above (Ribbeck 1897, frag. 3): *iterum Thyestes Atreum adtractatum advenit, / iterum iam adgreditur me et quietum exsuscitat.* In addition to bibliography, cited above, see Morford 2000, 173–174, on the possible connections between Varius' *Thyestes* and Seneca's *Thyestes.*

13. Tarrant 1985, 161: "The result may be 'untheatrical' by certain standards, but it is undeniably effective, displaying both Atreus' absolute control of the situation and his keen enjoyment of his power over Thyestes. The speech is also a pointed counterpart to Thyestes' opening monologue: while Thyestes' internal conflict withdrew him from his surroundings, Atreus remains intensely aware of every detail in the scene he is manipulating, from the pounding excitement of his own heart to the matted tangle of Thyestes' beard."

14. See Boyle 1997, 90–91, for an allusion in the play to the Julio-Claudian dynasty: "*Troades* thus exploits a myth of immediate contemporary import. The death of a civilisation, the dissolution of a culture, dramatized in *Troades,* has patent ramifications for the palimpsestic, dissolving world of late Julio-Claudian Rome."

15. See Conte 1994, 403–404, for the "spectacularization of literature": "In the face of this [elite's attempt to restore tragic drama] it is not suprising that

contemporary literature, poetry especially, tends, within certain limits and in certain aspects, to become a form of spectacle and to take on theatrical traits"; and Leigh 1997, 234–291, for allusion to the amphitheatre in the *Pharsalia*, and 281ff., for the inclusion of the sadistic voyeurism of the amphitheatre in Seneca's prose works. And see, most recently, Fitch 2002, 17–18, for the descriptive "dark foreboding" in the prologues to set the tone for the rest of the play.

16. Boyle 1997, 114.

17. Tarrant (1976, 343) translates, "He's got it [i.e., the mortal blow], it's all over with him." Tarrant connects the gladiatorial language in this passage with Roman comedy and with the *Hercules oetaeus*, in which the same expression is used by Hyllus to tell Hercules about the death of Deianara.

18. For the connections between the theatricality of the theatre and the arena, see Boyle 1997, 135–136: "By describing violent death verbally and representing it and the reaction to it theatrically Seneca is able to control the perception and evaluation of death in a way that the arena could do. Every *spectator* at the games saw different things. Seneca controls what they see and how they see it in the theatre, and furnishes them with a conceptual framework with which to judge it." On interpreting theatrical allusions outside the theatre, see Bartsch 1994, 1–35.

19. Fitch (2002, 13) conjectures a date during Nero's reign for the *Thyestes* and the *Phoenissae*. See Varner 2000, 119–136, for an analysis of the grotesque in the art of the Neronian period and for correspondences in the plays of Seneca; and Bartsch 1994, 36–40, 46–47, for horror and grotesque elements in Lucan's narrative. See, most recently, Fitch 2002, 18: "True, Seneca sometimes emphasises the groteque aspect of violence, in part for shock value and in keeping with the taste of his age. But even as the grotesquery thrusts the physicality of violence in our faces, it also underlines its human meaning."

20. See Coleman 1990, 44–73, esp. 63–73, for mythological role-play in the punishment of prisoners under the reigns of Gaius, Claudius, and Nero. On the realism of spectacle, see 68: "From reports of the gullibility of audiences we can conclude that by the time of the early Empire a considerable degree of realism must have been achieved in Roman spectacles of all types (i.e. not simply those involving fatal encounters in the arena)."

21. Once again, I quote Beacham's (1992, 124) term, which I first cited in chapter 2 in connection with Accius' use of gore in his tragic narratives.

22. Euripides' first play, entitled *Hippolytos kalyptomenos*, was considered scandalous for its promiscuous depiction of Phaedra. Sophocles wrote a *Phaedra* that seems to have restored a measure of dignity to Phaedra's character by having her believe that Theseus was dead before turning her amorous attentions to Hippolytus.

23. Self-determination of characters is also evident in the *Troades*, where Astyanax hurls himself from the cliff: *Troades* 792ff. A character taking an active role in his or her own death is also evident as early as Livius Andronicus, who describes Agamemnon's death in the *Aegisthus*: *ipsus se in terram saucius fligit cadens.*

24. On epigrams in general, see Rawson 1987.

25. See Boyle 1997, 133–137, for the presentation of theatricalized death in Seneca against the precepts of Horace *Ars poetica* 179–188 that violent scenes should remain offstage.

26. Cited is the text of Miller 1984.

27. See Seneca *Q Nat.* 3.27.13–15, where he uses the expression *pueriles ineptias.*

28. Goldberg (1996, 283) argues: "This loss of a popular audience could have spelled the end of tragedy as it certainly spelled the end of comedy, but it did not. Tragedy instead took on a new life in a new environment by reclaiming its literary heritage and becoming once again a vehicle for serious literary endeavor."

29. Most recently, Boyle (1997, 15, 104, 134) refers to the play as incomplete, as does Fitch (2002, 278), who argues for a late composition date. Tarrant (1978, 229–230), however, argues that the play is complete: "Because of its length and unique structure, the play has often been considered incomplete. The individual scenes, however, do not give the impression of being unfinished; the opening dialogue in particular has only one near-equal for length in all of the genuine plays, and the closing scene between Jocasta and her sons could hardly be spun out to greater length without losing its effectiveness. Furthermore, the mere insertion of choral interludes and the expansion of the middle scenes, while it might bring the play up to normal Senecan length, would not affect the unconventional structure of its episodes. It seems best to regard *Phoenissae* as an essay in a distinct subgenre of tragedy."

30. Likewise, the *Hercules* ends with a dialogue between Hercules and Theseus, the *Troades* with a dialogue between Hecuba and a messenger, the *Medea* with a dialogue betwen Jason and Medea, the *Agamemnon* with a dialogue between Clytemnestra and Cassandra, and the *Thyestes* with a dialogue between Thyestes and Atreus. Only two plays contain an extended speech that serves to provide closure to the dramatic events: the *Phaedra* and the *Oedipus*. Zwierlein (1988) ends the play with a dialogue between Eteocles and Jocasta, while Fitch (2002, 328–329), following Grottius, ends the play with a dialogue between Polynices and Eteocles.

31. This is also apparent in the *Troades,* in which Polyxena is onstage at least from lines 872 to 1008 and is addressed by Helen and Andromache, but remains silent.

32. Beare (1964, 234), however, describes pantomime as a performance genre distinct from tragedy: "The modern view that tragedy was decomposed, so to speak, into the dramatic recitations and the pantomimic dances is altogether artificial. The most obvious link of the pantomime with drama was the stage setting; its themes, taken from mythology, might naturally be tragic; at its highest level it may have appealed to that section of the public who would in other circumstances have been interested in tragedy; but our evidence is that the essential attraction of pantomime was the supple, artistic, expressive, passionate, sometimes exquisitely lascivious movements of the dancer—and what has such a performance to do with true tragedy?"

33. Using Medea's murder of her children as an example, Fitch (2002, 21) ar-

rives at a similar conclusion: "The action is not specifically verbalised in the text, so that someone reading or listening to the text alone could not be sure, until some four lines further on (975), that the action had actually occurred. Here, in fact, action is primary, and the words of the text allude to it. While such a scene could presumably have been managed somehow in recitation, the primacy of action leaves little doubt that Seneca is envisaging stage performance as he composes."

34. Seneca reveals his knowledge of mounted stage productions in his prose works, suggesting that even if he did not acquire practical knowledge of dramaturgy as a playwright, which is difficult to imagine, he was at least a seasoned spectator of full stage productions of tragedy and comedy. See in particular *Ep.* 76.31, 80.7–8; *De ira* 2.17.1; *Consol.* 10.1; and *Q Nat.* 7.32.3.

35. On the recitation of Seneca's tragedies, see the extensive treatment in Zwierlein 1966.

36. Beare 1964, 234ff. Beare does not take other aristocratic or independently wealthy dramatists into consideration in his somewhat naive approach to the problem of performance. In fact, he is extremely reluctant to consider Senecan tragedy in the context of performance: "We Anglo-Saxons believe that the plays were written for declamation, not for performance in the theatre. Moreover, we think little of them as plays" (351).

37. Ibid., 235.

38. Costa (1974, 5) also argues in favor of a dramatic recitation, presumably on the basis of Maternus in Tacitus' *Dialogus,* without citing actual evidence: "The old debate on whether the plays were acted or recited need raise little dust nowadays: in view of the known conditions of drama in the Neronian age discussed above and certain characteristics of the plays themselves, it is generally agreed that anything like a full-scale production is most unlikely, though of course the individual declaimer or actor in reciting the play, or extract from it, would have introduced whatever histrionic effects he liked of movement and gesticulation to enliven his own performance."

39. Herington 1966, 444: "Were the tragedies intended for acting on stage? We cannot, in method, be certain."

40. Ibid., 444: "Though I do not know of any evidence which indicates beyond doubt that any first-century play was written for recitation by a single voice, there are certainly indications that some plays were composed for recital rather than full theatrical production." Herington argues that the sight of a single speaker reciting the lines from several characters, especially *stichomythia,* would be ridiculous. His conclusion, then, of a multi-voiced dramatic reading lacks evidence: "That the verse was intended for speaking then, I have no doubt, and if that can be admitted, the conclusion inevitably follows that it was intended for speaking by 'different voices for the different parts'" (444).

41. Fantham 1982, 48: "There is, it seems to me, only one medium in which the action of Senecan tragedy comes through with complete clarity, and that is the written text. I would suggest then, that Seneca composed with the expectation that he would himself recite chosen passages, or would give a dramatized reading in cooperation with others: but ultimately the play would be known

through written copies, and only the readers would experience the plays as complete works." Fantham's suggestion begs the question, why could a dramatized reading not include a complete play? What is the evidence that had Seneca recited from his plays, he would have read only "chosen passages"? Tacitus' *Maternus* gives the impression that the whole play was read. I wonder whether the plays as they have come down to us, with no specific entry and exit notations, etc., are significantly different from those circulating from earlier tragedians in the time of Seneca. Furthermore, there are no other examples (except perhaps in the case of Ovid, but certainty is impossible) of a dramatist writing a tragedy with a view to its publication and not its performance.

42. Tarrant 1978, 218 n. 23: "In discussing Senecan drama, language relating to the theatre (for example, 'on stage' and 'off stage') is employed in a purely figurative sense, and carries no suggestion that Seneca's plays were intended for stage presentation."

43. Tarrant 1976, 7: "In interpreting *Agamemnon* I have assumed that Seneca wrote with recitation, not stage-production, in mind; by 'recitation' I mean public reading either by one person or by several persons dividing the roles among themselves. This is, I think, the most probable view, but its truth cannot be demonstrated."

44. See Tarrant 1978, 247ff. For inconsistent illusion, see Coffey and Mayer 1990, 16: "It must be conceded that Seneca's attempts in *Phaedra* to present the illusion of a staged drama are intermittent."

45. See Boyle 1997, 11, and his recent bibliography on the question of performability of the plays.

46. Sutton 1986, 62: "There is, in sum, no evidence that any Senecan play was actually produced in antiquity. But there is an equal absence of convincing internal evidence that their author did not write them with the expectation, or at least the hope, that they would be brought to the stage. Quite to the contrary, we have uncovered a number of reasons for thinking that he gave considerable, if not always equally successful, thought to their staging. There is no reason for denying Seneca the title of playwright in the full sense of the word."

47. Sutton 1986, 62 n. 42. The graffito is taken from *Agamemnon* 730.

# BIBLIOGRAPHY

Abbot, F. F. 1907. "The Theater as a Factor in Roman Politics under the Republic." *TAPA*: 49–56.

Abel, L. 1963. *Metatheatre*. New York.

Ahl, F.M. 1976. *Lucan*. Ithaca.

Aly, Wolfgang. 1936. *Livius und Ennius von Römisher Art*. Leipzig.

Anderson, James C., Jr. 1997. *Roman Architecture and Society*. Baltimore.

Anderson, William S. 1993. *Barbarian Play: Plautus' Roman Comedy*. Toronto.

André, J. 1949. *La Vie et l'oeuvre de C. Asinius Pollion*. Paris.

———. 1966. *L'Otium dans la vie morale et intellectuelle romaine*. Paris.

Archellaschi, André. 1990. *Médée dans le théâtre latin d'Ennius à Sénèque*. Collection de l'École Française de Rome 132. Rome.

Austin, Alan. 1978. *Cato the Censor*. Oxford.

Austin, R. G. 1963. *Vergili Maronis Aeneidos Liber Quartus*. Oxford. (Original ed., 1955.)

Bailey, C. 1962. *Lucreti De Rerum Natura Libri Sex*. Oxford. (Original ed., 1900.)

Balsdon, J.P.V.D. 1934. *The Emperor Gaius*. Oxford.

Barchiesi, M. 1962. *Nevio epico*. Padua.

———. 1969. "Plauto e il 'metateatro' antico." *Il Verri* 31: 113–130.

Barnes, T. D. 1981. "Curiatius Maternus." *Hermes* 109: 382–384.

Barret, Anthony A. 1990. *Caligula: The Corruption of Power*. New Haven.

Barrile, Resta, ed. and trans. 1969. *Accius, Lucius: Frammenti dalle tragedie e dalle preteste*. Bologna.

Bartsch, Shadi. 1994. *Actors in the Audience*. Cambridge, Mass.

Beacham, Richard C. 1992. *The Roman Theatre and Its Audience*. Cambridge, Mass.

———. 1999. *Spectacle Entertainments of Early Imperial Rome*. New Haven.

Beare, W. 1964. *The Roman Stage*. 3d ed. London.

Bergmann, Bettina, and Christine Kondoleon, eds. 1999. *The Art of Ancient Spectacle*. New Haven.

Betensky, A. 1978. "Neronian Style, Tacitean Content: The Use of Ambiguous Confrontation in the Annals." *Latomus* 37: 419–435.

Bettini, Maurizio. 1979. *Studi e note su Ennio*. Pisa.

Bieber, M. 1961. *The History of the Greek and Roman Theater*. 2d ed. Princeton.

Bilinski, Bronislaw. 1957. *Accio ed i Gracchi: Contributo alla storia della plebe e della tragedia romana Accad. Polacca di Scienze e Lettere Bibliot. di Roma.* Rome.

Bishop, J. D. 1985. *Seneca's Daggered Stylus: Political Code in the Tragedies.* Beitrage zur klassichen Philologie 168. Königstein.

Boissier, Gaston. 1857. *Le Poète Attius: Étude sur la tragédie latine*. Paris.

————. 1897. "L'Art poétique d'Horace et la tragédie romaine." *Rev. Phil.* 21.

Bosworth, A. B. 1972. "Asinius Pollio and Augustus." *Historia* 21: 441–473.

Boyencé, Pierre. 1940. "Sur Cicéron et l'histoire." *REA* 42: 388–392.

Boyle, A. J. 1983. "*Hic Epulis Locus*: The Tragic Worlds of Seneca's *Agamemnon* and *Thyestes*." In A. J. Boyle, ed., *Seneca Tragicus: Ramus Essays on Senecan Drama*, 199–228. Berwick, Australia.

————. 1994. *Seneca's Troades*. Trowbridge.

————. 1997. *Tragic Seneca*. London.

Bremmer, J. N. 1987. "Myth and Ritual in Ancient Rome: The Nonae Caprotinae." In Bremmer and Horsfall 1987, 76–88.

Bremmer, J. N., and N. M. Horsfall. 1987. *Roman Myth and Mythology*. London.

Brink, C. O. 1960. "Tragic History and Aristotle's School." *PCPS* 6: 14–18.

Brooks, Robert Angus. 1981. *Ennius and Roman Tragedy*. New York. (Diss., Harvard University, 1949.)

Burck, E. 1979. *Das römische Epos*. Darmstadt.

Burns, Elizabeth. 1972. *Theatricality: A Study of Convention in the Theatre and in Social Life*. London.

Bury, J. B. 1909. *The Ancient Greek Historians*. New York.

Calder, W. M., III. 1975. "The Size of the Chorus in Seneca's Agamemnon." *CP*: 32–35.

————. 1983. "*Secreti Loquimur*: An Interpretation of Seneca's *Thyestes*." In Boyle 1983, 184–198.

Cancik, Hubert. 1978. "Die republikanische Tragödie." In Eckard Lefèvre, *Das Römische Drama*, 308–347. Darmstadt.

Caratello, Ugo. 1979. *Livio Andronico*. Rome.

Carey, Earnest. 1961. *Cassius Dio*. Loeb Classical Library. Cambridge, Mass. (Original ed., 1914.)

Carney, Thomas Francis. 1961. *A Biography of C. Marius. Proceedings of the African Classical Associations*, suppl. 1.

Cecioni, Natale. 1993. "Octavian and Orestes in Pausanias." *CQ* 43: 506.

Clausen, W. V. 1992. *A. Persi Flacci et D. Iuni Iuvenalis Saturae*. Oxford. (Original ed., 1959.)

Coarelli, F. 1971–72. "Il complesso pompeiano di Campo Marzio e la sua decorazione sculturea." *Rend. Pont. Acc.* 44: 99–122.

Coffey, Michael. 1957. "Seneca, Tragedies 1922–1955." *Lustrum*: 113–186.

———. 1986. "Notes on the History of Augustan and Early Imperial Tragedy." In J. H. Betts, J. T. Hooker, and J. R. Green, eds., *Studies in Honour of T.B.L. Webster*, 1: 46–52. Bristol.

Coffey, Michael, and Roland Mayer. 1990. *Seneca: Phaedra*. Cambridge.

Cole, Thomas. 1992. "Initium mihi operis Servius Galba iterum T. Vinius consules. . . ." *YClS* 29: 231–245.

Coleman, K. M. 1990. "Fatal Charades: Roman Executions Staged as Mythological Enactments." *JRS* 80: 44–73.

Coleman, R. 1936. "Philosophical Aspects of Early Roman Drama." *CP* 31: 321–337.

Conte, Gian Biagio. 1994. *Latin Literature: A History*. Trans. Joseph B. Solodow. Baltimore. (Original ed., Florence, 1987.)

Corbeill, Anthony. 1996. *Controlling Laughter: Political Humor in the Late Roman Republic*. Princeton.

Costa, C.D.N. 1973. *Seneca: Medea*. Oxford.

———, ed. 1974. *Seneca*. London.

Coulton, C. C. 1940. "Marcus Junius Brutus and 'the Brutus' of Accius." *CJ* 35: 460–470.

Courtney, Edward. 1980. *A Commentary on the Satires of Juvenal*. London.

———. 1993. *The Fragmentary Latin Poets*. Oxford.

Cova, Pier Vicenzo. 1989. *Il poeta Vario*. Milan.

Dangel, Jacqueline. 1989. "Diverbia et cantica chez Accius: Versification et diction dramatique." *REL* 67: 191–212.

———. 1990. "Sénèque et Accius: Continuité et rupture." In Jürgen Blänsdorf, ed., *Theater und Gesellschaft im Imperium Romanum*, 107–122. Bonn.

———. 1995. *Accius: Oeuvres (fragments)*. Budé ed. Paris.

D'Anna, Ioannes, ed. 1967. *M. Pacuvii Fragmenta*. Rome.

D'Antò, Vicenzo. 1980. *I frammenti delle tragedie di L. Accio*. Lecce.

Dawson, H. 1968. "Whatever Happened to Lady Agrippina?" *CJ* 64: 253–267.

Degl'Innocenti Pierini, Rita. 1982. *Studi Su Accio*. Florence.

Della Corta, Fr. 1981. "La Tragédie au siècle d'Auguste." In H. Zehnacker, ed., *Théâtres et spectacles dans l'antiquité, Actes du Colloque de Strasbourg*, 5–7 November 1981, 227–243. Strasbourg.

Dewar, M. J. 1988. "Octavian and Orestes in the Finale of the First Georgic." *CQ* 38: 563–565.

———. 1990. "Octavian and Orestes Again." *CQ* 40: 580–582.

Dewitt, N. J. 1941. "Rome and the 'Road of Hercules.'" *TAPA* 72: 59–69.

Diehl, E. 1925. *Res Gestae Divi Augusti: Das Monumentum Ancyranum*. Bonn.

———. 1967. *Poetarum Romanorum veterum reliquiae*. Berlin.

Diggle, J. 1998. *Tragicorum Graecorum Fragmenta Selecta*. Oxford.

Dominik, William J. 1993. "From Greece to Rome: Ennius' *Annales*." In A. J. Boyle, ed., *Roman Epic*, 37–58. London.

———, ed. 1997. *Roman Eloquence: Rhetoric in Society and Literature*. London.

Douglas, A. E. 1968. *Cicero*. Greece and Rome Survey in the Classics 2. Oxford.

Duckworth, G. E. 1994. *The Nature of Roman Comedy*. 2d ed. Princeton.

Duff, J. Wight. 1953. *A Literary History of Rome*. Vol. 1. New York.

Dupont, Florence. 1985. *L'Acteur-roi ou le théâtre dans la Rome antique*. Paris.

———. 1988. *Le théâtre latin*. Paris.

Edwards, Catharine. "Beware of Imitations: Theatre and the Subversion of Imperial Identity." In Jas Elsner and Jamie Masters, eds., *Reflections of Nero: Culture, History and Representation*. London.

———. 1996. *Writing Rome: Textual Approaches to the City*. Cambridge.

Eichholz, D. E. 1962. *Pliny: Natural History*. Loeb Classical Library. Cambridge, Mass.

Elam, Kier. 1980. *The Semiotics of Theatre and Drama*. London and New York.

Erasmo, Mario. 2001a. *Archaic Latin Verse*. Newburyport, Mass.

———. 2001b. "Staging Brutus." In Elizabeth Tylawski and Charles Weiss, eds., *Essays in Honor of Gordon Williams: Twenty-Five Years at Yale*, 101–114. New Haven.

Ernout, A. 1957. *Recueil de Textes Latines Archaïques*. Paris.

Evans, E. C. 1950. "A Stoic Aspect of Senecan Drama, Portraiture." *TAPA* 81: 169–184.

Fantham, Elaine. 1982. *Seneca's Troades*. Princeton.

———. 1992. *Lucan, "De Bello Civili," Book 2*. Cambridge, Mass.

———. 1997. "The Contexts and Occasions of Roman Public Rhetoric." In Dominik 1997, 111–128.

Feeney, D. C. 1991. *The Gods in Epic*. Oxford.

Fisher, C. D. 1963. *Cornelii Taciti Annalium ab excessu divi Augusti libri*. Oxford. (Original ed., 1906.)

Fishwick, Duncan. 1987. *The Imperial Cult in the Latin West*. Leiden.

Fitch, John G. 2002. *Seneca: Tragedies*. Loeb Classical Library. Cambridge, Mass., and London.

Flower, Harriet I. 1995. "Fabulae Praetextae in Context: When Were Plays on Contemporary Subjects Performed in Republican Rome?" *CQ* 45: 170–190.

———. 1996. *Ancestor Masks and Aristocratic Power in Roman Culture*. Oxford.

Fornara, C. W. 1983. *The Nature of History in Ancient Greece and Rome*. Berkeley.

Forsythe, Gary. 1994. "Review of Erich S. Gruen's *Culture and National Identity in Republican Rome* (Ithaca, 1992)." *Bryn Mawr Classical Review* 5: 9–14.

Fraenkel, E. 1932. "Zur Medea des Ennius." *Hermes* 67: 355–356.

———. 1960. *Plautini in Plauto*. Florence. (= *Plautinisches im Plautus* [Berlin, 1922].)

Franchella, Quirinus. 1968. *Lucii Accii tragoediarum fragmenta*. Bologna.

Frank, Tenney. 1937. "Curiatius Maternus and His Tragedies." *AJP*: 225–229.

Frassinetti, P. 1954. *Fabula Atellana, saggio sul teatro popolare latino*. Genoa.

———. 1975. *Gli Annali di Ennio*. Genoa.

Frézouls, Edmond. 1981. "La construction du 'theatrum lapideum' et son contexte politique." In H. Zehnacker, ed., *Théâtres et spectacles dans l'antiquité, Actes du Colloque de Strasbourg*, 5–7 November 1981, 193–214. Strasbourg.

Gabba, Emilio. 1969. "Il 'Brutus' di Accio." *Dioniso* 43: 377–383.

Gardner, R. 1958. *Cicero: The Speeches; Pro Sestio and In Vatinium.* Loeb Classical Library. Cambridge, Mass.

Garton, Charles. 1972. *Personal Aspects of the Roman Theatre.* Toronto.

Geer, Russel Mortimer. 1935. "The Greek Games at Naples." *TAPA* 66: 208–221.

Gentili, Bruno. 1979. *Theatrical Performances in the Ancient World: Hellenistic and Early Roman Theatre.* Amsterdam.

Goar, R. J. 1987. *The Legend of Cato Uticensis from the First Century B.C. to the Fifth Century A.D.* Collection Latomus 197. Brussels.

Goldberg, Sander M. 1980. *The Making of Menander's Comedy.* Berkeley.

———. 1995. *Epic in Republican Rome.* Oxford.

———. 1996. "The Fall and Rise of Roman Tragedy." *TAPA* 126: 265–286.

———. 1997. "Melpomene's Declamation (Rhetoric and Tragedy)." In Dominik 1997, 166–181.

Gorton, Charles. 1972. *Personal Aspects of the Roman Theatre.* Toronto.

Gowling, Alan. 1995. *The Triumviral Narratives of Appian and Cassius Dio.* Ann Arbor. (Original ed., 1992.)

Graf, Fritz. 1992. "Gestures and Conventions: The Gestures of Roman Actors and Orators." In Jan Bremmer and Herman Roodenburg, eds., *A Cultural History of Gesture,* 36–58. Ithaca, N.Y.

Gratwick, A. S. 1982a. "Drama." In Kenney 1982: 77–137.

———. 1982b. "Ennius' Annales." In Kenney 1982: 60–76.

Griffin, Miriam T. 1992. *Seneca: A Philosopher in Politics.* Oxford. (Original ed., 1976.)

———. 1985. *Nero: The End of a Dynasty.* New Haven. (Original ed., London, 1984.)

Grimal, Pierre. 1953. *Le Siècle des Scipions, Rome et l'hellénisme au temps des guerres puniques.* Paris.

Gros, Pierre. 1987. "La fonction symbolique des édifices théâtreaux dans le paysage urbain de la Rome augustéene." In C. Pietri, ed., *L'Urbs: Espace urbain et histoire,* Collection de L'École Française de Rome, suppl. 98, 319–346. Rome.

———. 1998. "Porticus Pompei." In Steinby 1993–2000, 5:148–149.

———. 1999a. "Theatrum Pompei." In Steinby 1993–2000, 6:35–38.

———. 1999b. "Venus Victrix, Aedes." In Steinby 1993–2000, 6:120–121.

Gruen, Erich S. 1992. *Culture and National Identity in Republican Rome.* Ithaca, N.Y.

Gummere, Richard M. 1930. *Seneca: Ad Lucilium Epistulae Morales.* Loeb Classical Library. Cambridge, Mass. (Original ed., 1920.)

Hall, Edith. 1989. *Inventing the Barbarian: Greek Self-Definition through Tragedy.* Oxford.

Hammond, N.G.L. 1967. *Epirus.* Oxford.

Hammond, N.G.L., and H. H. Scullard, eds. 1970. *The Oxford Classical Dictionary.* 2d ed. Oxford.

Hanson, John Arthur. 1959. *Roman Theater Temples.* Princeton.

Harmon, A. M. 1936. *Lucian: De Saltatione*. Loeb Classical Library. Cambridge, Mass.

Helm, R. 1934. "Die Praetexta Octavia." *SPAW*: 283–347.

———. 1942. "Pacuvius." *RE* 18, pt. 2: 2159–2174.

———. 1954. "Praetexta." *RE* 44: 1569–1575.

Henry, D., and B. Walker. 1965. "The Futility of Action: A Study of Seneca's *Hercules Furens*." *CP* 60: 11–22.

Herington, C. J. 1961. "Octavia Praetexta: A Survey." *CQ* 11: 18–30.

———. 1966. "Senecan Tragedy." *Arion* 5: 422–471.

———. 1982. "Senecan Tragedy." In Kenney 1982, 519–532.

Hill, D. K. 1944. "The Temple above Pompey's Theater." *CJ* 39: 360–365.

Hinds, Stephen. 1998. *Allusion and Intertext*. Cambridge.

Hornblower, Simon, and Antony Spawforth. 1996. *The Oxford Classical Dictionary*. 3d ed. Oxford.

Horsfall, N. H. 1976. "The Collegium Poetarum." *Bulletin of the Institute of Classical Studies of the University of London* 23: 79–95.

———. 1994. "The Prehistory of Latin Poetry: Some Problems of Method." *Revista di filologia* 122: 50–75.

Hughes, Joseph J. 1997. "Inter tribunal et scaenam: Comedy and Rhetoric in Rome." In Dominik 1997, 182–197.

Hutchinson, G. O. 1993. *Latin Literature from Seneca to Juvenal: A Critical Study*. Oxford.

Jacobson, H. 1977. *Ovid's Heroides*. Princeton.

Jal, Paul. 1963. *La Guerre civile à Rome*. Paris.

Jocelyn, H. D. 1967. *The Tragedies of Ennius*. Cambridge.

———. 1969. "The Poet Cn. Naevius, P. Cornelius Scipio and Q. Caecilius Metellus." *Anticthon* 3: 32–47.

———. 1971. "Ennius as a Dramatic Poet." In *Ennius, Entretiens* 27, 41–88. Vandoeuvres-Genève.

———. 1972. "The Poems of Quintus Ennius." *ANRW* 1.2: 987–1026.

———. 1980. "The Fate of Varius' Thyestes." *CQ* 30: 387–400.

———. 1990. "Review of Pier Vincenzo Cova, *Il poeta Vario* (Milan, 1989)." *Gnomon* 62: 596–600.

Johnston, Patricia A. 1993. "Review of Richard C. Beacham, *The Roman Theatre and Its Audience* (Cambridge, 1992)." *CP* 88: 353–355.

Jona, Mario. 1962–63. "Cassio Parmense." *Atti dell' Accademia delle Scienze di Torino, Classe di scienze morali, storiche, e filologie* 97: 68–104.

Jones, Brian W. 1992. *The Emperor Domitian*. London.

Jory, E. J. 1970. "Associations of Actors in Rome." *Hermes* 98: 224–253.

———. 1986. "Continuity and Change in the Roman Theatre." In J. H. Betts, J. T. Hooker, and J. R. Oren, eds., *Studies in Honour of T.B.L. Webster*, 1:143–152. Bristol.

Keil, Heinrich. 1857. *Grammatici Latini*. Vol. 1: *Diomedes, Artis Grammaticae*. Lipsiae.

Kiessling, Adolf. 1914. *Q. Horatius Flaccus: Briefe*. Berlin.

Kenney, E. J. 1961. *Ovid: Amores*. Oxford.

————, ed. 1982. *The Cambridge History of Classical Literature.* Vol. 2: *Latin Literature.* New York.

Kent, Roland G. 1967. *Varro: De Lingua Latina.* Loeb Classical Library. Cambridge, Mass. (Original ed., 1938.)

Kerr, C. A. 1919. *Martial, Epigrams.* Loeb Classical Library. Cambridge, Mass.

Klotz, Alfred. 1953. *Scaenicorum Romanorum fragmenta.* Munich.

Konstan, D. 1983. *Roman Comedy.* Ithaca, N.Y.

Korfmacher, W. C. 1934. "Philosophical Aspects of Early Roman Tragedy." *TAPA* 65: li–lii.

Laidlaw, W. A. 1960. "Cicero and the Stage." *Hermathena* 94: 56–66.

Lanciani, Rodolfo. 1897. *The Ruins and Excavations of Ancient Rome.* Boston.

Lana, Italo. 1958–59. "L'Atreo di Accio e la leggenda di Atreo e Tieste nel teatro tragico romano." *Atti della Accademia delle Scienze di Torino II. Classe di Scienze Morali, Storiche, e Filologiche* 93: 295–385.

Lanowski, J. 1961. "Histoire des fragments des tragédies de Livius Andronicus." *Eos* 51: 65–77.

La Penna, A. 1970–71. "Cassio Parmense nella Storia del Teatro Latino." *Studi classici e orientali* 19–20: 286–292.

————. 1979. *Fra teatro, poesia e politica romana.* Turin.

Lebek, W. D. 1996. "Moneymaking on the Roman Stage." In Slater 1996, 29–48.

Lefèvre, E. 1971. "Der *Thyestes* des Lucius Varius Rufus. Zehn Überlegungen zu seiner Rekonstruktion." *AAWM* 9.

Leigh, Matthew. 1996. "Varius Rufus, Thyestes, and the Appetites of Antony." *PCPS* 42: 171–197.

————. 1997. *Lucan: Spectacle and Engagement.* Oxford.

Leo, F. L. 1878. *Annaei Senecae Tragoediae.* Vol. 1: *De Senecae Tragoediis Observationes Criticae.* Berlin.

————. 1910. *De tragoedia romana.* Göttingen.

————. 1913. *Geschichte der Römischen Literatur: Die Archaische Literatur.* Berlin.

Lindsay, W. M. 1968. *Early Latin Verse.* Oxford.

————. 1989. *T. Macci Plauti Comoediae.* Oxford Classical Text. Oxford. (Original ed., 1905.)

————. 1990. *P. Terenti Afri Comoediae.* Oxford. (Original ed., 1926.)

Lobel, E. 1949. "A Greek Historical Drama." *Proceedings of the British Academy* 35: 207–217.

Lowe, N. J. 1993. "Review of R. C. Beacham, *The Roman Theatre and Its Audience.*" *JRS* 88: 195–196.

Luce, T. J., and A. J. Woodman, eds. 1993. *Tacitus and the Tacitean Tradition.* Princeton.

Mackail, J. W. 1930. *The Aeneid.* Oxford.

Mckeown, J. C. 1979. "Augustan Elegy and Mime." *CPSP* 25: 711–784.

MacMullen, Ramsey. 1966. *Enemies of the Roman Order.* Cambridge, Mass.

Magno, Pietro. 1977. *Marco Pacuvio, i frammenti.* With introduction, translation, and commentary. Milan.

————. 1979. *Quinto Ennio.* Fasano di Puglia.

Malcovati, Henrica. 1923. "De C. Asinii Pollionis Carminibus." *Athenaeum,* n.s. 1: 131–136.

Malissard, Alain. 1990. "Tacite et le théâtre ou la mort en scène." In Jürgen Blänsdorf, ed., *Theater und Gesellschaft im Imperium Romanum,* 213–222. Bonn.

Manacorda, D. 1999. "Theatrum Balbi." In Steinby 1999, 6:30–31.

Manning, C. E. 1975. "Acting and Nero's Conception of the Principate." *G&R* 22: 164–175.

Manuwald, Gesine. 2001. *Fabulae praetextae: Spuren einer literarischen Gattung der Römer.* Munich.

Mariotti, Italo. 1960. *Introduzione a Pacuvio.* Urbino.

Mariotti, Scevola. 1951. *Lezioni su Ennio.* Pesaro.

————. 1955. *Il Bellum Poenicum e l'arte di Nevio.* Rome.

————. 1986. *Livio Andronico e la traduzione artistica.* Urbino.

Marshall, P. K. 1968. *A. Gellii Noctes Atticae.* Oxford Classical Text. Oxford.

Marx, F. C. 1963. Lucilii Carminum Reliquiae. Amsterdam. (Original ed., Lipsiae, 1904.)

Mellor, Ronald. 1993. *Tacitus.* New York.

Mickwitz, G. 1928. "Tragedien 'Octavia' och den tidigare 'fabula praetexta.'" *Eranos* 26: 234–242.

Millar, Fergus. 1984. "The Political Character of the Classical Roman Republic, 200–151 B.C." *JRS* 74: 1–19.

————. "Politics, Persuasion and the People before the Social War (150–90 B.C.)." *JRS* 76: 1–11.

Miller, Frank Iustus. 1984. *Ovid: The Metamorphoses.* Loeb Classical Library. Cambridge, Mass. (Original ed., 1916.)

Moore, Timothy J. 1998. *The Theater of Plautus: Playing to the Audience.* Austin.

Morford, M.P.O. 1967. *The Poet Lucan: Studies in Rhetorical Epic.* Oxford.

————. 2000. "Walking Tall: The Final Entrance of Atreus in Seneca's *Thyestes.*" *Syllecta Classica* 11: 162–177.

Morel, Willy. 1975. *Fragmenta Poetarum Latinorum Epicorum et Lyricorum. Praeter Ennium et Lucilium.* Stuttgart. (Reprint of 2d ed., 1927.)

Morris, Edmund. 2000. *Dutch: A Memoir of Ronald Reagan.* New York.

Morris, Edward P. 1911. *Horace: The Epistles.* New York.

Mueller, Lucianus. 1854. *Q. Enni Carminum Reliquae.* Petropolis.

————. 1884. *Quintus Ennius: Eine Einleitung in das Studium der römischen Poesie.* St. Petersburg.

————. 1885. *Livi Andronici et Cn. Naevi Fabularum Reliquiae.* Berlin.

Mynors, R. A. 1990. *P. Vergili Maronis Opera.* Oxford. (Original ed., 1969.)

Némethy, Geyza. 1903. *Vita A. Persii Flacci de Commentario Probi Valeri Sublata.* Budapest.

Nicolas, Alex. 1851. *De Cassio Parmensi Poeta.* Paris.

Nicolet, C. 1980. *The World of the Citizen in Republican Rome.* Berkeley.

Nikolaidis, A. G. 1985. "Some Observations on Ovid's Lost *Medea.*" *Latomus* 44: 383–387.

Otis, Brooks. 1970. *Ovid as an Epic Poet.* 2d ed. Cambridge.

Owen, S. G. 1963. *Ovid: Tristia.* Oxford. (Original ed., 1915.)

Pantzerhielm, Thomas S. 1945. "Die Octavia Praetexta." *SO* 24: 48–87.

Paratore, E. 1957. *Storia del teatro latino.* Milan.

———. 1969. "Indizi di natura sociale nel teatro latino." *Dioniso* 43: 37–58.

Parker, Holt N. 1999. "The Observed of All Observers: Spectacle, Applause, and Cultural Poetics in the Roman Theater Audience." In Bergmann and Kondoleon 1999: 163–179.

Paton, W. R. 1972. *Polybius: The Histories.* Loeb Classical Library. London and Cambridge, Mass. (Original ed., 1923.)

Pedroli, Lydia. 1953. *Fabularum Praextextarum Quae Extant.* Genoa.

Perrin, Bernadotte. 1916. *Plutarch: Sulla.* Loeb Classical Library. Cambridge, Mass.

———. 1919. *Cicero; Cato the Younger.* Loeb Classical Library. Cambridge, Mass.

———. 1920. *Antony; Marius.* Loeb Classical Library. Cambridge, Mass.

———. 1968. *Pompey.* Loeb Classical Library. Cambridge, Mass. (Original ed., 1917.)

Pickard-Cambridge, Sir Arthur. 1988. *The Dramatic Festivals of Athens.* Reissue of 2d ed. (1968), with supplement and corrections. Oxford. (Original ed., 1953; revised 1968 by John Gould and D. M. Lewis.)

Platner S., and T. Ashby. 1965. *A Topographical Dictionary of Ancient Rome.* Rome. (Original ed., Oxford, 1929.)

Pollard, N. 1999. "Theatrum Scauri." In Steinby 1999, 6:38–39.

Purcell, Nicholas. 1999. "Does Caesar Mime?" In Bergmann and Kondoleon 1999, 181–193.

Raaflaub, Kurt A. 1986. *Social Struggles in Archaic Rome.* Berkeley.

Radice, Betty. 1969. *Pliny: Letters and Panegyricus.* Loeb Classical Library. Cambridge, Mass.

Raven, David. 1969. "Tragedy." In John Higginbotham, ed., *Greek and Latin Literature,* 262–299. London.

Rawson, E. 1985. "Theatrical Life in Republican Rome and Italy." *Proceedings of the British School at Rome* 53: 97–113.

———. 1987. "On Moralizing in Roman Drama and the Roman Audience's Reception of Dramatic Sententiae." In Michael Whitby, Philip Hardie, and Mary Whitby, eds., *Homo Viator: Classical Essays for John Bramble.* Bristol.

Reggiani, Renato. 1987. "Rileggendo alcuni frammenti tragici di Ennio, Pacuvio e Accio." *Quaderni di cultura e di tradizione classica* 5: 31–92.

Rehm, Rush. 1992. *Greek Tragic Theatre.* London and New York.

Ribbeck, Otto. 1875. *Römische Tragödie.* Leipzig.

———. 1897. *Scaenicae Romanorum Poesis Fragmenta.* Vol. 1: *Tragicorum Romanorum Fragmenta.* 3d ed. Lipsiae.

———. 1962. *Scaenicae Romanorum Poesis Fragmenta.* Vol. 2: *Comicorum*

*Romanorum Praeter Plautum et Terentium Fragmenta.* Hildesheim. (Original ed., Leipzig, 1873.)

Richardson, L., Jr. 1992. *A New Topographical Dictionary of Ancient Rome.* Baltimore.

Richlin, Amy. 1997. "Gender and Rhetoric: Producing Manhood in the Schools." In Dominik 1997, 90–110.

Rolfe, J. C. 1924. *Suetonius.* Loeb Classical Library. Cambridge, Mass. (Original ed., 1914.)

Rosenmeyer, T. 1989. *Senecan Drama and Stoic Cosmology.* Berkeley.

Rostagni, Augusto. 1964. *Suetonio "De Poetis" e Biografi Minori.* Turin.

Rudd, Niall. 1989. *Horace Epistles Book II and "Ars Poetica."* Cambridge.

———. 1992. "Stratagems of Vanity: Cicero *Ad familiares* 5.12 and Pliny's Letters." In Tony Woodman and Jonathan Powell, eds., *Author and Audience in Latin Literature,* 18–32. Cambridge.

Rudich, Vasily. 1993. *Political Dissidence under Nero: The Price of Dissimulation.* London and New York.

———. 1997. *Dissidence and Literature under Nero: The Price of Rhetorization.* London and New York.

Santoro, A. 1922. "Di alcune imitazioni greche nell' Octavia." *Riv. Indo-Greco-Italica* 6: 19–22.

Saunders, C. 1913. "The Site of Dramatic Performances at Rome in the Times of Plautus and Terence." *TAPA* 44: 87–97.

Schiesaro, A. 2003. *The Passions in Play: Thyestes and the Dynamics of Drama.* Cambridge.

Scullard, H. H. 1973. *Roman Politics, 220–150 B.C.* Oxford.

Sedgwick, W. B. 1927. "Parody in Plautus." *CQ* 21: 88–89.

Segal, C. P. 1984. "Senecan Baroque: The Death of Hippolytus in Seneca, Ovid, and Euripides." *TAPA* 114: 311–325.

———. 1986. *Language and Desire in Seneca's Phaedra.* Princeton.

Shackleton Bailey, D. R. 1971. *Cicero.* London.

———. 1983. "Cicero and Early Latin Poetry." *ICS:* 239–249.

———. 1988. *Cicero's Letters to His Friends.* Atlanta. (Original ed., Penguin, 1978.)

———. 2001. *Cicero, Letters to Friends.* Loeb Classical Library. 3 vols. Cambridge, Mass.

Shipley Duckett, Eleanor. 1915. *Studies in Ennius.* Bryn Mawr College Monographs 18. Bryn Mawr, Pa.

Sifakis, G. 1967. *Studies in the History of Hellenistic Drama.* London.

Silk, M. S. 1996. *Tragedy and the Tragic.* Oxford.

Skutsch, F. 1899. "C. Cassius Parmensis." In *RE* 3: 1743–1744.

Skutsch, Otto. 1953. *The Annals of Quintus Ennius.* Inaugural lecture delivered at University College London, 29 November 1951. London.

———. 1963. "Enniana V." *CQ* 57: 89–100.

———. 1966. "Notes on Ennian Tragedy." *HSCPh* 71: 125–142.

———. 1985. *The Annals of Q. Ennius.* Oxford.

Slater, Niall W. 1985. *Plautus in Performance: The Theatre of the Mind.* Princeton.

————. 1996. "Nero's Masks." *CW* 90.1: 33–40.

Slater, William J., ed. 1996. *Roman Theater and Society.* Ann Arbor.

Snell, Bruno. 1971. *Tragicorum graecorum fragmenta.* Göttingen.

Steinby, E. M., ed. 1993–2000. *Lexicon topographicum urbis Romae.* Rome.

Stocker, A. F., and A. H. Travis. 1965. *Servianorum in Vergili Carmina Commentariorum Editionis Harvardianae.* Oxford.

Strzelecki, W. 1963. "Naevius and Roman Annalists." *RFIC* 91: 440–458.

Styan, J. L. 1975. *Drama, Stage and Audience.* Cambridge.

Sullivan, J. P. 1985. *Literature and Politics in the Age of Nero.* Ithaca, N.Y.

Sutton, Dana F. 1983. *The Dramaturgy of the Octavia. Beiträge zur klassichen Philologie,* vol. 149. Königstein.

————. 1986. *Seneca on the Stage.* Leiden.

Syme, Ronald. 1939. *The Roman Revolution.* Oxford.

————. 1958. *Tacitus.* Oxford.

Taylor, L. R. 1931. *The Divinity of the Roman Emperor.* Middletown, Conn.

————. 1961. *Party Politics in the Age of Caesar.* Berkeley. (Original ed., 1949.)

Tarrant, R. J. 1976. *Seneca: Agamemnon.* Cambridge.

————. 1978. "Senecan Drama and Its Antecedents." *HSCP* 82: 213–263.

————. 1985. *Seneca's Thyestes.* Atlanta.

Timpanaro, S., Jr. 1946. "Per Una Nuova Edizione Critica di Ennio." *SIFC,* n.s. 21: 41–81.

————. 1949. "Note a Livio Andronico, Ennio, Varrone, Virgilio." *ASNP* 2.18–19: 186–204.

Turner, Victor. 1982. *From Ritual to Theatre.* New York.

Ullman, B. L. 1942. "History and Tragedy." *APA* 73: 25–53.

Vahlen, Iohannes. 1963. *Ennianae Poesis Reliquiae.* Reproduction of 1928 ed. Amsterdam. (Original ed., Lipsiae, 1854; reprinted 1903 and 1928.)

Valsa, M. 1957. *Marcus Pacuvius, Poète Tragique.* Paris.

Varner, Eric R. 2000. "Grotesque Vision: Seneca's Tragedies and Neronian Art." In George W. M. Harrison, ed., *Seneca in Performance,* 119–136. London.

Vergrugghe, G. P. 1989. "On the Meaning of Annales, on the Meaning of Annalist." *Philologus* 133: 192–330.

Versnel, H. S. 1970. *Triumphus.* Leiden.

Villeneuve, F. 1941. *Horace: Épitres.* Budé ed. Paris.

Von Hessberg, Henner. 1999. "The King on Stage." In Bergmann and Kondoleon 1999, 65–75.

Wallace-Hadrill, Andrew. 1983. *Suetonius: The Scholar and His Caesars.* New Haven.

Walbank, F. W. 1945. "Polybius, Philinus, and the First Punic War." *CQ* 39: 1–18.

————. 1979. *A Historical Commentary on Polybius.* Vol. 3: *Commentary on Books XIX–XL.* Oxford.

————. 1981. *The Hellenistic World*. Brighton, Sussex.

————. 1985. *Selected Papers*. Cambridge.

Walker, B. 1952. *The Annals of Tacitus*. Manchester.

Walton, F. R. 1968. *Diodorus of Sicily*. Loeb Classical Library. London and Cambridge, Mass. (Original ed., 1957.)

Warde-Fowler, W. 1964. *Social Life at Rome in the Age of Cicero*. London. (Original ed., 1908.)

Warmington, E. H. 1982. *Remains of Old Latin*. Vol. 2: *Livius Andronicus, Naevius, Pacuvius and Accius*. Loeb Classical Library. Cambridge, Mass. (Original ed., 1936.)

————. 1988. *Remains of Old Latin*. Vol. 1: *Ennius and Caecilius*. Loeb Classical Library. Cambridge, Mass. (Original ed., 1935.)

Watt, W. S. 1982. *M. Tulli Ciceronis Epistulae*. Vol. 1: *Epistulae ad familiares*. Oxford.

Weichert, A. 1836. *De L. Varii et Cassii Parmensis vita et carminibus*. Grimae.

Weinstock, S. 1971. *Divus Julius*. Oxford.

Wickham, E. C. 1959. *Q. Horati Flacci Opera*. Oxford Classical Text. Oxford. (Original ed., 1901.)

Wiles, D. 1991. *The Masks of Menander*. Cambridge.

Williams, G. W. 1968. *Tradition and Originality*. Oxford.

————. 1978. *Change and Decline*. Berkeley.

————. 1992. "Poet and Audience in Senecan Tragedy." In T. Woodman and J. Powell, eds., *Author and Audience in Latin Literature*. Cambridge.

Williams, R. D. 1992. *The Aeneid of Virgil, Books 1–6*. New York. (Original ed., London, 1972.)

Winniczuk, Lidia. 1961. "Cicero on Actors and the Stage." In *Atti del I Congresso Internazionale di Studi Ciceroniani, Roma, Aprile 1959*, 1:213–222. Rome.

Winstedt, E. O. 1925. Cicero: Letters to Atticus. Vol. 3. Loeb Classical Library. Cambridge, Mass. (Original ed., 1918.)

————. 1927. *Cicero: Letters to Atticus*. Vol. 1. Loeb Classical Library. Cambridge, Mass. (Original ed., 1912.)

Wiseman, T. P. 1979. *Clio's Cosmetics: Three Studies in Greco-Roman Literature*. Leicester.

————. 1988. "Satyrs in Rome? The Background to Horace's *Ars Poetica*." *JRS* 78: 1–13.

————. 1994. "The Origins of Roman Historiography." In *Historiography and Imagination: Eight Essays on Roman Culture*, 1–22. Exeter.

————. 1995a. "Afterword: The Theatre of Civic Life." In Ian M. Barton, ed., *Roman Public Buildings*, 151–155. Exeter. (Original ed., 1989.)

————. 1995b. *Remus: A Roman Myth*. Cambridge.

————. 1998. *Roman Drama and Roman History*. Exeter.

Woodman, A. J. 1988. *Rhetoric in Classical Historiography*. London.

————. 1993. "Amateur Dramatics at the Court of Nero." In Luce and Woodman 1993, 104–128.

Wolf-Hartmut, Friedrich. 1948. "Ennius-Erklärungen." *Philologus* 97: 277–301.

Wright, F. W. 1931. *Cicero and the Theater.* Smith College Classical Studies 11. Northampton, Mass.

Wright, John. 1974. *Dancing in Chains: The Stylistic Unity of the "Comoedia Palliata."* Rome.

Zehnacker, Hubert. 1981. "Tragédie prétexte et spectacle romain." In idem, ed., *Théatres et spectacles dans l'antiquité, Actes du Colloque de Strasbourg,* 5–7 November 1981, 31–48. Strasbourg.

Zillinger, W. 1911. *Cicero und die altrömischen Dichter.* Würzberg.

Zorzetti, N. 1980. *La pretesta e il teatro latino arcaico.* Naples.

Zwierlein, Otto. 1966. *Die Rezitationsdramen Senecas.* Meisenheim am Glan.

———. 1988. *L. Annaei Senecae Tragoediae.* Oxford Classical Text. Oxford. (Original ed., 1986.)

# INDEX

Accius, L., 9, 18, 22, 30–34, 36, 40, 42–51, 43, 54, 55, 67, 68, 82, 123, 129, 138, 145–148; *Aeneadae sive Decius,* 54, 55, 67, 68–71, 73; Atreus, 101, 102, 104–108, 116, 117; *Brutus,* 4, 43, 54, 55, 59, 62, 63, 67, 73, 91–101, 110, 138; *Clytemnestra,* 7, 86, 87–89, 91, 110; *Eurysaces,* 6, 7, 95; *Medea sive Argonautae,* 5, 45–50; *Tereus,* 98–100
actor(s), 3–8, 11, 14, 30, 32, 52, 79, 82, 90, 91, 101, 117–124, 136, 137, 138; actor-audience, 8, 121–123, 127, 129, 137–139
*aemulatio,* 2
Aeneas, 56, 58, 103
Aeschylus, 35, 51; *Persians,* 53, 59–63, 72, 94
Aesopus, 7, 83, 95, 96
Agrippina, 56, 59, 112, 119
Ajax, 99, 117
Alexander the Great, 90
allegory, 29
allusion: dramatic, 5–7, 51, 90, 91, 101, 109, 122; metatheatrical, 22; mythological, 81, 82, 90, 101, 102, 109–111, 117, 129, 138; off-stage, 3, 91, 138; onstage, 56, 91;

political, 82, 91, 101–103, 109–112, 120, 121; theatrical, 4, 33, 79, 91, 101, 102, 103
Antigone, 134
Antonius, Gaius, 97, 98
Antony, Mark, 97, 98, 103, 109, 111
Apollonius Rhodius, 45
Appian, 90
*Argonautica,* 43, 45, 49
Atilius, 1
Atossa, 59–63, 72
Atreus, 101–117, 124
audience, 4–8, 13, 15, 27, 28–33, 35, 44, 51, 52, 56, 68, 73–75, 79–83, 89–91, 95, 96, 101, 118, 120–122, 124, 136, 137
Augustus, 4, 51, 80, 82, 84, 100, 102, 104, 109–112, 116, 120, 138, 149

Battle of Sentinum, 54
Beare, W., 136
Bilinski, Bronislaw, 82
Boyle, A. J., 8, 122, 123, 128, 136
Brutus, L. Junius, 55, 73, 82, 91–101
Brutus, Marcus Junius, 96–100, 103
Brutus Callaicus, D. Junius, 54, 92, 94, 96, 97, 100, 103
Burrus, S. Afranius, 120

Gracchus, Sempronius, 150;
  *Thyestes,* 101
grotesque, 129, 133

Hellenistic, 46
Hercules, 118
Herington, C. J., 136
Hippolytus, 127, 129–134
Horace, 42, 43, 54, 103, 111
Hortensius, Q. Hortalus, 33

*Iliad,* 43, 45
illusion, dramatic, 4, 122, 129, 136, 138
imagines, 76, 77, 79
*imitatio,* 2
interpolations (actors'), 6, 7, 91

Jocasta, 134, 135
Julio-Claudians, 67, 77, 84, 103, 117, 138
Julius Secundus, 116
Juvenal, 119

Kronos, 134

La Penna, A., 53
Lentulus, L., 74
Licinius, 1
Livius, M., 69
Livius Andronicus, L., 2, 9–14, 16, 18–20, 29, 30, 42, 137, 139, 142; *Aegisthus,* 11–13; *Equos Troianus,* 86, 90
Livy, 56, 69, 77, 92
Lucan, 123, 152
Lucilius, 36, 42
Lucretia, 100
*ludi,* 3, 77, 79, 83, 89; *ludi Apollinares* (169 B.C.E.), 102; *ludi Apollinares* (57 B.C.E.), 6, 94; *ludi Apollinares* (44 B.C.E.), 96–99

Macro, 112, 113
Maecenas, 103

Marius, M., 86
Medea, 124
Menander, 1
metatheatre, 4, 5, 9, 19, 22, 28–34, 44, 46, 50–52, 82, 137
metatragedy, 8, 81, 82, 122–139
Metelli, 15
mime, 29, 32, 33, 51, 78, 79
Moschion, 53, 72

Naevius, Gn., 2, 9, 14–20, 29, 30, 52–56, 67, 86, 90, 137, 139, 142; *Bellum Punicum,* 15; *Clastidium,* 15, 54, 55, 67, 92, 110; *Danae,* 16–18; *Equos Troianus,* 15, 86, 90; *Romulus sive Lupus,* 54, 56, 67
Neptune, 129
Nero, 8, 43, 44, 56, 59, 63, 66, 67, 82, 85, 112, 114–115, 117–121, 123, 129, 138
Nobilior, M. Fulvius, 18
Novius, 43

Octavia, 56, 59, 63
*Octavia,* 54, 56, 58, 59, 63, 66–68, 74, 94, 112, 114–116, 123
Octavian. *See* Augustus
Odysseus, 99
Oedipus, 118, 134
orator, 31
Orestes, 111, 118, 119
Ovid, 44, 45, 50, 52, 111, 123, 131–134, 150; *Medea,* 44, 45, 138

Pacuvius, M., 1, 4, 9, 18, 30, 32, 33, 34–42, 43, 50, 51, 54, 55, 57, 123, 138, 144, 145; *Antiopa,* 1, 37–42; *Paullus,* 54, 55, 67, 68, 92, 99
pantomime, 8, 123, 134, 135, 137
Paullus, L. Aemilius, 54, 55, 77
performance text, 7, 32, 75, 91, 138
Persius, 42, 152
Persius, King of Macedonia, 54

Petronius, 120
Phaedra, 127, 129, 130, 134
Phrynicus, 53; *Sack of Miletus,* 72
Piso, G. Calpurnius, 119
Plato, 1
Plautus, 4, 15, 29
Pliny, 83, 85, 86, 117, 119
Plutarch, 3, 32, 56, 84
Pollio, C. Asinius, 50, 74, 103, 150
Polybius, 69, 76, 77
Polynices, 134, 135
*pompa,* 77, 79
Pompeii, 137
Pompey, Sextus, 109
Pompey (Gn. Pompeius Magnus), 6,
    7, 74, 80, 82, 83–91, 95, 110,
    112, 120
Pompey's theatre. *See* theatre
Pomponius, 43
Pomponius Secundus, 50, 123, 151;
    *Aeneas,* 54, 56, 67; *Atreus,* 101,
    112
Poppaea, 59, 63, 66, 118
Porphyrion, 109
*praetextae. See fabulae praetextae*
Propertius, 103
Pseudo-Acro, 109
Pseudo-Seneca, 54, 56, 66–68, 74,
    94, 112, 114, 116, 151
Pydna, 57

Quintilian, 34, 42, 45, 103, 112

realism, 7, 8, 33
reality: audiences', 4, 9, 51, 79, 80,
    91, 101, 138, 139; competing real-
    ities, 5, 52, 68, 81, 123, 138; dra-
    matic, 9, 14, 33, 50–52, 91, 135;
    offstage, 4, 5, 14–16, 30, 33, 35,
    51, 52, 57, 68, 75, 79, 81, 91, 129,
    137, 138; onstage, 4, 7, 16, 33, 79,
    82, 101, 122, 137, 138; outside of
    theatre, 44, 122, 137, 138; rhetori-
    cized stage reality, 5, 129, 137; the-
    atricalized, 7, 33, 43, 44, 80, 82,
    101, 122, 128, 138

recitation, 135, 136
Remus, 56, 57
rhetoric, 5, 18, 30, 31, 33–35, 37,
    38, 42–44, 46, 123, 130, 134,
    137, 138
rhetoricized mentality, 123
role-playing, 31
Romulus, 56, 57, 96

Santra, 149
Scaurus, M. Aemilius, 112, 117, 150;
    *Atreus,* 101
Scipio Africanus, 18
semiotics, 51, 68, 79, 81, 82, 89, 90
Seneca, 8, 9, 33, 42, 45, 50, 51, 59,
    68, 81, 82, 119, 120, 122–139,
    151; *Agamemnon,* 118, 128, 136,
    137; *Oedipus,* 127; *Phaedra,* 127–
    129, 131, 133, 134; *Phoenissae,*
    134, 135, 137; *Thyestes,* 101,
    112–114, 124; *Troades,* 126
Shakespeare, 4, 99
Slater, Niall, 5
Sophocles, 43
spectacle, 43, 45, 128, 129, 135,
    137, 138
Spurius Maecius Tarpa, 83
stage, 2–5, 7–9, 15, 19, 29–32, 35,
    68, 118–121, 135–138
Strabo, C. Julius, 50, 148
Suetonius, 8, 18, 59, 78, 79, 85, 99,
    118, 119
Sulla (L. Cornelius Sulla Felix), 51
Sutton, Dana F., 136

Tacitus, 43,
Tarquin(s), 54, 55, 62, 63, 66, 82,
    91–94, 96, 97, 101
Tarrant, R. J., 125, 136
Temple of Minerva, 18
Temple of Venus Victrix, 183, 184
Terence, 1, 54
Tertullian, 83
theatre, 3–8, 10, 11, 14, 15, 18, 33,
    44, 56, 57, 75, 121, 122, 135, 137;
    of Balbus, 83; of the dead, 76; of

Marcellus, 83; of Pompey, 15, 51,
80, 82, 83–91, 102, 109–111,
123, 138; of Scaurus, 84, 85, 87
theatricality, 3, 4, 18, 31–33, 35, 45,
68, 80, 82, 118, 121, 122, 129,
137, 138; offstage, 8, 18, 30, 32,
33, 35, 44, 53, 68, 117, 120, 137;
onstage, 14, 33, 35, 117, 135, 137;
theatricalized tragedy, 33, 45, 68,
121, 122
Themistocles, 72, 73
Theseus, 129, 134
Thrasea Paetus, 120
Thyestes, 101–117, 119, 124, 134
Tiberius, 85, 116, 117

Tiridates, 85, 123
tragic parody, 30
Troy, 58
Tullius, Servius, 95, 96

Varius Rufus, 4, 44, 45, 50, 80, 82,
91, 103, 150; *Thyestes,* 4, 44, 80,
82, 91, 101–104, 109–112, 138
Varro, 100
Vergil, 103, 120
Vidumarus, 54
Vindex, 120
voyeurism, 125, 126

Xerxes, 61, 72